DANCE, ACCESS AND INCLUSION

The arts have a crucial role in empowering young people with special needs through diverse dance initiatives. Inclusive pedagogy that integrates all students in rich, equitable and just dance programmes within education frameworks is occurring alongside enabling projects by community groups and in the professional dance world where many high-profile choreographers actively seek opportunities to work across diversity to inspire creativity. Access and inclusion is increasingly the essence of projects for disenfranchised and traumatised youth who find creative expression, freedom and hope through dance. This volume foregrounds dance for young people with special needs and presents best practice scenarios in schools, communities and the professional sphere. International perspectives come from Australia, Brazil, Cambodia, Canada, Denmark, Fiji, Finland, India, Indonesia, Jamaica, Japan, Malaysia, New Zealand, Norway, Papua New Guinea, Portugal, Singapore, South Africa, Spain, Taiwan, Timor Leste, the UK and the USA.

Sections include:

- inclusive dance pedagogy
- equality, advocacy and policy
- changing practice for dance education
- community dance initiatives
- professional integrated collaborations

Stephanie Burridge lectures at LASALLE College of the Arts and Singapore Management University and is the Series Editor for *Celebrating Dance in Asia and the Pacific* (Routledge).

Charlotte Svendler Nielsen is Associate Professor and Head of Educational Studies at the Department of Nutrition, Exercise and Sports, research cluster 'Embodiment, Learning and Social Change', University of Copenhagen, Denmark.

DANCE, ACCESS AND INCLUSION

Perspectives on Dance,
Young People and Change

*Edited by Stephanie Burridge and
Charlotte Svendler Nielsen*

Routledge
Taylor & Francis Group

LONDON AND NEW YORK

First published 2018
by Routledge
2 Park Square, Milton Park, Abingdon, Oxon OX14 4RN

and by Routledge
711 Third Avenue, New York, NY 10017

Routledge is an imprint of the Taylor & Francis Group, an informa business

British Library Cataloguing-in-Publication Data
A catalogue record for this book is available from the British Library

Library of Congress Cataloging-in-Publication Data
A catalogue record for this book has been requested

ISBN: 978-1-138-67407-3 (hbk)
ISBN: 978-1-138-67408-0 (pbk)
ISBN: 978-1-315-56151-6 (ebk)

Typeset in Bembo
by Deanta Global Publishing Services, Chennai, India

CONTENTS

Note: The country indicated is where the study is located and not necessarily where the writer lives or comes from.

ACKNOWLEDGEMENTS

This book is supported by Dance and the Child International (daCi) and the World Dance Alliance (WDA). Dance and the Child International is a non-profit association, founded in 1978, dedicated to the growth and development of dance for children and young people on an international basis. The World Dance Alliance serves as the primary voice for dance and dancers throughout the world, and encourages the exchange of ideas and the awareness of dance in all its forms.

Co-editor Dr. Stephanie Burridge is grateful for the generous support of the National Arts Council Singapore for a Research and Development grant towards the research and editing of this volume.

The editors would like to acknowledge the outstanding contributions that the authors have made to this book, which is a vibrant account of dance access and inclusion across continents and countries. Finally, the editors would like to thank Routledge for their foresight in commissioning this volume and their understanding of the complexity of assembling such a rich and diverse collection of authors for the anthology.

CONTRIBUTORS

Imogen Aujla (MSc, PhD) is a Senior Lecturer in Dance and Course Coordinator of the MSc in Dance Science at the University of Bedfordshire. She originally trained as a dancer before specialising in dance science and later dance psychology. Her research interests cover both the optimisation of performance among elite dancers, and the impact of recreational dance on the health and well-being of non-dancers. She has a particular interest in the psychological factors that drive participation in dance. She sits on the publications committee of the International Association for Dance Medicine and Science, and has published and presented her research internationally.

Raimon Àvila has been teaching movement at Institut del Teatre since 1988, and body awareness at ESMUC (Escola Superior de Música de Catalunya) since 2001. He studied contemporary dance in Barcelona and completed his performance studies at Maurice Béjart's school MUDRA in Brussels (1983). He is the author of several books on artistic practice (drama, poetry) and research fields, including: *Kylian, Somniador de Danses*, 2002; *Moure i Commoure, Consciència corporal per a Actors, Músics i Ballarins*, 2011; *Impulsos, Emoció i qualitat de moviment en l'intèrpret escènic*, 2016.

Jordi Baltà works as a freelance researcher and trainer in cultural policy and international affairs, with a special interest in cultural diversity, the place of culture in sustainable development and international cultural relations. He regularly works for the committee on culture of United Cities and Local Governments (UCLG) and the Asia-Europe Museum Network (ASEMUS), and is a member of the UNESCO Expert Facility on the Convention on the Diversity of Cultural Expressions. Prior to this, he worked at the Interarts Foundation and coordinated the European Expert Network on Culture (EENC) between 2011 and 2014.

Adam Benjamin was joint founder and Artistic Director of Candoco Dance Company and founder of Tshwaragano, the first South African dance company integrated both racially and physically. He has choreographed for community and professional companies worldwide. A Rayne Choreographic Fellow and associate artist of the Place, he now teaches at Plymouth

University. He was awarded a National Teaching Fellowship in 2013 and was named a Change Maker in 2015 by the South Bank Centre. His book *Making an Entrance: Theory and Practice for Disabled and Non-disabled Dancers* (Routledge, 2002) is considered a seminal text in the field of integrated dance.

Elaine Bliss (PhD) is a Senior Tutor in Geography at the University of Waikato, Hamilton, New Zealand. She has recently completed her PhD thesis, titled 'Performative Methodologies: Geographies of Emotion and Affect in Digital Storytelling Workshops.' She trained at and maintains a close relationship with the Centre for Digital Storytelling (and an international digital storytelling community of practice). She teaches an interdisciplinary course in digital storytelling at the University of Waikato and is co-director of Digital Storytelling Aotearoa, a Hamilton-based organisation that facilitates digital storytelling workshops, primarily within the community sector.

Ralph Buck (PhD) is an Associate Professor at the University of Auckland and is an award-winning teacher and academic leader. His research has been featured at the UNESCO Second World Conference on Arts Education. He is on the International Editorial Boards of Research in Dance Education (RIDE) and Journal of Dance Education (JODE) and has collaborated with UNESCO in raising the profile of arts education around the world. He initiated, advocated for and planned UNESCO's International Arts Education Week and is on the Council for the World Alliance for Arts Education. His research and publications focus on dance teaching and learning, and community dance.

Stephanie Burridge (PhD) lectures at LASALLE College of the Arts and Singapore Management University. She was Artistic Director of Canberra Dance Theatre (1978–2001) and was awarded the first Choreographic Fellowship at the Australian Choreographic Centre. She is Series Editor for Routledge's *Celebrating Dance in Asia and the Pacific*, Research and Documentation Network Co-Chair for WDA Asia Pacific and Co-Editor of *Dance Education around the World: Perspectives on Dance, Young People and Change, with a Foreword by Sir Ken Robinson*, with Charlotte Svendler Nielsen (Denmark). She has been living with multiple sclerosis since 1998.

Gemma Carbo Ribugent (PhD) is Director of the UNESCO Chair in Cultural Policies and Cooperation at the University of Girona. With a PhD in Education, she has also gained an Advanced Studies Diploma in Culture and Law, a Master's in Cultural Management and a Bachelor of Arts in History. She lectures at the University of Girona and is coordinator of the Virtual Master's in Cultural Management (UOC-UdG-UIB) and the postgraduate programme: 'Education and culture, management programs and projects.' Her research explores the relationship between cultural policy and education, education and cultural diversity, and education and creativity. She is the President of ConArte International.

Chung-shiuan Chang obtained an EdD at Teachers College, Columbia University in 1991, with her research focus on children's creative dance. She was a founding member of Neo-Classic Dance Company, led by Dr. Liu Feng-hsueh, a respected choreographer and dance scholar in Taiwan. She has been a full-time teacher at the Taipei National University of the Arts (TNUA) since 1992. At TNUA, besides teaching, she has been the Chair of the Dance

Department, Dean of the Dance School and the Dean of Academic Affairs. Currently, she is the vice president at TNUA.

Philip Channells of Dance Integrated Australia is considered one of Australia's foremost artists in disability-inclusive dance practice. His choreographic credits include: *PERFECT (im)PERFECTIONS – stories untold*, *The Main Event* (2014), *Skin-deep, Enter & Exit* (2013), *Second Skin, inPerspective #1, Lythophytes & Epiphytes* (2012), *Next of Kin – no ordinary status family* (2010). Through his international networks, he builds collaborative environments conducive to creativity and social inclusion.

Sue Cheesman is a teacher, choreographer and researcher who is a Senior Lecturer in Dance Education at the University of Waikato, Hamilton, New Zealand. She has an eclectic background in dance with emphasis on contemporary and has worked in the field of integrated dance for many years, particularly in relation to the work of Touch Compass Dance Company. Recent research has centred on: writing articles in relation to her own teaching practice within community and educational settings; dance and disability; and dance education and choreography, particularly in relation to site-specific work.

Anthony Meh Kim Chuan is the founder and Managing Director of Dua Space Dance Theatre, and the artistic director of Shuang Fu Performing Arts Troupe under Shuang Fu Disabled Independent Living Association. He graduated from The Hong Kong Academy for Performing Arts in dance, was a former dancer of Taiwan Cloud Gate Dance Theatre, Nai-Ni Chen Dance Company and GGD Dance Company in New York, USA. His contributions to dance have enabled him to receive numerous awards and recognitions, such as The Cultural Character of the Year 2010 from Global Golden Brand Awards, and World Chinese Model 2011 from World Chinese Venture Model Association.

Filomar Cortezano Tariao has had an international and versatile professional career in dance and theatre spanning two decades, performing for Gus Giordano Jazz Dance Chicago, Ballet Philippines, Powerdance, Singapore Repertory Theatre, Filipiniana Touring Dance Company and Hong Kong Singers, among others. He graduated as a full-scholar from the Hong Kong Academy of Performing Arts. A Doctor of Medicine and a licensed physician, he left his practice to pursue a greater passion. He is a full-time Senior Lecturer at Nanyang Academy of Fine Arts and leads the Asian dance and somatic practices modules.

Laura Evans is from the UK, but currently lives in Cambodia, where she is Co-Director of Epic Arts. She manages the Inclusive Arts Course at Epic Arts and is advisor to Epic Encounters, a fully inclusive performance company. She graduated from York University in 2002 with a BA Honours degree in Dance and was awarded the Ede and Ravenscroft Award for Outstanding Achievement. She has worked as a dance tutor and arts manager for over fifteen years and specialises in inclusive arts practice. She holds a Master's degree in Applied Theatre and wrote the book *Inclusive Arts in Action: An Exploration of the Inclusive Arts Practices at Epic Arts*, published by Epic Arts in 2015.

Naomi Faik-Simet is a dance researcher with the Institute of Papua New Guinea Studies and specialises in research on Papua New Guinea's traditional and contemporary dance. She has published extensively for local and international journals on issues concerning the diverse forms of Papua New Guinea's dance heritage. Recently, she has been involved in research investigating the transmission of creative knowledge embedded in tradition as a method of pedagogy. Her work with Agnes Aimo, a teacher/choreographer for disabled children, is part of this research and is shared in this volume.

Rachel Federman-Morales (MA, BC-DMT) started her movement career as a professional ballet dancer. She has been practising dance/movement therapy since 1997 with diverse populations. For the last eleven years she has dedicated her clinical practice to children with severe disabilities caused by cerebral palsy. She directs, teaches and choreographs dance collaborations and has been featured in the 'Circle of Care, The Arts in Medicine' documentary and 'Arts & Culture Spot' on WHYY PBS TV, highlighting her work on dance and disability. She was selected from amongst twenty-six Philadelphians to be part of 'How Philly Moves,' a 50,000-square-foot mural installed at the Philadelphia International Airport.

Eva García is an expert in the creation and production of performing arts projects in unusual contexts and with unusual groups. She holds a degree in Textual Interpretation (ESAD, Córdoba) and obtained a Master's in Advanced Studies following her stay with Augusto Boal in Brazil (2000). In 2004 she established transFORMAS, an organisation that aims to develop professional performing arts productions through community projects. Since 2012 she has been the coordinator of the annual Conference on Social Inclusion and Education in the Performing Arts, organised by INAEM (Spanish Ministry of Education and Culture).

Leng Poh Gee holds a Master's of Arts (Performing Arts) from University of Malaya and Bachelor of Science (Human Development) from Universiti Putra Malaysia. He is a Lecturer at the Dance Department, Cultural Centre (School of Performing Arts), University of Malaya, where he is the former Head of Department (2011–2013). He was the Vice President of My Dance Alliance (2011–2016) and dance notation facilitator to the Johor Heritage Foundation (2011–2012).

Gianti Giadi is a choreographer/dancer and Director who graduated with a Bachelor of Arts (Hons) from LASALLE College of the Arts (Singapore); upon graduation, she joined LASALLE as a part-time lecturer. She is trained in many dance genres, including Indonesian traditional dance. She has also participated in the American Dance Festival, where she trained under Keith Thompson and Abby Yager from Trisha Brown Dance Company. She is currently an Artistic Director of GiGi Art of Dance, GiGi Dance Company and She Foundation in Jakarta, Indonesia. Passionate about her Indonesian roots, she aims to find a new voice in traditional Indonesian arts and culture with a contemporary statement.

Miriam Giguere (PhD) holds a Bachelor of Arts in psychology, an MA in Education (University of Pennsylvania) and a PhD in dance (Temple University). She directs the dance programme at Drexel University. Her research has been published in *Journal of Dance Education, Research in Dance Education* and *International Journal of the Arts and Education,* among others. She is the 2009 recipient of the American Educational Research Association Arts and Learning SIG national dissertation award, and keynote speaker for Dance Education

Conference 2010 (Singapore). She is author of the textbook *Beginning Modern Dance* and Associate Editor for the journal *Dance Education in Practice*.

Annie Grieg was the Artistic Director of Tasdance from 1997–2015, during which time she developed the company into a vital force in the cultural landscape of Tasmania, contributing to national arts practice. She has worked in many capacities: Course Director with the National Aboriginal and Islander Skills Development Association; freelance teacher and video maker; dance lecturer at the University of Tasmania; and Performing Arts Program Officer with Arts Tasmania. She was president of Ausdance NSW and a former National Vice-President of Ausdance, the Australian Dance Council. She received the Services to Dance Award in 2014.

Avril Huddy is a Lecturer in dance at Queensland University of Technology. Her diverse dance career includes performing, producing, establishing and curating with regard to independent performance venues, tour management and teaching across the three tiers of the Australian education system. She is a STOTT Pilates instructor and Feldenkrais Practitioner. Her approach to dance pedagogy and curriculum incorporates her extensive theoretical and embodied knowledge with her professional dance experience. She received a 2009 Australian Learning and Teaching Council Citation for Outstanding Contributions to Student Learning.

Nick Hughes has been Company Manager of Restless Dance Theatre since 1998. He has a Bachelor of Arts degree in Drama and Sociology from Birmingham University. Arriving in Australia from England in 1973, Nick became a founder professional member of the Popular Theatre Troupe based in Brisbane, making political theatre and performance events. In 1982, he became the founding Artistic Director of Harvest Theatre Company, based on Eyre Peninsula in South Australia. He has taught acting and directing, written twenty-eight theatre scripts and written extensively on community-based forms of arts practice.

Liisa Jaakonaho is a Finnish dance pedagogue, dance movement therapist, artist and researcher. In her doctoral research at Theatre Academy of the University of the Arts Helsinki, she investigates ethical questions in and around arts-based work that operates in the boundary areas between arts, education and health/social care. She is also involved in a multidisciplinary research project, ArtsEqual in the Arts@School research team.

Veronica Jobbins (MA, FRSA) is Head of Learning and Participation (Dance) at Trinity Laban. She originally trained as a specialist dance teacher, working in London schools for many years, including serving as the advisory dance teacher for the Inner London Education Authority. She was instrumental in the formation of the National Dance Teachers Association, taking an active interest in promoting and developing dance in schools throughout her career. She regularly writes for dance and arts journals and presents at conferences in the UK and abroad, serving on several dance, arts and education boards, panels, and working groups concerned with youth dance and dance in the curriculum.

Shu-hwa Jung (PhD) majored in drama at the University of Exeter, UK in 2008. Now, she is Associate Professor in the Graduate Institute of Arts and Humanities Education at Taipei

National University of the Arts. She has worked for professional theatre for nearly thirty years. In 1999, due to the education reform initiative, the government put performing arts into the national curriculum within the compulsory education system; since then, she has focused on the field of 'Applied Drama/Theatre', specifically on subjects such as, 'Drama in Education', 'Theatre in Education', 'Community and the Sociology of Arts', 'Community Theatre' and the development of youth theatre in Taiwan.

India Lennerth has extensive experience as a performer and has both danced in independent contemporary works and been employed as a commercial dancer. She has worked in schools across South Australia directing productions, performances and school dance programs. In 2011 she completed a Master's in Teaching. She has worked as a tutor for Restless Dance Theatre across many of their workshop programmes, including Growth Spurt, Leaps and Bounds, SCOSA, Dot to Dot, Links and Youth Ensemble.

Kate Marsh Following a career as a dance artist and teacher, she has worked in a variety of settings both in the UK and internationally, including with Candoco Dance Company. In 2009 she completed a Master's in Dance by Independent Study at De Montfort University (Improvisation and Widening Participation in Dance). This sparked an interest in dance research and she is now undertaking a full-time PhD studentship at Coventry University researching leadership in relation to dancers with disabilities. She is also currently touring a duet with dance artist Welly O'Brien, titled *Famuli*.

David Mead (PhD) is a British freelance dance practitioner and writer. He teaches and choreographs regularly at universities and schools in Taiwan and the UK, including the Chinese Culture University, Taipei, and the pre-professional dance department at the city's Shuang Yuan Junior High School. He has an MA in Ballet Studies from Roehampton University and a PhD in Dance Studies from the University of Surrey, where he researched creativity in dance education, focusing on the Cloud Gate Dance School in Taiwan. He is a critic and writer for *Dancing Times*, contributor to other international publications and editor of *SeeingDance.com*.

Lesley Ovenden (née Hogg) completed her MA in Dance Studies at the University of Surrey, England. Her dissertation is titled 'Dance for Dyspraxic Children: An Investigation into the Potential for Dance Tuition to Improve the Abilities of Dyspraxic Children.' Her case study focused on the Special Needs Dance Project of the Royal Academy of Dance in London, where she trained as a ballet teacher and gained the Licentiate of the Royal Academy of Dance. Her research focuses on the empowerment of dancers with (dis)abilities. She is the New Zealand representative of daCi.

Tone Pernille Østern (PhD) is a dance artist/choreographer and Professor in Arts Education with a focus on dance at the Programme for Teacher Education, Norwegian University of Science and Technology. Her 2009 PhD in dance art is from the Theatre Academy at the University of the Arts Helsinki, Finland. Since 2010 she has been Head of the Department for Arts, Media and Sports Teaching and Learning at the Programme for Teacher Education, and she is the leader of a Master's degree in arts education.

Jackie Prada has assisted with (since 2004), and, following the completion of a Bachelor of Arts in Therapeutic Recreation in 2011, administrated and choreographed, adapted and integrated dance programs at the Carousel Dance Centre. She was involved in the development and creation of the integrated dance company at Carousel and has taught dance as part of a university course at Arts Express, an integrated arts camp. She was part of the most recent daCi conferences in Taipei and Copenhagen, where she explored ideas related to the provision of integrated performance opportunities and programme options for persons with disabilities.

Emma Redding (MSc, PhD) is Head of Dance Science at Trinity Laban Conservatoire of Music and Dance, London, UK. She trained as a dancer and has performed professionally for a number of contemporary dance companies such as the Hungarian based company Tranz Danz and for Rosalind Newman's DanceHKNY in Hong Kong. Her research interests include training methodologies, injury incidence and prevention, developing interdisciplinary screening programmes, pedagogical considerations in technique class, and the physiological requirements of training and performance. She has published in journals such as *Journal of Dance Medicine and Science*, *Journal of Strength and Conditioning Research* and *Social Behaviour and Personality*, and is past-President and a member of the Board of Directors of the International Association for Dance Medicine & Science (IADMS).

Nicole Reinders is a PhD candidate in the Department of Kinesiology and Physical Education at Wilfrid Laurier University, Canada. Her primary research interest is exploring the effects of recreational dance programmes for special populations, including young adults with Down's Syndrome and children with Autism Spectrum Disorder. She has been a dancer and dance instructor for most of her life and hopes that her research will help to make recreational dance classes more accessible to people with special needs.

Carolyn Russell-Smith is a Jamaican dance educator, consultant, founder and Artistic Director of Khulcha Theatre School of Dance and Khulcha Dance Company. She is Jamaica's national representative for daCi, a member of the Jamaica Association of Dance and Drama Educators (JADDE), member of CID, the National Dance Council for UNESCO, and a pioneer member of the Caribbean Examination Council's (CXC) Theatre Arts (Dance) examination. Awards include the Manchester's Heroes Day Award for Culture in 2005 and Rotary Club of Mandeville's award for community involvement in 2013. She is a graduate of Edna Manley College and past student of the Laban Centre, Goldsmiths College, University of London.

Michelle Ryan joined Meryl Tankard in Canberra and Adelaide as part of Meryl Tankard's Australian Dance Theatre where she was a performer for over seven years, followed by projects in Europe as Tankard's assistant. On returning to Australia, she was a founding member of Splintergroup and worked at Dancenorth for five years in various capacities. Appointed Artist Director of Restless Dance Theatre in 2013, she has created two works for the company. She worked on the film *Michelle's Story*, directed by Meryl Tankard, which premiered at the 2015 Adelaide Film Festival and won the People's Choice Award for Best Short Film, screening on national television in March 2016. She was inducted into the South Australian Women's Honour Roll in 2015.

Gerard M. Samuel (PhD) is currently Director in the School of Dance, University of Cape Town; Editor of the *South African Dance Journal*; and Chair of *Confluences* – an international dance conference based at UCT. He was a dancer at NAPAC Ballet Company and the Playhouse Dance Company during Apartheid. He held senior management posts for the Playhouse Company until 2006. His notable choreographies include *Prabhati* and *The Man I Love*.... He has also produced *Place of Grace*, a dance film. He is an advocate of disability arts in South Africa and in Copenhagen with his LeftfeetFIRST Dance Theatre. He recently completed his PhD researching 'Othering in Contemporary Dance in South Africa.'

Urmimala Sarkar Munsi (PhD) is an Associate Professor of Theatre and Performance Studies at the School of Arts and Aesthetics at Jawaharlal Nehru University, New Delhi, India. She is the vice president and the co-chair of the Research and Documentation Network of the World Dance Alliance – Asia Pacific. Her current research focuses on marginalization and living traditions, politics of performance, gender and dance, and performance as research (PaR). She is the Co-Editor of the peer-reviewed web journal JEDS (*Journal for Emerging Dance Research*).

Barbara Snook (PhD) is a professional teaching fellow and professional research fellow at the University of Auckland. She is currently engaged in researching the use of an arts-rich pedagogy in primary school classrooms. She was the Caroline Plummer Fellow in Community Dance at the University of Otago in 2008. She is a successful author of dance textbooks widely used in Australia and New Zealand and was the recipient of an Osmotherly Award for services towards the development of dance education in Queensland Australia in 2007. Her early career was as a high school teacher of drama and dance.

Sachiko Soro is a composer and choreographer with Fiji's internationally renowned independent dance company VOU. After completing a Bachelor of Music in Composition and a Bachelor of Performing Arts in Dance at the University of Auckland she returned home to Fiji to continue her passion and spread the magic of music and dance from the Pacific across the globe.

Kym Stevens is a Lecturer in Dance Education at the Queensland University of Technology and has worked as a dance teacher artist in both NSW and QLD, in primary and secondary schools, and continues to develop arts implementation strategies in QLD schools. In 2016 she was involved in the *Counterworld* community dance project, a youth dance work involving 140 dancers from across the Sunshine Coast in Queensland, Australia. Her research areas include dance curriculum implementation, arts teacher training pedagogies, cultural dance education teaching approaches and the development of creative skills for the twenty-first century.

Cheryl Stock (PhD, AM) has enjoyed a forty-year career as dancer, choreographer, director, educator, researcher and advocate. She is a past Secretary General of World Dance Alliance and Adjunct Professor in the Creative Industries Faculty, Queensland University of Technology, where she was previously Head of Dance and Director of Postgraduate Studies. Artistic Advisor and Founding Director of Dancenorth, she has created over fifty dance works and undertaken twenty collaborative exchanges in Asia. Her publications/practice encompass interdisciplinary, site-specific performance, contemporary Australian and Asian dance, and practice-led research. She has been honoured with an Order of Australia and a Lifetime Achievement Australian Dance Award.

Charlotte Svendler Nielsen (PhD) is Associate Professor and Head of Educational Studies at the Department of Nutrition, Exercise and Sports, research cluster 'Embodiment, Learning and Social Change,' University of Copenhagen, Denmark. She is Co-Editor of *Dance Education around the World: Perspectives on Dance, Young People and Change* (Routledge, 2015) and Coordinator of the Danish part of the European Observatory of Arts and Cultural Education linked to UNESCO. In her research in primary and secondary schools, the question of inclusion/exclusion and the different needs and experiences of children and young people (physical, cultural, social, personal) are always in focus in relation to exploring their possibilities for learning.

Luciana Veiga has studied arts since 1979. She has taught dance in different variations throughout her career; as a teacher of classical dance since 1994 in private schools, as an educator for the Mesquita Education Department (Brazil) from 2011 and as a teacher in the Special Education School for teens and adults since 2014, amongst other posts.

Madalena Victorino is a Portuguese choreographer, teacher and arts project developer. She graduated variously in Contemporary Dance, Composition, Choreography and Pedagogy of the Arts from: the Place, London School of Contemporary Dance; the Laban Centre, Goldsmiths College, University of London; and from Exeter University. Based in Lisbon, over the last three decades she has created a unique arts practice evidenced by the creation of many cultural and artistic projects with a community focus that involves discourse between professional artistic practice and society in general, throughout the country.

Sarah Whatley (PhD) is Professor of Dance and Director of the Centre for Dance Research (C-DaRE) at Coventry University. Her research interests include dance and new technologies, dance analysis, somatic dance practice and pedagogy, and inclusive dance practices; she has published widely on these themes. The AHRC, the Leverhulme Trust and the European Union fund her current research, which is broadly focused on the impact of digital technologies on cultural heritage, and dance and disability. She is also Editor of the *Journal of Dance and Somatic Practices* and sits on the editorial boards of several other journals.

INTRODUCTION

Stephanie Burridge and Charlotte Svendler Nielsen

Sharing the space to dance, to imagine, to make friends, to work together, to put on a show or simply enjoy the moment. The journeys of dance in this book are diverse. Differently abled bodies create new movement vocabularies and pedagogical dialogues with their teachers, choreographers and fellow dancers. These conversations embody a diversity of narratives, contexts and cultures that are revealed through experiencing dance and journeying from empathy to empowerment. These journeys are not experienced alone. Parents, carers, teachers, artists, families and friends work alongside NGOs, government departments and policy makers, all inching towards an equitable future where access to and inclusion in artistic and cultural practice, according to the United Nations Convention of the Child (2006),[1] is a basic human right. Others are on a collision course where discrimination and historical and cultural prejudices impede and restrict the creative potential of the expressive body and different lived experiences. The 2006 UNESCO Road Map for Arts Education strives to highlight the importance for all young people of the world of gaining *access* to the practice of the arts, including dance, in formal and informal educational settings, for their overall education as human beings, but also for the vast potential of the arts to contribute to resolving social and cultural challenges. The 2006 objectives include learner-centered approaches ensuring relevance, promoting universal values and equity in terms of access and outcomes, social inclusion and individual rights. Students' lives, aspirations and interests, as well as those of their families and societies, should be recognised and respected. Central to the significance and importance of the arts is the tenet to empower young people with the locally germane abilities required for them to function successfully in their society and culture. To fulfill this quest there is a need for trained and motivated artists and teachers in dance education.

Based on these general principles, we have selected contributions as examples of practice and research in the field of dance education which give insights into, and question how, to foster quality education in dance for young people with a diversity of needs. The sections feature: inclusive dance pedagogy; equality, advocacy and policy; changing practice for dance education; community dance initiatives; and professional integrated collaborations. Inherent values, advocacy, pedagogy beyond technique, diversity, participation, new spaces for creativity, partnerships, self-realisation and creating body-mind connections are some of the fields explored in the book.

Nomenclature and the scope of the field are contested throughout the world and in this text the terminologies that education departments, governments and organisations use to define it include dance for special needs, the disabled, differently abled bodies, inclusive dance and more. The spectrum for discussion in these areas has been considerably widened in this volume to include examples of dance programmes and projects for young people in crisis, migrant students and those in isolated communities. Access and inclusion is increasingly the essence of projects for disenfranchised and traumatised youth who find creative expression, freedom and hope through dance.

International agencies and NGOs contribute to efforts in Cambodia for instance, while private dance schools from Australia to Indonesia, Canada to the UK, and from Jamaica to India are committed to the transformative power of dance to affect lives and make change. The arts have a crucial role in empowering young people with special needs through such diverse dance initiatives. Inclusive pedagogy that integrates all students in rich, equitable dance programmes within education frameworks are occurring alongside enabling projects by community groups and in the professional dance world where many choreographers actively seek opportunities to work across diversity to inspire creativity, contribute to positive experiences and enrich the lives of a broad range of dancers. Established companies like the UK's world-renowned Candoco Dance Company and Restless Dance Theatre in Australia are integral to the story, alongside powerful creative practices led by artists working in Fiji, Japan, Malaysia, Norway, Portugal and Singapore, for example.

Education is the key to changing mindsets and enabling access to, and inclusion in, dance practice across all schools and communities. This book includes chapters from advocates and game-changers in the field who have spent decades pushing the agenda for opportunities for young dancers with special needs. They have inspired changes across the globe as evidenced in new education practices and policies in, for example, Australia, Canada, Denmark, Finland, New Zealand, Norway, Singapore, South Africa, Spain, Taiwan and the United States. Individual efforts by teachers with belief and passion to engage students and implement changes towards inclusivity in communities in Brazil, Jamaica, Japan, Malaysia, Papua New Guinea and Timor-Leste, among others, are recounted in the chapters and narratives.

A rich aspect of this collection of writing is the emergence of a diversity of approaches to pedagogy, logistics and negotiations across cultures. Respecting cultural differences in practice, teaching and learning can open up international conversations and embrace new ways of working as we learn from each other and expand the possibilities for young people through dance. Some of the writers seek to move beyond recreation and socialisation – to give professional training and performance opportunities for differently abled dancers. All dancers strive to achieve, improve, perfect and challenge themselves either in a tertiary dance training course, or community or school group. Best practice may require adapting a range of learning paces and abilities in an inclusive dance class of diverse participants rather than prejudging and categorising dancers in an assumption of what they can do – not all disabilities are immediately obvious and pedagogy should make adjustments to benefit all. Surprises are in store as the shared learning journey begins.

The chapter authors base their work on different theoretical perspectives approaching issues of dance and special needs through extensive research. Case narratives are situated within diverse social frameworks and often represent a specific cultural perspective.

Some recount projects and activities while others take a broader perspective – a common thread to all contributions the book is that they explore change, processes and transformations that come about in the lives of young people through dance.

PHOTO Stephanie Burridge   **PHOTO** Charlotte Svendler Nielsen

Note

1   Available at https://www.un.org/development/desa/disabilities/resources/general-assembly/convention-on-the-rights-of-persons-with-disabilities-ares61106.html [Accessed 28 November 2016].

PART I
Inclusive dance pedagogy

PHOTO The Dance Laboratory (Norway)
Dancer: Mari Flønes
Choreographer: Tone Penille Østern
Photographer: Jøran Værdahl

1.1

MAKING NO DIFFERENCE

Inclusive dance pedagogy

Sarah Whatley and Kate Marsh

Introduction

This chapter discusses how developing a range of pedagogical strategies ensures that dancers of all abilities can access dance in further and higher education, as a preparation for a professional career in dance. Beginning with an overview of some of the factors that have shaped an inclusive dance pedagogy, and a discussion on the terminology that has supported or inhibited inclusion, the chapter will describe actions for best practice within the dance studio, where dancers with and without disabilities can lead, learn and develop together. We will examine the merits of adaptation and translation, and outline the principles behind a range of teaching methods illustrated through examples of activities. Evaluative commentary will discuss the effectiveness or otherwise of these approaches in removing perceived barriers to participation for those with different abilities. We argue that rethinking and adjusting teaching and learning methods to accommodate differently abled dancers results in better experiences for all dancers, calling for a radical pedagogy that promotes equal access to dance as a route into professional practice.

Access and inclusion

Accessing a training course in dance at a further or higher education level is always more challenging for dancers with disabilities. These challenges result from perceptions that are held by all involved in the individual student's journey: the educational institution and teaching faculty, career advisers, family and friends, and the student him- or herself. It is perhaps surprising that in the twenty-first century there is still some way to go before barriers to participation are dissolved and our dance training programmes are fully accessible to talented and motivated students. Many dance curricula do not overtly discriminate against the differently abled dancer but that does not always mean that the curriculum is accessible, appropriate and inviting to those students who may perceive themselves to be discriminated against. Moreover, there continues to be anxiety amongst many who design and teach courses in dance about how to accommodate and support disabled students.

The common perceptions of who can and should be able to access dance training need changing if disabled students are to feel able to apply for courses, can learn in an inclusive environment and can be role models for others to follow. The prejudices that still lurk, often unspoken, in the dance studio and are re-inscribed in the 'perfected' dancing body in the name of 'excellence' and 'quality', and which persist through an aesthetic of similarity coupled with flawlessness, grace and elegance, do no service to any dancer, disabled or non-disabled, and neither do they move the art form forwards. There are dance artists who challenge this very successfully in their work. Catherine Long, for example, in *Impasse* (2014) consciously explored an aesthetic of awkwardness and the 'monstrous', which set out to challenge the fear of loss, of not being 'whole' that is associated with disabled dance.[1] But Long's work is not yet penetrating the institutions that preserve a dominant dance aesthetic that is blind to diverse dancing bodies. Long demonstrates that every dancer has the potential to develop a unique virtuosity worthy of value and praise. Moreover, differently abled dancers show how no bodies are static; we are all unique and all in transition, gaining and losing functions, and capacity for movement. An aesthetic grounded in inclusion would facilitate the shift that has been called for in the "discourses of legitimacy" (that still marginalise the bodies and artistic contributions of disabled dancers) (Irving & Giles, 2011).

Building a diverse student community in a dance training environment requires a strong inclusive ethos but the emphasis on dancers developing a virtuosic technique, predicated on a normative aesthetic, privileges some dancing bodies over others. The dance training environment can therefore fuel 'ableism' and 'disablism', whereby 'ableism' is associated with the perfect body, designating disabled people as inferior to non-disabled people, reinforcing bias and discrimination, and which a radical approach to teaching dance tries to resist. However, there are unavoidable realisms to this resistance. Students with any physical, sensory or cognitive impairment are frequently in a tiny minority within a dance programme. Often, if the only student in a cohort of non-disabled students, in a context that is traditionally built upon homogeneity of body types rather than heterogeneity, a student who is differently abled is hypervisible. Moreover, non-disabled students are usually unfamiliar with the experience of dancing alongside and working with students with disabilities so careful orientation and induction is needed for all students, particularly if the disabled student needs assistive technologies in the studio, such as wheelchairs or seeing dogs, etc. Another challenge lies in the indivisibility of the dancer's body from the dance, presenting something of a paradox. If the dancer's disability is visible then disability is once again made hypervisible; disability becomes performative and hence the familiar condition of the disabled person always 'performing' their disability (Garland Thomson, 2009). Conversely, if the disability is unseen, then the dancer may find herself treated no differently than any other non-disabled students. Whilst full integration may be desirable the absence of any appropriate adaptation or mitigation may present different problems.

Rethinking the teaching of dance 'technique'

Technical training continues to be a main strand of activity within a dance programme and this often calls for the dancer to work towards a 'neutral' body – stripping away prior learning and privileging the natural, which tends towards essentialising the normate dancing body. But assuming there is a neutral body is problematic and the disabled dancer with a unique body or impairment will find little relevance in a course of study that promotes the acquisition of a flawless and "multipurpose hired body [that] subsumes and smooths over differences" (Foster, 1997: 256). The dancer will also need to find an individual approach to technical development and may come with little or no prior learning on which to draw whereas most non-disabled students come from an experience of mainstream education and with prior experience of what it means to learn in a dance context – the format of class, the etiquette, behaviour, etc. – so there is already an imbalance in the studio, the primary learning space for the dancer. Consequently, including students with disabilities takes time, resources, willingness and systems in place (such as Learning Support Assistants [LSAs]) to provide the right level of support for each student. If an LSA is to provide support then it works best if it begins from induction onwards, wherein all students learn the value of partnering and peer support and students with any impairments are given space to speak to their peers about their disability and their needs, if appropriate, including any 'rules' around a seeing dog or other aid in and around class. Importantly, by working together as creative collaborators throughout their studies, the interest in bodily difference as an exotic spectacle (Mitchell & Snyder, 2006: 157) is diminished.

Building an inclusive learning experience is therefore dependent on the employment of particular teaching strategies to accommodate the different physicalities and abilities of the students. But despite what is inscribed in law, specifically the 2001 Special Educational Needs and Disability Act, that education providers have a duty not to treat disabled students less favourably and a duty to make reasonable adjustments to ensure that people who are disabled are not put at a substantial disadvantage compared to people who are not disabled, there remain barriers for disabled dancers entering training programmes, sometimes due to reluctance on the part of the institution to make the necessary adaptations and adjustments.

Where teaching, learning and assessment methods have been considered and perhaps adjusted to ensure compliance, tutors have recognised that changes that are made for the disabled students are frequently positive for all students. An accessible dance curriculum is about good course design, good teaching and assessment methods and a student-centred approach to all aspects of course delivery.

Thus far, we have referred to 'inclusive' or 'integrated' dance as descriptive 'labels', and 'translation' and 'adaptation' as teaching strategies. These terms are often contested, as are the wider labels and categories that persist within the discourse on dance and disability. Indeed, the language used to describe, discuss and represent disability has a history of dividing opinion. The etymology of key words and phrases associated with impairment gives an insight into shifting perceptions of disability over periods of history. The term 'Handicapped', widely rejected in current UK discourse, holds negative connotations and has been rejected, in particular, by individuals and organisations championing the rights of people with disabilities. A brief inspection of the history of this term indicates that it is synonymous with themes of burden or carrying extra 'weight'.[2] 'Inclusion' is a label that often defines a mode of working, viewing and interaction, but which is not always helpful to those involved. But both 'inclusive' and 'integrated' are terms frequently used within the professional dance context to signal where disabled people work alongside non-disabled people. Inclusion as a mode of working and thinking can be implicit in the dancers' working environment. Working methods can vary widely but at the core is an interest in exploring both common ground and individual difference. Set within a broader context of an inclusive ethos, the label 'inclusive' thus suggests a relational aesthetic, which can be empowering (feeling part of an inclusive 'movement') or it might limit judgment and openness to what is being viewed. Inclusion is therefore a fluid term that benefits from continual questioning so that the terms 'inclusion' and 'inclusive practice' are used or applied thoughtfully and knowingly, acknowledging the situatedness of the term and its implications. An inclusive label also avoids any erasure of or making invisible disability but may draw attention to disability rather than emphasising the *dance*. Related to the label 'inclusive' is the real distinction between disability and impairment, which points again to the complexities of terminology. Consequently, there is considerable debate about the positive and negative aspects of these terms but as they continue to be in common circulation within the sector they are terms used to point to the fundamental philosophy of equal participation.

Disability versus impairment

It is generally acknowledged, following the social model of disability (Finkelstein, 1993)[3] that disabled dancers are dancers with impairments who are (more accurately) disabled by the environment and structures in which they live, so 'disabled dancers' is somewhat unhelpful; it promotes the objectification of a group of people and reinforces the categorisation of disabled people as 'other'. The term non-disabled refers to the artists who have not disclosed any disability but it can imply a binary between one group and another. Dancers with disabilities sometimes choose to describe themselves as 'differently abled', but any label is contingent, imprecise and can infer allegiance with an objectification of a group of people. Whilst care with language is important, some dancers will feel proud of a disability label. The term can offer a sense of belonging to a wider community, which can be empowering; a community which finds form within the dance sector as well as within the wider context. The unpacking of terminology and its associated meaning and interpretation has been and continues to be central to the rights and voices of people with a disability or impairment.

There is also a valid discussion to be had around 'disabled' versus 'impaired'. Mike Oliver offers a useful definition of impairment as "individual limitation" and disability as "socially imposed restriction" (1993: 17). Even within these definitions there seems to be a potential further discussion around the terms 'limitation' and 'restriction'; the point here is that the debate is key. Historically individuals with impairment were relatively passive in the language used to talk about their own bodies and terminology originated from medical definitions of impairment. Argument over terminology, critical discourse from a range of communities, disabled and non-disabled, activists and policy makers, can only put a greater focus on the voices of people with disabilities. But fear of saying the 'wrong' word can lead people to say nothing, which stifles debate, halts progression, and leads to assumptions and polite skirting around the issues. Probably the most effective means for progression and shifting perceptions is to communicate about disability.

Adaptation or translation?

Adaptation and translation as descriptive terms or procedures raise additional questions. Translation is more often seen as positive, each dancer responding to and translating tasks and information to suit their own individual physicality, in order to achieve an equal outcome. The task, exercise or sequence is offered as a way of developing particular mechanical, creative or interpretive skills, not as a copying, mimicking or imitation exercise. But adaptation implies that there is an optimum way of performing a task and any dancer with a different body will need to adapt it to his/her own body, reinforcing the difference and implication of 'other', which can be equated with a lack, or deficit, when compared with the 'original' performed by the 'whole' dancing body. Good teaching will enable each dancer, disabled and non-disabled, to work to push their own limits and to develop a technically secure and expressive body, avoiding any hierarchical privileging of one body over another.

Communication, verbal and non-verbal, is thus core to promoting a non-discriminatory learning environment. Too often, a dancer with an impairment is left to find his or her own adaptations in a class or workshop, maybe because the language used to talk about impaired bodies feels like such a controversial area. The body in this instance is frequently not referred to at all. But talking about each individual body in dance makes clear that there is no 'one size fits all'. Speaking about different bodies sometimes means getting it 'wrong' or being corrected, but will acknowledge the essential choice of the individual to decide the language of her own body and her experiences.

Pedagogical strategies

In a dance teaching context, we propose that disability should make no difference, or at least difference should be celebrated rather than erased. Encouraging all participants to approach their dance training in a curious and questioning way ensures that there is open dialogue about the purpose of each component of their training. The dance 'technique' class is probably where most doubts are raised about the way in which dancers with impairments can gain an equal experience. Partly due to resources and class sizes, an individualised experience for each student is unrealistic but with planning and preparation each participant can work towards their own goals. Technique is an important resource for the dancer but is not inherently dependent on moving a specific body part or making a specific shape in space or moving in a specific direction that presupposes that all dancers possess (for example) the same physicality, or the same sensory engagement with the space around them and with other dancers. Technical proficiency can be developed through a variety of tasks that may diverge from traditional programmes and teaching syllabi that have been developed often to serve the needs of a particular individual dancer or group of dancers, but which over time have become generalised and in turn, have tended to develop dancers who aspire towards a generalised technically proficient body (the *corps de ballet* model[4]). Individual difference and the natural idiosyncrasies of every dancer's body are thus neutralised, as noted earlier. The value of translation for every dancer is diminished, replaced by a desire for similarity and uniformity. The challenge is thus to develop strategies that enable dancers to dance with their whole body, however it moves and with attention given to the reality of the individual body *as it is*. Students are thus encouraged to develop their technique and creative ability as appropriate for their own abilities. Students are not learning to dance *despite* their disability. Technique should therefore be predicated on bodies moving how real bodies move rather than adapting to a normative model of the dancing body.

Traditional approaches to technique can be changed in a positive way by a group of dancers with different physicalities or sensory impairments. But changes can raise questions about the veracity of the technical training. Jurg Koch has developed a system that offers an alternative to the traditional technique class for classes where there are students with different abilities. His *Universal Design of Instruction* model has been developed through his work with Candoco Dance Company and through teaching in higher education, mostly in the United States. Rather than taking an approach whereby movement is adapted to suit individual dancers, his approach allows all class participants to work with the same principles, using them in a way that is specific to their own needs and which allows them to push themselves. The approach is designed for application in any context, providing dance skills for students and a clear set of assessment criteria for tutors. As Koch outlines: "It is in this way that disability and disabled students become a part of the full spectrum of diversity in our dance studios, our universities and our societies, rather than being isolated as an 'issue' or group to be taught outside the 'regular' curriculum."[5]

The model is a valuable example of how to equalise the class, enabling each dancer to find their own response to tasks rather than beginning with an established class content, which is then adapted for dancers with different physicalities. There is no 'standard' way of performing a task which each dancer aspires to assimilate, with those unable to physically reproduce the same movement left to adapt the task to their own body and ability. It offers a way of integrating students of all abilities. The model is dependent on Koch's own insight into this method and may not transfer so easily to other tutors with less experience of different dancing bodies. When the starting point is a desire to achieve technical excellence tutors may need support in how to adopt and adapt this approach to meet the needs of different training contexts.

Discussing needs and assessing the appropriate level of support is key; each student is likely to have a different need so support is organised on an individual basis. An experienced supporter will work sensitively with the student to provide the appropriate level of intervention and mediation whilst showing awareness of the other students in class. Those with dance experience provide the most effective support but ground rules are important to encourage independence so the student retains agency and control whilst learning to work with a partner in class. The LSA can become a signifier of dependency, inadvertently reinforcing the student's experience of being overwhelmed by the weight of managed support, which can inhibit and infantilise the student (particularly where it upholds the binary of 'normal' supporter and 'non-conforming' disabled student).[6]

Importantly, a careful assessment of the student's range of movement potential is useful to ensure that the student is appropriately challenged throughout the programme. Ideally this is a process that is undertaken by a physiotherapist or other trained body worker but with great care to ensure that the process is non-judgemental, avoids labelling disability as pathology and is designed to facilitate an open exchange between all those involved. Tutors often tend to avoid making physical demands on disabled students in class, which can lead to students finding the work unchallenging, resulting in complacency or a tendency for the student to be reluctant to work beyond what feels 'comfortable'. Students, tutors and LSAs all benefit from a clear knowledge about what the student can move on his/her own, what parts of the body can bear weight, what can support weight and where a student experiences genuine physical limitations (Whatley, 2013: 8–9).

Teaching dance – a radical pedagogy?

Nothing in what constitutes good teaching could be considered radical on its own terms but what is radical is that the changes that are necessitated by including students with disabilities in mainstream dance teaching are changes that benefit all students, disabled and non-disabled. Good teaching practice involves thinking about how to describe movement and avoiding the tendency towards ocularcentrism, which can disable a student with a sensory impairment. Words related to sight as synonyms for words equating to knowledge can be disabling, like phrases such as 'Gaining an insight into' and 'Do you see what I mean?' As an experiential art form, the visual bias in language can be less than useful for dancers, particularly those with visual impairment.

Rather than asking students to 'open their eyes' the students can be asked to 'open the senses' and 'be aware of the room'. The use of 'hands on', combined with verbal cueing, can communicate more effectively movement principles and set sequences. Equally, the student can use hands to track body design and LSAs can take on the role of guide to support students as they move through and in space. The idea of witnessing another dancer moving does not have to rely primarily on the sense of sight. Other strategies might be used such as 'orientating' whereby the visually impaired student takes a guided walk around and in the space before beginning class to locate exits and notable landmarks. For wheelchair users, asking dancers to work on 'vertical release' rather than 'standing release' clarifies what is being asked of the students and allows for those dancing in wheelchairs to engage with this activity through the 'sitting bones'. Minor translations of set material can be made to reduce the challenge of elevation and changes of direction as another version of a sequence. By making 'translation' a normal part of the learning process, so all students learn to translate, dancers with disabilities are not expected to respond any differently to a task. For example, the class could be guided through a movement task or sequence, following clear anatomical descriptions (thus allowing for individual variation) and then asked to translate the phrase by taking it onto the knees, or to sitting, or without sight or by altering the spatial or dynamic structures. The task of translation is thus a challenge for all students, not only those with a non-normative body or sensory impairment. It removes any assumption that a student is dancing *despite* a disability and the tendency to regard the student with a disability as either a hero (overcoming a disability) or a victim of disability. All students are thus encouraged to dance with the whole body however it moves, noticing the body *as it is* and not in comparison with an imagined normative body.

Conclusions and looking to the future

The image of the 'normative' body is ingrained in our understanding of being human. It is an image that is presented to us through many channels throughout our lives; education, employment, the media – representations of difference in these contexts are largely from a position of segregation. We live in a world where the 'normal' body rules. We are 'accepting' of difference, charitable even, but there is still an underlying narrative of curiosity and freakishness relating to the 'different' body.

On the subject of the narrative of different bodies, Rosemarie Garland-Thomson suggests that "Conservative shapes make conservative stories. Extraordinary shapes require extraordinary stories" (2009: 167). There seems to be a fascination with difference; we question how difference occurs, captivated by stories of difference. Whether through 'tragedy' or 'fate' we want to know the story behind the difference. By staring and asking questions the different body becomes spectacle and somehow unreal. Being confronted with difference highlights the fragility of 'normality'. In a desire to conform and 'fit in' we disassociate our 'normal' selves from the differentness of others.

Difference is a marker of impairment, it is a characteristic of the disabled person – in medical terms impairment is often referred to as an anomaly, something to be fixed or normalised. This legacy of being perceived or labelled as different has informed the experience of impairment. But being different makes us who we are. Education has a key role in addressing how we deal with and accept difference, without making difference normal. In our embodied experience of life we are both of these opposing terms at any time and in any context. Ironically, the emphasis on physical intelligence developed through dance should ensure that dancers are most attuned to physical difference. Consequently, dance education is the ideal site for foregrounding these issues and for disturbing 'the ground on which the dominant history of mainstream dance has been developed' (Smith, 2005: 76).

Traditional class structures are generally built upon a presumption of a non-disabled, non-impaired dancing body, so assumed structures may need to be reconsidered. For example, not all students will take the same time to prepare for studio-based work, warm-up time may need to be adjusted and additional time taken prior to the session to change clothing or wheelchair or other mechanical aid. 'Crip time' (Kuppers, 2014) means that time is different; providing an equal amount of preparation time can result in an unequal experience. Class structures can therefore be modified whilst continuing to include familiar activities including demonstration, translation (to focus on the anatomical purpose of the exercise or phrase rather than attempting to reproduce the same visual form), repetition (where appropriate, encouraging students to notice and avoid the tendency to work submaximally and too comfortably) and variation (to open up new possibilities, whilst retaining the sense of common purpose in class) (Whatley, 2007: 12-13).[7] Working in partnership with other students and not always the LSA is important for the student to discover more about her own movement range, whilst not attempting to emulate or replicate the movement of their non-disabled partner. The value of observation is important in recognising habits and areas of weakness.

Communication between everyone within the learning environment can clarify working conditions but attempting to normalise the experience for the disabled dancer can mean inadvertently overlooking the needs of the non-disabled dancers. Adjustments are as necessary for the non-disabled learners as for those with disabilities.

Admission tutors and teaching faculty may also require training. With more awareness, the work of disabled dancers and the politics of disability in dance will feature more within the broader dance curricula so that students are familiar with the discourse of disability and can debate the problematics of labels, discriminatory practices and aesthetic prejudices. Education will enable dancers to have a political voice; disability should not be seen to be something to be overcome, to be hidden or disguised through performance. Collectively, disabled dancers would then be empowered to challenge the "history of the dominant western theatre dance tradition [which] has reflected a particularly pervasive social coding of the body that enforces a corporeal hierarchy serving to invalidate differentiated, heterogeneous, and physically impaired bodies" (Smith, 2005: 76).

For all of us directly involved in the management, design and teaching of dance, a useful reminder comes from Phelan who observes that "consciousness of disability awakens us from our untested beliefs in embodiment: disability consciousness transforms one's worldview because it reorders the invisible and visible frames that illuminate our worlds" (Phelan, 2005: 324). Eventually, inclusion will become the norm based on a post-disability culture in which disability is no longer always seen as reductive but promotes a poetics of disability.

Notes

1   *Impasse* was a reformulation of the solo *Stalemate* originally choreographed and performed by Doran George in 2009. George and Long described how *Impasse* explores performative and theoretical implications of how bodies generally, and they themselves specifically, are configured differently

within ideas of dis/ability. See http://www.ugeducation.ucla.edu/uei/docs/dsminor/Catherine%20 Long%20Poster.pdf

2   There is one school of thought suggesting that handicapped is derived from 'hand in cap' a description of 'cripples' begging. Another theory relates to the term handicapped as disadvantaged in some way (take the golfing metaphor for example). Whatever the definition, it is not a term promoting positivity and equality.

3   The social model of disability suggests that it is the organisation of society for able-bodied living that discriminates against disabled people (Finkelstein, 1993: 36).

4   The *corps de ballet* is a group of dancers who all dance in unison as a tight unified group, regarded as the lowest rank within the ballet company.

5   Jurg Koch has led many workshops that introduce his pedagogy base in the Universal Design model; see for example http://www.candoco.co.uk/event/professional-development-workshop-with-jurg-koch/ [Accessed April 2, 2017].

6   What is yet to be commonplace is a situation where more experienced disabled dancers contribute to the role of supporting disabled students.

7   For examples of dance exercises translated for different abilities, see Whatley (2007).

References

Finkelstein, V. (1993) 'The "social model of disability" and the disability movement'. Available at http://disability-studies.leeds.ac.uk/files/library/finkelstein-The-Social-Model-of-Disability-and-the-Disability-Movement.pdf [Accessed 16 May 2016].

Foster, S. (1997) 'Dancing bodies'. In J. Desmond (ed.), *Meaning in Motion: New Cultural Studies of Dance*. Durham & London: Duke University Press (pp. 235–258).

Garland-Thomson, R. (2009) *Staring – How We Look*. Oxford: Oxford University Press.

Irving, H. R. & A. R. Giles. (2011) 'A dance revolution? Responding to dominant discourses in contemporary integrated dance'. *Leisure/Loisir*, 35(4), (pp. 371–389).

Kuppers, P. (2014) 'Crip time'. *Tikkun*, 29(4). Available at http://tikkun.dukejournals.org/content/29/4.toc [Accessed May 16, 2016].

Mitchell, D. & S. Snyder. (2006) *Cultural Locations of Disability*. Chicago: University of Chicago Press.

Oliver, M. (1993) *Disabling Barriers – Enabling Environments*. London: SAGE Publications.

Phelan, P. (2005) 'Reconsidering identity politics, essentialism, and dismodernism'. In Sandahl, C. & P. Auslander (eds.), *Bodies in Commotion: Disability and Performance*. Ann Arbor: University of Michigan Press (pp. 319–326).

Smith, O. (2005) 'Shifting Apollo's frame – challenging the body aesthetic in theater dance'. In Sandahl, C. & P. Auslander (eds.), *Bodies in Commotion: Disability and Performance*. Ann Arbor: University of Michigan Press (pp. 73–85).

Whatley, S. (2007) 'Dance and disability: the dancer, the viewer and the presumption of difference'. *Research in Dance Education*, 8(1) (pp. 5–25).

Whatley, S. (2013) *Strategies for Inclusion in Dance: Disability, Performativity and Transition Into and Out of Higher Education*. VSA Kennedy Centre. Available at http://education.kennedycenter.org/education/vsa/resources/Whatley_Sarah_Strategies_for_inclusion_in_dance.pdf [Accessed April 2, 2017].

1.2

DEVELOPING INCLUSIVE DANCE PEDAGOGY

Dialogue, activism and aesthetic transformative learning

Tone Pernille Østern

In this chapter I discuss the aesthetic and pedagogical approach developed through the six-year-long (2003–09) artistic and art educational research and development project the Dance Laboratory[1] (Østern, 2009) in Trondheim, Norway. Today the Dance Laboratory is a performing community dance company with differently bodied dancers, with and without disabilities [Photo 1.2]. The artistic and pedagogical research journey, which included both determination and activism, that I undertook together with the group pushed me towards developing a spacious, dialogical, critical, transformative and inclusive dance pedagogy.

Meeting, wondering and bringing ideas along

The process that led me to the development of the Dance Laboratory, today a community dance company with differently bodied, adult dancers, started with my meeting with Candoco Dance Company[2] during my studies in the United Kingdom in the middle of the 1990s. At that time, the newly established Candoco Dance Company was Europe's first professional dance company to include dancers with and without disabilities. My meeting with their work made a huge impression on me, and from that meeting I took with me a wondering about what, how and for whom dance could be. Since then, this wondering has come to be the focal point around which my professional life as a dance artist, teacher and researcher has pivoted. Life brought me to Norway, where I have lived since 1999. Norway is a Nordic, socio-democratic, geographically long country with around 5 million inhabitants in total. Dance is a young art form in Norway, but as an art form dance in this country has experienced a rapid development from around the 1970s onwards. The idea of inviting dancers with and without disabilities into the world of contemporary dance was still new at the beginning of this millennium in Norway, and the Dance Laboratory was the first organisation of its kind in Norway. The Dance Laboratory, where I am no longer the artistic leader,[3] continues to be a space for wondering, investigating and discovering in dance. Based on my experiences from my research and development project, and my continuous work afterwards, I seek to draw various threads together and investigate and discuss the research question: 'What aesthetic and pedagogical aspects turn dance pedagogy into inclusive dance pedagogy?'

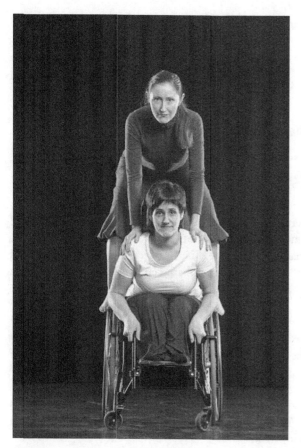

PHOTO 1.2 The Dance Laboratory
Dancers: Elen Øyen and Anne Marit Ligaard
Development of inclusive dance art and pedagogy class
Photographer: Jøran Wærdahl

Seeing beyond, world- and word-making

Seeing beyond in this context (which for me was/is a body-phenomenological endeavour) is about seeing beyond traditional and often tacit categorisations and ideas about dance and dancers. For an artist and dance teacher that means confronting ideas both 'inside' and 'out there' that are deeply rooted in dance worlds (and words), and in the surrounding society. Put simply, it is never enough to categorise people and know already who they are, how they are capable of dancing or choreographing, and how they will learn. On the contrary, the often tacit feeling that, for example, 'I know what a person in a wheelchair is like', should raise an internal alarm. This feeling of 'knowing already' is often rooted in conventional and disempowering assumptions about people using wheelchairs. People are bodies, but they are not body categories that hold fixed characteristics of how they are capable of moving, dancing, learning, creating and contributing. It seems very easy to make up categories based on the body (like male/female), but this means pushing people together in simplistic ways. Disability history tells that this is disempowering, devastating and dangerous (Benjamin, 2002; Sandahl & Auslander, 2005). In seeing each other as body categories, we continue creating dualistic dance worlds. In seeing beyond the worlds (and words) of categorisations, we have the possibility to create new dance worlds, more critical and inclusive language, and, eventually, more inclusive dance pedagogy.

The Dance Laboratory and the MultiPlié dance festival

In 1999 I moved to Trondheim in Norway, and in 2001 I, together with a dancer colleague[4] and the support of the municipality, set up a pilot project which would eventually lead to the Dance Laboratory. We called it 'Mixed Ability Project' and it attracted six participants, with and without disabilities. We worked in an improvisation-based manner for one semester, with me as the teacher-choreographer – a completely new experience for me. I found the semester exciting, challenging and thought-provoking and wondered if it was just me, or if the work had also been of special interest for the others. I asked the participants to send me their written evaluations. One of the young women with cerebral palsy and who used a wheelchair wrote:

> I am in a very good mood after each class. I feel that I have been able to show who I am. I also feel that I have been accepted as I am. It feels very good to be able to show who I am in a new way, in the dance. It is good that people get to know me through the dance.

This woman is Vera, who even now at the time of writing this article, fifteen years later, is a dancer at the Dance Laboratory. Another young, non-disabled amateur dancer (today a professional dance artist living in Oslo) wrote:

> The most important aspect is maybe that I have developed a conscious relationship to the fact that you don't need to be able-bodied to dance, not even to perform dance. I believe that the performance showed the audience that dance embraces a lot and that there are actually very few limits. In addition, I think that the performance expressed something about relationships between human beings.

This feedback which I received from the group was what finally prompted me to go on with the work and find out more, thereby leading to the PhD project and the start of the Dance Laboratory in 2003. That first autumn, there were only two participants (Vera and Anna, a non-disabled dancer working professionally with dance, both still in the Dance Laboratory) and it was difficult to recruit people to the project. The idea of combining dancers with and without disabilities seemed strange back then in the city, and as I ran around to cafés and other places to promote the new group there was little interest. Still, though not without difficulties, the group grew, and already by spring 2004 there were eight participants. Today the community dance company the Dance Laboratory has sixteen dancers, and a beginner's Dance Laboratory with twelve participants has also started up. I left as the artistic leader in 2012, but am in contact with the group in the role of researcher (and audience and friend).

Alongside the development of the community dance company, a new event called MultiPlié dance festival[5] grew, simply out of the need for somewhere to show our work. At that time, the established dance and theatre venues in this city were not very keen on opening up their stages to differently bodied dancers. Our first choreography with the pilot project in 2001 was shown on a cold and rainy afternoon in a basement in a closed school eight kilometres outside the city centre with, including me as the choreographer-teacher, eight people in the audience. In order to become visible, it was clear that we needed to develop our own performing venue. MultiPlié dance festival, first organised with an extremely small budget but with keen support from the municipality in 2004, is the festival that bends and stretches ideas about dance and dancers. Today, the biennale is Norway's third largest dance festival, arranged by the regional dance agency DansiT,[6] with a clear artistic view on challenging and expanding ideas about dance and dancers. It has hosted national and international dance artists oriented towards stretching and changing ideas about dance and dancers, like Philip Channells (Australia), Mickaël Philippeau (France), BewegGrund (Switzerland), Stopgap (UK) and Mia Habib (Norway).

Spacious, dialogical, transformative and inclusive dance pedagogy

I will now discuss aspects that work towards turning dance pedagogy into inclusive dance pedagogy, which are aesthetic and pedagogical (Figure 1.2). A pedagogical approach to dance teaching will be inseparably twinned with the same aesthetic approach to the movement material that is being produced. The aesthetics gives birth to the pedagogy, or vice versa (see Engelsrud, 2006). I present and discuss each of these aspects, together creating what I have experienced to be an inclusive approach to dance pedagogy.

Spacious teaching

Space is an important element in dance and, in dialogue with critical postmodern theories of space, I claim that inclusive dance pedagogy needs to be spacious. The critical postmodern human geographer Edward Soja (1996), in dialogue with critical sociologist Henri Lefebvre (1974/1991), proposed a model of thirdspace, which embraces the plurality of spatial understandings. Thirdspace offers a framework of addressing the complexity of contemporary social spatiality through the trialectics of perceived, lived and conceived space. The extension of spatial understanding that Soja offers is of interest when it comes to seeing beyond in dance, striving towards a more inclusive dance pedagogy. Perceived space is measurable and quantifiable spatial information. Lived space

FIGURE 1.2 Aesthetic-pedagogical aspects working towards the development of inclusive dance pedagogy

refers to how the space is directly lived through kinesthetic experiences. Conceived space is about how social reality is spatialised, and as Soja states, there is *no unspatialised social reality* (Soja, 1996: 46, original emphasis). The perspective of conceived space receives epistemological power, including when it comes to stretching dance pedagogy into inclusive dance pedagogy. McDowell (1999: 5, here in Munjee, 2014: 134) notes that, depending on personal history and social codes connected to class, gender and race (and, I add, ability), occupants of the same perceived space may live in very different 'places'. Translated to a dance situation: dancers with disabilities can have very different experience of, or access to, a 'traditional' dance space than (so called) non-disabled dancer bodies.

As I was analysing the 2004 video material from the Dance Laboratory, very slowly, and in dialogue with critical and postmodern theory about space, I managed to see how we, as dance teacher and dancers, moved not only in perceived space or lived space, but also in conceived space. As we were improvising, and as I was teaching in the beginning of the project, the teaching choices I made were influenced by tacit, social codes of 'helping' a person with a disability more than the non-disabled dancers, for example. I could see that I more often, and completely without awareness of it in the teaching situation, made more choices on behalf of the dancers with a disability than of the others. In that way, I also 'shrank' the space around them. I was reproducing the conceived space created around the dancers with a disability, instead of challenging it. I had to really make an effort, and it took me some years to see beyond, and allow myself to change, in dialogue with theory that created new perspectives. In that way, my teaching practice could also change, and I became a more inclusive dance teacher. I became aware that when teaching, I moved not only in a flat, perceived, physical space, but in a spacious space, which has both lived, cultural and political dimensions. Inclusive dance pedagogy is a spacious endeavour, and thereby also holds the potential to disturb, interrogate with, and protest against, the embedded social codes regarding dis/abilities in conceived space.

Valuing difference, meeting and dialoguing

Maybe the most important aspect in order to create truly inclusive – and challenging – dance pedagogy is to see difference among dancers as central and valuable, not additional. Difference is not an ingredient that can be put on top of an already existing dance activity, if the goal is to create inclusive dance art and pedagogy. Instead, the whole inclusive dance project needs to start from a genuine interest in difference and what that can give rise to in terms of aesthetic, artistic and pedagogical processes and products in a dance community comprising different individuals. The meeting between different dancers is essential for inclusive dance pedagogy to become truly inclusive. What the individual dancers in this dance community learn, they learn from the community, in dialogue with each other. The dancers learn in individual, and not categorical, ways. However, the individual dancers are deeply connected in their learning processes. They affect each other and as the individuals learn and change, so does the group. The learning processes taking place in the Dance Laboratory are dependent on every single individual who contributes to that community. Remove one, and the meaning potential changes (Østern, 2009: 271).

In connecting inclusive dance pedagogy to Hannah Arendt's (1958) philosophy of plurality, action and freedom, the political aspects and the activism connected to the push towards a more inclusive dance pedagogy become explicit. Central in Arendt's philosophy about the active life (*vita activa*) is the view that action as a free subject is never possible without plurality (Biesta, 2014: 134).

For Arendt (1958), becoming-a-subject is an action (and not an essence), and freedom to act as a subject can only take place in spheres characterised by plurality among subjects. Dance contexts with differently bodied dancers are such spheres characterised by plurality. Arendt enters a clear political sphere in stating that to exist politically means to exist together in plurality, and to exist politically is what is genuinely human. Biesta (2014) connects Arendt's philosophy to the question of democracy in pedagogy and underlines that real pedagogical communication is a radically open and undefined process. Translated to the question of inclusive dance pedagogy, this implies a process that is always in the act of deconstruction and reconstruction of what, how and who in dance. According to Biesta, democracy is at the core of pedagogy and is also what is at stake in pedagogical situations. In this context, and based on my experiences with the Dance Laboratory, I would say that the valuing of truly and genuinely dialogical meetings between differently bodied dancers is at the core of, and also what is at stake in, inclusive dance pedagogy.

Transformative learning

In this project, I followed eight differently bodied dancers' (and also my own as the choreographer-teacher) meaning-making processes in dance over time. Through a hermeneutic-phenomenological approach and analysis, in close dialogue with the dancers/research participants as well as Jack Mezirow's (1991) theory about transformative learning, I showed how the participants (and I) went through rather profound transformative learning processes as they/we were dancing and finding out together.[7] The most profound change among some of the dancers/research participants[8] concerned their view on what and how dance can be and the view on 'the Other', both connected to dance and in life outside the dance studio. Their view on who can be a potential dancer or choreographer changed profoundly, and their ideas about the aesthetics (the forms) of dance expanded greatly. When inclusive dance pedagogy really works as an inclusive activity, challenging and changing traditional ideas about dance and dancers, it holds the possibilities of aesthetic transformation, transformative learning and depth in learning and teaching processes.

Depth in education, in contrast to more shallow education, concerns the whole person and the whole teacher. Francois V. Tochon (2010) describes how depth in education implies a sense of purpose and deep, transformational learning, involving a sense of one's deep identity. Depth in education is always in the making, and the learning processes affect both learners and teachers. Ideas equivalent to the idea of depth are found in art educational practices and theory about embodied learning, contemporary dance pedagogy and in art educational thinking in general (for example Anttila, 2013; Østern, 2015).

Tochon's idea of depth in education also fits well together with Mezirow's (1991) transformative learning theory. Mezirow describes how transformative learning has a process, which starts with a disorienting dilemma (such as meeting new dancers and dance contexts), and then uses that experience of imbalance as an opportunity for discovering new perspectives (such as expanded views on what dance can be). Transformative learning takes place when these perspectives are fundamentally challenged. This change of meaning perspectives might be experienced as deep learning. Transformative learning experienced as deep learning in an inclusive dance pedagogical context can, for example, be a radically new and expanded understanding of what dance is and who can be a dancer.

Improvisation as a key entrance to 'how' in an inclusive dance pedagogical context, has an important function in opening up for transformative, meaning-making processes in dance (Benjamin, 2002; Cooper-Albright, 1997). As dancers and choreographer-teachers take part in, and contribute to, inclusive dance pedagogical contexts through improvisation-based approaches, they have the possibility of stretching, expanding and changing ideas and practices about dance and dancers. Participation in inclusive dance pedagogy may (depending on how it is carried out) give rise to transformative learning and the experience of depth.

Concluding remarks – not only inclusion, but active change

In this chapter I have presented and discussed aspects that I, through a six-year-long research and development project with differently bodied dancers, and in dialogue with an inclusive dance field and relevant theory, developed as important in order to turn dance pedagogy into inclusive dance pedagogy. These aspects are seeing beyond word-making and world-making, spacious teaching, valuing difference, meeting and dialoguing, and transformative learning. To see beyond what you already think you know about dance and dancers, open up for new possibilities and see difference among dancer bodies as a value, is an important step towards inclusive dance pedagogy. This takes open-minded meetings and dialogue between dancers understood as equals, with real interest in one another's possibilities and movement ideas. It is the teacher's or choreographer's task to make the dance space a spacious and generous one. The process of turning dance pedagogy into inclusive dance pedagogy also invites new word-making as old concepts might become insufficient. The development of inclusive dance pedagogy might contribute to creating new dance worlds, where more and different dancers are to be found as dancers, choreographers and teachers. At best, inclusive dance pedagogy contributes to an experience of deep learning by the involved dancers and teachers.

Based on my experience, to initiate, develop, stand up and argue for inclusive dance art and pedagogy is hard and sweaty, but also very meaningful, work that takes determination and the willingness to change. I am not completely satisfied with the concept 'inclusive dance pedagogy', but it is the best I can come up with right now on this ongoing journey. The development of inclusive dance pedagogy is about, as I already have pointed out, both word-making and world-making. These two concepts cling together. Inclusion is good, and necessary, but not enough. To create a dance pedagogy that is truly inclusive requires activism, determination and willingness to change oneself as well as others, dance worlds and dance words.

Notes

1   www.danselaboratoriet.no
2   www.candoco.co.uk
3   Ingeborg Dugstad Sanders has been the artistic leader since 2012.
4   Arnhild Staal Pettersen.
5   MultiPlié dance festival has been arranged by DansiT, the regional dance agency in Sør-Trøndelag county, since 2008. www.dansit.no
6   www.dansit.no
7   For details about methodology, see Østern (2009).

8   The eight dancers did not go through the same transformative learning processes, and they changed in individual, not categorical, ways. As I do not have the space in this chapter to go into depth about these changes, I refer to Østern (2009: 214–262).

References

Anttila, E. (2013) 'Dance pedagogy in the contemporary world'. In A. K. Ståhle (Ed.), *Close Encounters. Contemporary Dance Didactics: Exploration in Theory and Practice* (pp. 13–30). Stockholm: Dans-och cirkushögskolan.

Arendt, H. (1958) *The Human Condition*. Chicago: University of Chicago Press.

Benjamin, A. (2002) *Making an Entrance. Theory and Practice for Disabled and Non-Disabled Dancers*. London: Routledge.

Biesta, G. (2014) *Utdanningens vidunderlige risiko* [The beautiful risk of education]. Transl. by Ane Sjøbu. Bergen: Fagbokforlaget.

Cooper Albright, A. (1997) *Choreographing Difference. The Body and Identity in Contemporary Dance*. Hanover: Wesleyan University Press.

Engelsrud, G. (2006) *Hva er kropp*. Oslo: Universitetsforlaget.

Lefebvre, H. (1974/1991) *The Production of Space*. Translated by D. Nicholson-Smith. Malden, MA: Blackwell.

Mezirow, J. (1991) *Transformative Dimensions of Adult Learning*. San Francisco: Jossey-Bass.

Munjee, T. (2014) 'Appreciating "Thirdspace". An alternative way of viewing and valuing site-specific dance performance'. *Journal of Dance Education*, 14(4), pp. 130–35.

Østern, T. P. (2009) *Meaning-Making in the Dance Laboratory. Exploring Dance Improvisation with Differently Bodied Dancers*. Helsinki: Theatre Academy.

Østern, T. P. (2015) 'The Dance Project: perfect (im)perfections as a deep educational experience of plurality'. *Nordic Journal of Dance*, 6(1), pp. 36–47.

Sandahl, C. & P. Auslander (Eds.) (2005) *Bodies in Commotion. Disability & Performance*. Michigan: The University of Michigan Press.

Soja, E. W. (1996) *Thirdspace: Journeys to Los Angeles and Other Real-and-Imagined Places*. Malden, MA: Blackwell.

Tochon, F. V. (2010) 'Deep education'. *Journal for Educators, Teachers and Trainers*, 1, pp. 1–12.

1.3

BEYOND TECHNIQUE

Diversity in dance as a transformative practice

Philip Channells

Introduction

How is authentic movement and expression manifested? To what extent is creative process both educational and transformative? What are some of the examples in my dance teaching and choreographic work where profound transformation has occurred?

Through my teaching and choreographic work in the Beyond Technique Residency I collaborated with disabled artist Daniel Monks on the evolutionary stages of his site-specific dance for screen solo work, *Black Weeping Rock* [Photo 1.3]. I have captured some of Daniel's responses from an interview I conducted in 2013 in which he shares his personal story of acquiring a disability at age 11. It is evident in both his physical and written responses that his professional development with Dance Integrated Australia has had a positive effect on both his personal and professional life. This narrative investigates and analyses aspects of this transformative journey.

The creative process – searching for authenticity

Beyond Technique is a disability-inclusive dance workshop/master class, which I have led throughout various regional and metropolitan centres in Australia as well as overseas. This workshop is designed to challenge and inspire differently abled participants of all ages and cultural backgrounds to search for, and embody, authentic movement expression. By this, I mean the movement that is generated from the investigations unique to the artists creating the material so that they look like themselves, not some altered versions of others.

Participants who have engaged in Beyond Technique over the years have included non-performers and non-stereotypical dancers, emerging and professional artists with different physicality and life experiences, arts workers engaging in community arts practice, and academics interested in researching and experiencing creative processes focused on inclusion and diversity. In searching for authenticity, I often choose improvisation tasks over set routines to generate different movement vocabulary unique to the ensemble I collaborate with. This way of working places the participants in their own creative driving seat through a supportive

PHOTO 1.3 *Black Weeping Rock*
Dancer: Daniel Monks
Photographer: Philip Channells

approach that can sometimes result in a life affirming and transformative experience. This was the case for Daniel Monks. In an interview in 2013, I asked Daniel about his accident.

> At age 11, they discovered a large tumour in my spinal cord, filling 90 per cent of my spinal cord cavity. From the biopsy, there were severe complications, and I was left originally quadriplegic, but then over three months in the hospital, my left side gradually came back, my right leg partially, and my right arm very minimally. Six months after that initial biopsy, we went to Sydney where my tumour was removed by [a specialist] who saved my life.

Professional development opportunity

Daniel began his dance journey as a participant in the 'Catalyst Dance Master Class Series' (2013) in Sydney. With no pre-conceived ideas of what it was, he plunged headfirst into the project. Daniel wrote this poem for the *Second Skin* project in Sydney:

Under my skin I live.
My skin may distort, may break, may fracture, may rot, may deform – but my soul will
      forever be unblemished.
With every tear, my soul only grows; deeper, wider, richer.
No matter what happens to my skin, I remain strong, true and free.
I am limitless.

Daniel was then awarded an 'Amplify Your Art' grant through Accessible Arts, the peak arts and
disability organisation in New South Wales. The grant enabled him to undertake a professional
placement over ten months with me. This placement provided Daniel with access to a series of
workshops and residencies around Australia including: the Beyond Technique Residency #2,
where he began devising his first site-specific, solo dance for the screen, the *Bundanon Local
Project: No Time Like Now*, shadowing filmmaker Sam James and I in the making of the video
installation work *Hyperreal Tales* (2016); and *The Corner Dance Lab* (2014), where he worked
alongside other emerging and established dance artists from across Australia and internationally.

Dance as a transformative tool

In the making of *Black Weeping Rock*, I witnessed Daniel connecting to his past through creative investigations originating from his accident. Observing him throughout this process and
later spending more time living and working together, I gained a deeper sense of Daniel, the
person. I witnessed him tackling lifelong fears, coming to terms with the things about himself and his life he was unable to change. Through this process, I saw Daniel accepting and
celebrating the person he has become today. I asked Daniel what it was like to work with
experienced dance artists:

> Life changing ... Even just being involved in the disabled art community in such an
> incredible, intimate way helped to further break down my misconceptions about dis-
> ability and open me up even further. It was a hugely emotional and cathartic experi-
> ence for me ... And discovering through the work that the way I move isn't lesser than
> the ideal, it's simply a different way of moving – and is unique, beautiful and worthy
> in itself – allowed me to trust and embrace my body even more.

As I watched ...

Motionless and covered in what appeared to be a shallow grave, the dried eucalyptus leaves
and forest debris covered the dancer only exposing his head, which I saw from a side-on
view. As if time stood still, moments later I watched his hidden, stretched out, lifeless body
slowly emerge from under a rock enclave. As he emerged, gasping for air, the crackling
sound of the leaves folding and ripping under his body provided the audience with a natural
soundscape punctuated with sunlight peering through the bushes and trees. With the sound
of tiny bird calls, the quiet trickling of water in an almost dried-up creek bed and the feeling
of faint wind on skin, the audience became part of Daniel's ecology, yet distanced from his
inner world and thoughts.

   Once fully emerged from the debris, Daniel slid head first, upside down towards the bank
of the creek. The anguish on his face, his heavy breath and the discomfort and awkwardness

his physicality first presented us with was reflective of the accident itself and the life journey Daniel has embarked upon since. He appeared standing upright in an open area where vines from fig trees acted as his stolen limbs and a river rock became his final resting place where he sat still, gazing skyward in contemplation.

IT'S ALL ABOUT ME – a work in progress

The starting point for this work was associated with his coming to terms with his physical disability. Alongside two other pieces, *Black Weeping Rock* has been translated into a short experimental dance film in the making, which forms part of a triptych by filmmaker Tim Standing. Building upon this initial research, Daniel brought his work from the bush land to the theatre to discover potential multiple formats for sharing his story. This work in development is titled *IT'S ALL ABOUT ME – Daniel Monks* and is part of an ongoing series of solo works by disabled artists.

For this creative development I worked one on one with Daniel across two weeks investigating new movement vocabulary generated from ongoing structured improvisations and writing tasks. Together we focused on researching a format through which to present the experience of merging Daniel's childhood trauma and adult life in a way that is educational, profoundly engaging and entertaining. What is most important to me when I'm navigating new creative territory is, first and foremost, to discover authenticity; to encourage deep learning and growth. Daniel commented on his experience of working with Dance Integrated Australia:

> The exploration of my authentic physical expression in projects like *Black Weeping Rock* and *IT'S ALL ABOUT ME* not only enabled me to come to a greater understanding of my body and the hidden capabilities it has, which has benefitted my practice, as well as my day-to-day life, but also helped me to embrace my body as a unique physicality with valuable expression, no lesser than that of an able-bodied person's, despite my physical impairments.

Conclusion

Dance Integrated Australia lays a foundation from which emerging artists launch their careers. A newly connected community of dancers, choreographers and cross-art-form collaborators who value, challenge, redefine and inform our different perspectives on contemporary life is the core of its work. Daniel's journey from a non-dancer to an exceptional one is just one example of the manifestation of profound personal transformation I have witnessed during the past twenty years. Not only has Daniel gained a renewed sense of self and appreciation for life, he continues to engage in dance in a professional capacity between the many stage and film projects he commits to. It is through witnessing the evolution of Daniel's career that I strongly believe that dance is not only educational but life-changing.

1.4

EXPLORING THE RELATIONSHIP BETWEEN DANCE AND DISABILITY

A personal journey

Jackie Prada

Regardless of how accepting and welcoming a studio is, there is a perception of what a dancer should look like. I don't necessarily mean that the dancer should look like their ability; I think I interpret other's thoughts that way from my own experiences and who I participated with. It is also about feeling successful in order to enjoy myself. It is important to note that I don't claim to speak for all people with disabilities. I sometimes wish I knew someone with similar challenges to me. Even with a positive attitude it can be tricky being the only one with this kind of challenge in a group. There is maybe something about people with physical disabilities, or those close to them, being more self-conscious.

As a dancer with mild cerebral palsy, affecting the left side of my body, I have an embodied perspective of the role of dance as a tool for identity development and community inclusion. The first time the adapted dance program was run I was about five years old and the program had more of a physiotherapy approach. I am not sure if my parents and teachers believed that I might not be able to dance in an average program. I briefly participated in an adapted dance class at KidsAbility, and I was also taking a class at Carousel Dance Centre, Ontario, and have been doing so ever since. I take advanced modern dance and I used to take ballet. I have been doing all the organizing and administration for the adapted dance and integrated programs at Carousel since graduation, but have helped with the 'Dance for EveryBody' classes since early high school. I have also choreographed pieces with members of this group. At the time of writing, we have more students who have developmental disabilities than students with physical disabilities.

It can be harder to learn to teach students who use wheelchairs because you must have someone willing to try so that a teacher can learn. That is what is great about Carousel's programs – they provide the opportunity to mix with peers with and without disabilities, which is ideal for allowing people to be themselves. We shouldn't think there is anything wrong with either and the current participants have shown me this.

When I am around new people in some situations, whether or not they know about my different abilities, it can feel awkward. Strangely, or not so strangely, it is like people with disabilities and those without are afraid of each other and the unknown; feelings get pushed below the surface and masked such that they may be perceived as something else, like indifference or other negative emotions. Part of my perspective comes from the groups I have interacted with, the activities I have participated in, and the goals I have pursued. The only leisure activity I joined in with others with a disability was for a very brief time when I was little. With some activities, like skiing and swimming, I did private lessons because groups didn't work as well for learning and private lessons in a public environment worked better. For some, the arts and dance might be their only way of escaping and feeling empowered, and offer the chance to be social and develop relationships. Dance is an embodied individual experience and music can be a part of it. This is the easiest way to describe why I believe people with different abilities could have more dance opportunities and become involved in developing further prospects. Performing and being in front of an audience has an impact on people and builds community. Performing and creative movement with props were some of my favourite parts of dance.

The following discussion includes some of the inclusive dance opportunities at Carousel, which is a large, non-competitive educational-based dance school focusing on creative dance, ballet, modern dance, and jazz. The studio has existed for over thirty years and has over 500 students normally. The studio has been fully accessible for several years, allowing further development of our programs for people with disabilities. The directors of Carousel are very involved in the development of, and teaching on, the program and have been running our adapted dance program, Dance for EveryBody (for children and teens who have developmental and/or physical disabilities), for over five years. The classes focus on modern, creative dance and jazz. Performance, both formal and informal, is a large part of Carousel. At the end of each year there is a big recital with the main section based on a story like *Peter Pan*, so each piece has a meaning within a theme. The students in both the children and teens Dance for EveryBody classes have become an anticipated and well appreciated part of the year-end show.

In fall 2011 after I graduated, I started to look at more performance opportunities for Dance for EveryBody besides the yearly recital. The way that I pursued this was through a program that is in addition to their weekly class. 'Dance Company' is an integrated performance opportunity for students who are enrolled in the Dance for EveryBody program. Our Dance Company (made up of students wanting extra performance opportunities from the regular dance school) rehearses on Saturday afternoons and performs at two extra performances that are only performed by company members. Castings for the pieces are mixed in age, which was a part of the structure that existed in Dance Company before Dance for EveryBody was involved. This structure helps provide a welcoming environment and support. Dance Company is the main way that older students start to get to know a few of the Dance for EveryBody participants. For example, some of the dancers are involved in an inclusive recital piece based on the popular video game Tetris.

Dance Friends is an opportunity for children, teens and adults of all abilities to dance, build friendships and have fun together. Each class has a theme, with creativity in pairs or groups, choreography, and a craft or an activity. This program is an hour and a half (a bit longer than most classes). It runs for four to six weeks each year after the recital, before summer. We show parents what we have worked on at the end of each week. The quick creative projects with props and music often look like they have been in development for more than one session. This class is different, maybe because of the mix of ages, or because of the different activities – it has the most enjoyable, relaxed, inclusive atmosphere. I have participated in this program, so for once I have direct experience, rather than experience only as an assistant or choreographer. Depending on numbers or what the activity is, the teacher also participates. The activities in this class are different; maybe it's the creativity mixed with games and crafts that make participants without disabilities feel less responsible, like assistants, and participation just comes naturally.

Throughout this narrative I have shared some of my perspectives as an academic, a dancer and a person with physical challenges. Dancing has given me the chance to become less concerned with what others think of me since the studio offers an opportunity to participate and engage in an experience that is focused less on competition and more on the enjoyment of dance as an expressive form of art. For individuals with a disability, dance participation can become an important contributor to shaping their identity, while also providing an inclusive social setting enabling relationship opportunities.

1.5

'SOWING DANCE' – BODY MOVEMENT FOR CHILDREN FROM SIX MONTHS TO THREE YEARS OLD

The experience in Mesquita, Brazil

Luciana Veiga

'Sowing Dance' is a pedagogical project for the inclusion of dance as an artistic language for the six month to three year old age groups in public schools in Rio de Janeiro, Brazil. The project takes place in Mesquita city, a town about forty kilometers from Rio de Janeiro. In Brazil the guidelines in the school curriculum allow for at least one artistic language to be taught from nursery through to high school. Dance, in the first stage of early childhood education, is called 'Body and Movement', and from three years of age on it is called 'Dancing'.

In many schools throughout Brazil, teaching takes place in designated sessions; morning or afternoon for children of kindergarten and elementary school age, and evening for older students. The network encompasses full-time daycare and a comprehensive-education-model school. In my first year working in Mesquita (2012), I worked in four schools because I needed to build my schedule around the time available in different schools. The beginning of this journey was difficult because this city, located forty kilometers from where I live in Rio de Janeiro, made me dependent on public transportation, which unfortunately is difficult in Brazil and sometimes dangerous. It was also hard because there were no financial resources for teaching; for example, I purchased all materials used in my classes and created my own teaching resources. In my third year, I was invited to implement dance classes as a pilot project in the first segment of early childhood education, in two networks of kindergartens.

'Body and Movement' for children six months to three years old

I give 'Body and Movement' classes once a week in each nursery school with one half-hour class for each group [Photo 1.5a]. The groups have a maximum of fifteen children and most of these students are in school full-time. The basis of the class is the practice of motor skills; the challenge is to include artistic and aesthetic knowledge into this program. The classes are divided by age, into six months to twelve months, thirteen months to twenty-four months, and then separate classes for two and three year olds.

PHOTO 1.5A Warming up
Children in Mesquita dance class
Photographer: Luciana Veiga

Education framework and arts curriculum development

Brazil has a framework for education in nurseries called Parâmetro Educação Infantil (Childrens' Education Frame). This document mentions 'movement education' and even with the understanding that babies do not practice dance at all, the class is named 'dance class'. This document is the basis for establishing the arts within the school curriculum. After the dance program had commenced, it was decided to also include a session each of music, drama, visual arts and storytelling once a week. In addition to the existing content of the main document, studies of psychomotor skills, aesthetic development and sensorial development are required to develop it further.

Most teachers in Brazil are not exclusively attached to one school but work in at least two schools and sometimes in different cities. There are meetings with the whole group once every two months and between this official meeting we share experiences at lunch time, by email, phone calls, and social networking. As teachers, we need to respect and pay attention to the experiences that come from different professionals, not only teachers. Teachers welcome children in the early morning and deal face to face with the families at this time; however, support staff like janitors and cooks live in Mesquita, so they personally know many of the children enrolled in the schools and can help the teachers through their knowledge of the community context and personal backgrounds. Because of my short time in the school, these connections with the community that other staff can share have been invaluable. For instance, I have found out that some of the families have no water at home and can only shower at school. This leads to medical conditions and influences their psycho-motor development.

Pedagogy

In the nursery classes, musical instruments, balls and props are used to facilitate games and learning activities. Sensory stimulation with fabric of different textures is incorporated and,

PHOTO 1.5B Sensory stimulation with fabric
Children in Mesquita dance class
Photographer: Luciana Veiga

over time, the activities progress, although the focus remains on one form of stimulation at a time [Photo 1.5b]. The two- and three-year-old age groups can explore their own movement with the props, but extra musical instruments and new activities like using the hula hoops can also be added. These older groups learn to enter the room in an orderly fashion at the beginning of the classes, mark places with masking tape or colored paper, and work in different configurations for sitting activities such as circles, lines or pairs. There is a gradual distribution of materials like fabric and satin ties in the circle, for instance, in a clockwise direction. The children develop spatial understanding of the center and the periphery through picking up props in the center of the circle and then moving back to their place at the edge. Exploring lateral movement, different body levels, expanding and collapsing forms, and showing and hiding materials are all part of the class, along with rhythm exercises. As locomotor skills develop, jumps, turns and further kinesthetic exploration occurs as they move on to developing creative dance through improvisation with a selection of different music. Music is an integral part of the dance programs and children learn to explore movements inspired by recorded music or by playing instruments in groups, responding to weak and strong sounds, experiencing silence, movement, and stillness.

Conclusion

Over two years of the program, the best achievement was the inclusion of other artistic languages into the curriculum in 100% of Mesquita's nurseries. All the staff at the schools and the city secretary for education felt empowered by this positive policy for the very young. The implementation of the arts in the curriculum of the nurseries also inspired them to include activities that connect the school to the families and wider community, for example regular meetings with families for the nursery and other classes; dance activities for students and relatives for the two- and three-year-old age group; and a museum visit with families to support the concept of diversity.

This is the early beginning of an arts policy in a public school that opens the possibility of access; it implies teaching and learning for children, arts teachers, coordinators, and the children's families too. In 2014, only dance classes took place in two nurseries in Mesquita; now the children have dance, drama, music, visual arts and storytelling – a dream come true.

1.6

DANCE FOR CHILDREN WITH DEVELOPMENTAL DYSPRAXIA

The impact of projects of the Royal Academy of Dance, London

Lesley Ovenden (née Hogg)

The aim of a case study I conducted at the Special Needs Project of the Royal Academy of Dance in 2003[1] was to determine the extent to which a child with developmental dyspraxia may benefit by attending these dance classes. Dyspraxia is an impairment which affects motor planning, language, perception and thought. I focused on a twelve-year-old girl who was diagnosed as dyspraxic and as having Asperger's syndrome. She had attended the special needs dance class for two years and had a range of needs that could be addressed by dance tuition. She had problems with verbal communication, poor muscle tone, difficulties with balance, coordination and motor planning, and was easily distracted. She had perceptuo-motor problems, in particular difficulties with proprioceptive feedback, spatial awareness, directionality and bilateral integration. Her observed strengths were an ability to imitate a teacher's actions when the teacher was directly in front of her, an emerging ability to perform homologous actions, an ability to respond to some metaphoric imagery and an ability to establish a rapport with significant adults. She had expressed her desire to remember her own dances.

Background

The project originated in 1990 with the aims of providing dance tuition to children with special needs and training dance teachers to include these children in their classes. The special needs encountered by the project teachers included learning and behaviour difficulties, visual and hearing impairment, health problems, and several syndromes. A team of dance teachers, specialising in ballet and other forms of Western theatre dance, taught the classes at the Royal Academy of Dance headquarters and in schools for the visually and hearing impaired.

Observations of child (referred to as A) with developmental dyspraxia in dance class

The class partly followed the structure of a classical ballet class. Lessons began with standing exercises, initially bilateral then crosslateral actions. Next were barre exercises such as pliés, battement tendus and battement en cloches. Exercises lying on the floor designed to strengthen the core and stretch muscles followed. After this came jumping and locomotor movements such as skipping, leaping, galloping forwards and sideways. The class concluded with a warm down section, often using a parachute to facilitate a calming response while performing developmental movements such as log rolls.

The area of the room that A occupied has a bearing on her capacity to focus on the teacher giving instructions. She was able to focus when she was directly facing the teacher at fairly close proximity. It could be that the range of her field of vision is limited and that she had difficulty attending to auditory cues. A's actions were performed momentarily after the teacher's and, consequently, not in time with the music because she seemed to rely on imitating the teacher's actions. This time lag in performance seemed to emphasise A's reliance on imitation rather than employing her own memory of the sequence.

Balance and posture

A had difficulty standing still with her legs and feet together and arms by her side. Her head was usually tilted forward causing a concave shape in the torso. Her eyes were often downcast and her eye focus was seldom directly ahead at eye-level. This distortion in body alignment is a factor that affected her static and dynamic balance. Low muscle tone and poor visual perception and proprioception may also contribute to A's difficulties with posture and balance, which impacts on all her movements. When A attempted homologous movements initiated by both lower limbs, such as a rise on to the balls of the feet with legs together in a parallel position and hands on the shoulders with the elbows relaxed down, she was able to imitate the teacher's action. She initiated the rise from the balls of the feet, leaving the torso, limbs and head inert. Standing exercises involving balancing on one leg caused A to lean to one side. Lack of pelvic stability is a factor. When taking her arms out to the sides at shoulder level to assist balance, her arms were bent at the elbows with drooping wrists. Both the standing and working legs were slightly bent. A's actions could be described as gestural rather than postural as they are initiated by the periphery. A was not observed to extend her reach fully into her personal kinesphere.

Barre exercises

A's dominant effort quality in pliés was suddenness. It seemed that she observed the teacher's final position more than the transition from one position to the next. In a demi-plié in first position, A was able to remain almost upright in stance. In a grand plié, she inclined her torso forward, causing a concave shape. When attempting to extend her leg to the side (second position), her leg was bent and ankle relaxed and her effort was slightly sudden. This again suggests that she observed the finishing position rather than the transition. In battement tendus derrière, her torso inclined forward more than was required to maintain balance and her legs were bent. It is probable that limited proprioception impeded her awareness of positions beyond her range of vision.

Floor exercises

When asked to lie prone with her hands under her shoulders and raise her head and shoulders, A demonstrated considerable flexibility in the lumbar spine. The students had asked the teacher if they could do 'dolphins and seals', meaning this exercise. A imitated the sound of a seal, which another child was making, and seemed to enjoy 'being' a seal.

Locomotor movements

A has been observed to volunteer to perform a 'log roll' over a parachute that is laid on the floor. Her difficulty in lying supine in a perpendicular position results in an inability to roll her body as one unit. After the teacher had held her hands together and feet together to promote the concept of moving as one unit, she rolled on to the leading side of the body, leaving the other arm and leg in place and then joined the following arm and leg to the leading arm and leg. A was able to travel sideways by stepping sideways and joining feet, when she was directly in front of the teacher. She also had some success at 'grapevine' steps, which involve crossing one leg behind, then in front. Her torso was slightly turned towards the direction of travel. When she was at the back of the studio and was asked to travel laterally, A faced the side and walked forward. This indicates that A was totally relying on the visual cue of the teacher's demonstration, had directionality difficulties and had not memorised the action she had performed at the front of the studio.

When interviewed by the author, A said she liked listening to a range of popular music at home and dancing to this, but was distressed that she could not remember what she had done. A said that she enjoyed a sequence of steps she had learnt, which resembled actions from the 'Sailor's Hornpipe' dance. This sequence was observed by the author and taught to the class three months prior to the interview. A described her recall of this sequence by demonstrating the folding of the arms, similar to the action used in the 'Sailor's Hornpipe'. She was not able to describe this verbally without prompting from the dance teacher. This seems to indicate that she had developed some movement memory and that the metaphoric imagery and role-play used in this instance aided her long-term memory.

Teaching methodology

The observed lessons are based on teaching dance movements rather than teaching the children to develop their own ideas in dance, and as such, are more concerned with dance training than dance education. Direct teaching, mostly using verbal cues and some metaphoric imagery, was the dominant approach employed in the observed classes.

Conclusion

In recent years, the Royal Academy of Dance has replaced the Special Needs Project with RADiate. A attended a special school, which closed in 2004. Since the school closed and the support of the Special Needs Project stopped, it is unlikely that she has continued dancing. A expressed a desire to initiate her own choices in music and movement linked to imagery. RADiate needs to support dance students to develop their own ideas, rather than imitating teacher-directed movements, for this twelve-year-old to be empowered through dance. There is a need for greater recognition of students with special needs as being differently abled and contributing their own sense of identity to dance classes and performances. For a child with special needs, whether this be developmental dyspraxia, autism spectrum disorder or another learning difficulty, the Royal Academy of Dance has continued to provide learning opportunities through dance. Progress towards integration, and further recognition of the contribution students with different abilities can make to dance classes, would enable the Royal Academy of Dance to better prepare these students for life in an inclusive society.

Note

1   Hogg, L. (2003) *Dance for Dyspraxic Children: An Investigation into the Potential for Dance Tuition to Improve the Abilities of Dyspraxic Children.* (Unpublished Masters Dissertation). University of Surrey, England.

PART II
Equality, advocacy and policy

PHOTO Wheelchair Dance Collaboration
Photographer: Joel Schwartz

2.1

VALUES AND PRINCIPLES SHAPING COMMUNITY DANCE

Ralph Buck and Barbara Snook

We enter the large activity room and we all sit in a circle. 'We' is Barb and Ralph, and a group of university students working with a group of adolescents with special needs at a local high school in Auckland, New Zealand [Photo 2.1]. Ralph yells out, "Come on, make the circle bigger, everyone has to see everyone else". Barb greets the students with hugs and ensures that the university students are mingling amongst the high school students. We settle into the circle, then Ralph, as a warm-up exercise, begins to tickle Andrew, a boy with Down Syndrome. We all do the same and the circle dissolves into a mass of laughing bodies, rolling, kicking, crawling, and yes, getting warm. The session carries on in this manner for an hour, concluding with biscuits, juice and farewells … till next week.

PHOTO 2.1 Auckland University students and dancers working together
Photographer: Tracey Holdsworth

As we bus back to the university, we sit next to each other and chat about how the session went, refining ideas, noting who was fully engaged, what works and what does not in such a lesson. Our discussion, like we have had many times, drills down to big questions. What are we achieving in these visits? What drives our approach to teaching and learning dance in this seemingly chaotic, non-technique, non-hierarchical, non-product type lesson? We reflect on the values and principles that drive our teaching, and really, how we live outside of the classroom as well. We reflect on the morning's class at the local secondary school, and agree that an important and often unstated aspect of our pedagogy that might be useful to share is a reflection on the values and principles that underpin it. In this chapter, we outline the key values informing our pedagogy, then note ongoing issues within special needs education, closing with the emergence of community dance education practices and research.

Values and principles

Every teacher holds values. We bring our values into the classroom, the studio, the gym and diverse community contexts. Our values consciously and unconsciously shape how we teach and learn. Values held and how they are enacted inform what we, as teachers, aim to achieve, and how we go about it. Values are formed from social and cultural forces that help shape individual teachers within their cultural, personal and political contexts. Jennifer Nais (1996) notes the classroom management skills and values of teachers and states, "one cannot help teachers develop their class-room and management skills without also addressing their emotional reactions and responses and the attitudes, values and beliefs that underlie these" (p. 294).

Our values are presented in the paragraphs below. We illustrate the values by staying with our experience with students at a local high school. But before we discuss values, it is useful to briefly note our theoretical position. In so doing, we declare 'how we see the world' and reaffirm that what we do is not random nor without deep consideration and thought. A social constructivist epistemology (Eisner, 1998) drives our methodology and enables engagement as we aim to construct possibilities for learning for our students in a meaningful way. We are concerned with meaning but we are also looking for questions. A constructive methodology supports the concept of learning through an interactive dialogue and also allows reflection on learning experiences. Through engagement with participants, a body of knowledge is formed.

Equity

We aim to provide all learners with equal access to education. The best image that illustrates this value is everyone sitting in a circle. This simple act invites everyone to feel equally seen and equally important, and is necessary for the circle to actually be a circle. Making the circle is not always easy. It is surprising how many people feel uncomfortable with 'being visible' in this way, though once they understand that the circle itself provides their security and that they are key in helping others feel secure, they relax. It is about giving and taking equally, and all one has to do is be present in mind and body. It sometimes takes a while for this understanding to take place.

It took Sam, a young boy with autism, three lessons to sit in a circle. It took Lillian, a young, Chinese International Master's student, two lessons to recognise that sitting in a circle was an okay way to commence a dance lesson. Both Sam and Lillian had to review their personal meanings of 'joining in', of 'dance' and of being a 'visible part of a group', but for very different reasons. We acknowledge that it is not easy for everyone. But this is what we do, this is what we aspire to in our dance classes.

Democracy

We aim to recognise the integral role of dialogue, agency and safety in dance education. After tickling each other, Ralph turned to Trudy, a student in the class, and asked "What will we do today?" Trudy proudly said, "Let's do Michael Jackson's moonwalk." Ralph asks if she can moonwalk and Trudy, with pride, says she can. Ralph promises that we will moonwalk at the end of the class. And we do, to everyone's delight.

Our dance classes are full of dialogue, spoken and embodied; the interaction of ideas, the sharing of personalities, the giving and taking of weight and space, all create dialogue and in turn make meaning. As constructivists, this is a cornerstone of our dance lesson, the construction and ongoing reconstruction of meaning. When we invite dialogue, we invite voice and this helps participants feel that they have agency in informing/determining what will happen and how a process and product unfolds. Teaching for agency requires construction of a lesson in a careful manner, working in small groups where the focus is on collaborative problem solving as a strategy that often allows for individual agency. Again, it is not easy for everyone and practice is required.

Diversity

We recognise that we are all diverse learners. When we look around our circle, we see students from diverse cultures; students with very different personalities and interests; and students with diverse abilities. Each student brings something to the dance classroom and it is the teacher's choice to see and value diversity. At times as teachers we overrule diversity and expect everyone to, for example, pay attention, freeze, do a specific move. Given this reality we, however, always provide a lesson structure that provides scope for individuality. In small groups of threes we ask the students, who are well and truly mingled by now, to make three shapes that represent a storm. There are rules: the students must have two feet, one hand and one back touching the floor, must all be connected in some way, and must move from high to low, or low to high. The limitations actually provide scope for diversity. The limitations also invite problem solving and invite each student to consider their body, culture and interests as resources. It always surprises us how creative the students become in including the girl in a wheelchair, or the boy with cerebral palsy.

Curiosity

Barb yells "Freeze." The room stops. Everyone is holding their breath, "What will she ask us to do next?" Barb smiles and in her quiet but devilish manner, asks the students to retrograde their small sequence and add a 'surprise' move. We constantly fuel our lessons with questions, challenges, tasks that extend thinking and learning. In this way students remain fresh to the process, they remain curious and they eagerly explore solutions to presented problems/challenges.

Fostering curiosity is about fostering an interest in finding out something, an interest in other people, an interest in pushing ourselves harder. Typically, students respond to positive feedback or the desire to master the particular challenge.

In our classroom the students make short 'storm' sequences. They have all been very focused on their own sequence. But it's time to share, to 'perform' their sequence with others. Immediately, new concerns ripple around the room. We hear statements like, 'How do we finish?', 'What happens after you jump?' We also see the students begin to look beyond their circle to see the room is full of like-minded dancers, busy working with incredible intensity and laughter.

Perseverance

"One more time, can we do it again?" yells Josh. Like so many children, Josh wants to have another opportunity to master his sequence. He is striving for a personal sense of achievement and success. We allow time in the one hour sessions for students to explore, practice, share, review and do again. It is clear that students, irrespective of ability and interest, want to work at doing the best they can. The reward is the intrinsic feeling of 'I did it' and feeling recognised by peers. After a certain age, the students no longer need 'stars', 'rewards' or 'bribes'. They're keen to work at something, to persevere, seeing that personal satisfaction. When we all do the Troika, a large, group Russian Folk dance, we get it wrong. We do it again. We persevere to get the right foot on the right beat. It's hard. We alter the moves to make it easier. We do it again. We do it slowly and then to the music. We imagine the snow, that we are horses pulling sleighs, and we begin. We finish and everyone collapses into applause. They persevered and they did it. Was the lesson about learning a dance? No, it was about learning to persevere.

Participation

We walked in ready to dance. Margaret wheeled in in her wheelchair. Andrea, a nineteen-year-old girl with Down Syndrome, sidled up to Ralph and said "Oh that poor woman in the wheelchair, how will she be able to join in?" Andrea then states firmly, "Don't worry Ralph, I'll look after her".

We all have assumptions and expectations about who is a dancer and even what dance is. We often see disability/ies before we see the person and yet when we consciously open up a dance lesson and plan in accord with the people in the room, it is more than apparent that participation is possible.

Margaret is completing her Master's thesis and has been a professional dancer within a mixed ability dance company. We have discussed with Margaret how her participation in dance is informed by her wheelchair. Margaret is candid in her response, that she is more than a dancer in a wheelchair. We note that people are complex; Margaret is also a young woman with diverse interests, aspirations and concerns. Participation in dance is maximised when we maximise our awareness of who the learners are and how they can be activated. Doing this may require opening up the teacher's imagination for finding new and engaging means for involving everyone.

In this lesson, Andrea remained true to her word, she partnered Margaret all morning. Andrea participated in a new way. In this lesson she wanted to take a 'leadership' or 'teacher' role, and participated wonderfully. Within a dance lesson there are many roles to play and hence more scope for participation. It is the teacher's duty to 'see' and 'feel' opportunities for students to participate.

Fun

Trudy wanted to perform Michael Jackson's moonwalk in this lesson. We had also canvassed opinion and found that others wanted to 'show' their dances as well. We allow time for five minutes of show and tell at the end of the lesson. Everyone is talking, everyone is having fun, everyone feels safe to perform, laugh, join in, improvise. We all love 'doing'. We all now know that joining in and giving it a go is the 'product' of the lesson. We smile knowingly, recognising that process, process, process and product creates the fun and when we see 100 per cent engagement from every person in the room, we feel success. When we hear the volume of conversation and laughter, we feel success. Trudy does her moonwalk, we all join in and laugh at our own attempts and in doing so admire Trudy's skill in performance. The lesson finishes. Veronica, the school-based classroom teacher, applauds and loudly says, "You're all wonderful and see you next week."

Reflection

We begin our plan for next week's visit to the local high school where our university students teach and learn with the students with special needs. Again, we ask, "Why do our values matter?" Laughingly, Barb states, "Values are like the foundations of a house. They are invisible, yet shape all choices made in the classroom; they determine the look, feel and design of the lesson." Ralph agrees and adds that there is no right or wrong set of values. The important thing is that the teachers are conscious of their values and how they shape their teaching and hence, how they invite access and inclusion. This seems especially important for learners with special needs as teachers strive to draw on individual creativity and enjoyment. We acknowledge, however, that this knowledge is important in all teaching.

Dance for learners with special needs

We have opted to use the term 'learners/dancers with special needs' to place emphasis on the fact that all learners/dancers have particular needs. We accept that the terms shift and that the term 'students with disabilities' and 'dance and the disabled' are common terms used in the literature, but again we choose to focus on abilities and needs rather than disability. However one describes the activity, 'Dance and Disability' is an area that has gained increasing acceptance in the classroom and on the stage. Anne Hickey Moody (2009) states, "To move beyond the theory and practice divide, to leave the mind-body distinction behind us, to affirm lives rather than to negate them, are among the wise principles of our age" (p. 1).

Particular dance companies use the words 'integrated' or 'inclusive' in their company title and, in so doing, raise the profile of the dancers but also unintentionally marginalise some of the dancers and disrespect their unique contributions. This is not to say that a dancer's special needs/disabilities should be ignored or disguised in performance, but rather, a nomenclature is yet to be found that comfortably acknowledges diversity of ability within dance companies. Questions of aesthetic hierarchies bubble under the surface, where ultra-flexible and lean female and male balletic images dominate. These images create tensions and possible conflict in terms of what is good dance or not, what do funding organisations fund or not, who is a professional dancer and so on. Peter Brinson (1991) challenged able-bodied assumptions about disability and made the point that the number of disabled people in our society runs into millions and we "overlook the fact that they comprise not only a significant audience, but also a creative resource of dance-making which expands our restricted notions of dance" (p. 190). It is not only able-bodied people who carry bias and limited perceptions, however. The experience of disability may be associated with a sense of loss, and as Linda Ross, cited in Boswell, Glacoff, Hamer, McChesney and Knight (2007) noted, "increased isolation often accompanies the experience of disability" (p. 33), where people are more likely to avoid activities such as dance as they would need to communicate and work cooperatively with others. People with "a physical disability, are often caught between conforming to existing standards or role definitions which society (or the local culture) dictates and exploring the promise of new alternatives" (Dent, 1994: 11). If the community around a disabled person is unlikely to experience dance themselves, then disabled people are unlikely to be drawn to dance. Biases that exist in dance are just as likely to influence the thinking of the disabled as able-bodied people, who are often heard to make the statement, "Oh, I can't dance". We could therefore assume that people with disabilities may think the same way. As so often happens, meanings of dance continue to fall back to limited assumptions of who is a dancer and what do they do. Images of the highly skilled balletic form prevail. If this remains true for the majority of society, it is understandable that it will take time for dancers with special needs to see themselves as dancers, or for wider society to accept a new aesthetic. Eluned Charnley (2011) makes a case for more opportunities in dance for people with disabilities. Her article focuses on barriers, and there are many; she does, however, suggest that, "professional training opportunities are opened up which challenge and enable physically disabled dancers to reach their full potential" (p. 3). This issue regarding provision of training for dancers with special needs is, for example, being explored by a semi-professional dance company in New Zealand (Touch Compass).

When examining why dance is important, we reflect upon the view that dance may be more important to dancers with special needs than to able-bodied/minded dancers as dance provides a vehicle for creative communication and expression that might not always be readily available to them. As a participant with disabilities in Boswell, Hamer, Knight, Glacoff and McChesney's (2007) study stated, "Meaning in life can be transformed by the creative process" (p. 37). Another participant in the same study went so far as to say, "I'd say it has played a central role in my life. I mean, more than relationships. There's something really important about creativity (dance)" (p. 37).

Community dance

Since the early 1980s the term 'community dance' has increasingly found a place within dance practice and literature. Defining community dance has always been something of a challenge. We question the term 'community dance'. Is this a Western construct, or is it all about participation? "Since the mid-1980s there has been critical debate about the purpose, practice and defining values of community dance" (Amans, 2008: 3). A continuing dialogue is a way forward, and as we journey in this diverse and complex field, we are more informed through the flow of writing in journal articles and books. Conferences in community dance are offered globally, and above all, we have opportunities to participate in community dance and develop an embodied understanding of the many ways it is practiced/offered.

Community dance in the United Kingdom has been a success story "where structures have been embedded into institutions to support the delivery of dance to a broad section of the population" (Houston, 2008, p. 11). Similarly, in Australia and New Zealand community dance has emerged as a relevant umbrella term that focuses attention upon maintaining access to, and participation in, dance for a broad variety of people. Twenty-five years ago, Brinson (1991) wrote:

> Dance is now more evident in our culture than it was twenty-five years ago. Community dance classes with a range of dance styles, small touring dance companies, dance on television, and the emergence of regional and local youth dance companies, indicate a driving level of interest.
>
> *(p. 161)*

Fifty years on, community dance has found more traction in institutions and society. The University of Auckland introduced a Master's in Community Dance in 2015; the University of Otago, the University of Waikato and the University of Auckland all offer courses in community dance. DANZ (Dance Aotearoa New Zealand) facilitates and promotes many community dance events. Currently community dance reaches out into hospitals, prisons, cultural communities, organisations for children and youth with special needs, the elderly, to people living with cancer or other illnesses, the well, the unwell, people wanting to dance for fun or people wanting to deliver a serious message. Community dance can be about the environment and can deliver messages about gender, inclusion or pride. Community dance offers opportunities to engage with people, valuing diversity and developing within participants a sense of self-worth and confidence. Chance (2000) sums up the practice of community dance thus:

> It may be based in a cultural tradition … It may have a political or social agenda and be about raising awareness of the social conditions of a community … It may simply be about people coming together to have a good time.
>
> *(p. 1)*

Reflection on felt change in the curriculum

Tertiary institutions offering dance have grown in New Zealand and Australia over a thirty-year period. Many tertiary dance students have the opportunity to study dance education and community dance, providing a broad understanding and appreciation in many areas of dance. This has assisted in breaking down hierarchical barriers that have existed between professional dance, dance education and community dance, with dance education and community dance historically at the bottom of the ladder. The arts are an important part of the school curriculum in both countries, and although a government policy drive for literacy and numeracy tends to push the arts into the background, we believe that there is an awareness of the arts that is new. Schools try to meet the requirements of the curriculum and even though it may sometimes be tokenistic and superficial, it is a step forward to have the arts as a key learning area and no longer hidden, as was the case with dance in Physical Education for many years in New Zealand. The importance of creativity is acknowledged through the introduction of the New Zealand and Australian arts curricula. Dance's inclusion in these arts curricula has removed the focus from limited forms of technique. Key in the emergence of dance in the arts curriculum is the role dance plays in engaging with diverse learners, especially learners with special needs.

Research provides us with a window into government initiatives in dance that align with UNESCO's vision for the arts, the Seoul Agenda (2010). While currently in the UK dance does not have a place within the curriculum for all students, conversations continue and the Department for Culture, Media and Sport states that "arts can tackle not only symptoms of social exclusion, but also its causes" (2003: 28). Patricia Sanderson (2008) suggests that while attitudes towards dance still vary, a major finding of her research into dance education implies "that the arts should be more widely available in schools so that all children and young people can have access to aesthetic experiences that have the potential to improve the quality of life" (p. 467). This is a widely held belief in countries that support dance in the curriculum.

As stated at the outset of this chapter, change in society is a constant and, similarly, so is the case with dance. While this chapter discusses the case for access and inclusion, we ask, "Who is a dancer and what is dance?" Never before has dance been more evident within communities across so many areas, genres, styles and bodies. Dance in the twenty-first century appears to have moved its focus towards imagination, creativity and relationships, therefore leading to a place of broader access and inclusion.

Community dance offers a future for promoting access to and inclusion in learning, both in formal school situations and informal community contexts. Within education and the arts, change is a constant. Education and the arts are at the heart of every society. They both reflect where we have been and where we as a society are going. Most important, however, is that civic leaders, politicians, children, mothers and fathers by and large believe that both education and the arts provide the means for us to find a better way to live, to build a better society for future generations. This is our aim as teachers, and the initial account of this chapter has provided a snippet of our personal journey as teachers in this area.

References

Amans, D. (2008) *An Introduction to Community Dance Practice*, London, Palgrave Macmillan.

Boswell, B., M. Hamer, S. Knight, M. Glacoff & J. McChesney. (2007) 'Dance of disability and spirituality', *Journal of Rehabilitation*, 73(4), pp. 33–40.

Brinson, P. (1991) *Dance as Education: Toward a National Dance Culture*, London, The Falmer Press.

Chance, S. (2000) 'Editorial: Communities dancing', *Dance Forum, Journal of the Australian Dance Council*, Winter 1, pp. 7–18.

Charnley, E. (2011) 'Towards a new vision of dance', *Animated Magazine*, Winter, pp. 25–27.

Dent, P. (1994) 'The perceptions of six women with disabilities of their self-directed occupational role as dancer', Master's Thesis, San Jose State University.

Department for Culture Media and Sport. (2003) *Regional Cultural Data Framework, a Report by Positive Solutions*. Business Strategies, Burns Owens Partnership and Andy C. Pratt, London, DCMS.

Eisner, E. (1998) 'The enlightened eye: qualitative inquiry and the enhancement of educational practice', Upper Saddle River, Prentice Hall Inc.

Hickey Moody, A. (2009) *Unimaginable Bodies: Intellectual Disability, Performance and Becomings*. The Netherlands, Sense Publishers.

Houston, S. (2008) 'Dance in the community'. In Amans, D. (Ed.), *An Introduction to Community Dance Practice*, Hampshire, Palgrave Macmillan.

Nais, J. (1996) 'Thinking about feeling: the emotions in teaching', *Cambridge Journal of Education*, 26(3), pp. 293–306.

Ross, L. (1995) 'The spiritual dilemma: its importance to patients' health, well-being, quality of life and its implications for nursing practice', *International Journal of Nursing Studies*, 32, pp. 457–468.

Sanderson, P. (2008) 'The arts, social inclusion and social class: the case of dance', *British Educational Research Journal*, 34(4), pp. 467–490.

UNESCO. (2010) 'Programme of the Second World Conference on Arts Education', Paper presented at the programme for the Second World Conference on Arts Education, Seoul.

2.2

THE UGLY DUCKLING

Stories of dance and disability from Denmark and South Africa

Gerard M. Samuel

The collapse of apartheid in South Africa saw many barriers to learning removed and a fight for equal education for children with disabilities advanced. But questions around dance performance by the disabled seemed to remain. Unpacking the issues of histories, aesthetics and norms for people with disabilities becomes heightened by oppressive laws. In the case of South Africa, understanding how apartheid statutes propped up a colonial hierarchy and thus cultural superiority is to discover how privileging of only certain bodies that were permitted to dance operates. The notion of 'black is beautiful' and svelte dancing bodies take on a particular meaning in this context where the majority of the populace were defined as 'the Other'. Black children with disabilities in South Africa were shockingly maltreated. My research conducted in the late 1990s revealed that the number of schools for disabled allocated to white learners was more than double allocated to that of black learners (Samuel, 2012). But the momentous transition period also saw greater opportunities arise for South African artists and teachers 'of colour' (such as myself), who were previously tethered to engage in international arts and education projects. The cultural boycott which was a part of the anti-apartheid movement that many in Europe (and elsewhere) had supported, was a powerful mechanism to bring about social transformation. It also had the effect of limiting the exchange of new ideas and best practices in pedagogic and artistic spheres. The birth of democracy in 1994 saw a flurry of cultural exchange.

As a South African artist caught up in the heady revolution to demand human rights, I am part of that generation who engaged in dialogue with the Performing Arts Council to bring about social transformation in and through the performing arts. The Playhouse Company in KwaZulu-Natal where I was employed was amongst the first such arts councils undergoing transformation and ready to support teachers of Dance Studies in the mid-1990s. At this time dance as a subject had only just been introduced into all public schools in South Africa. Part of these teachers' development programmes included exploration of 'disability arts' and an interest in 'integrated arts', terms that will be contextualised below. UK-based dance educators, such as Jasmine Pasch and Edward Salt, were part of an influx of visionaries willing to travel and share their expertise and knowledge with South African counterparts. Some, such as Gisele Turner, who had worked with pupils who were deaf, and

John Mthethwa's KwaZulu-Natal Ballroom Dance Association for the Disabled, had already opened a path towards making dance more accessible to the people with disabilities in Durban.

I was fortunate to travel to Europe in the 1980s. For many South Africans, the expression 'travel abroad' was a euphemism for travelling[1] to Europe as local travel to, for instance, neighbouring African countries such as Swaziland and Mozambique was considered to be less valued. In the mid-1990s I met arts teachers and pedagogues from Denmark as part of the wave of international agencies, embassies and anti-apartheid lobbyists who were eager to support the rebuilding of our fractured country. Through the generosity of the Danish Cultural Institute I began sharing my experiences – exploring dance in a variety of colleges, schools for disabled children, after-school centres and clubs for young people with disabilities, especially in the Copenhagen area. I questioned the manner in which disability arts operated in each of our cultural spaces.

This chapter will chart my offerings in dance and integrated arts projects in Denmark and South Africa not only to celebrate the series of events that were undertaken for more than a decade, but to provide an outsider's vantage point. I reflect on a five-year-long dance-theatre project – *Who says, the ugly duckling?* – the departure point of which was that discrimination of the disabled is abhorrent. The partnership with Lene Bang Larsen and 'Klubvest' in Albertslund, Copenhagen, and my own LeftfeetFIRST Dance Theatre in Durban, South Africa, remain the most ambitious and rewarding international collaborations that I have led and will be unpacked below. I will take stock of the processes that led to this dance project being undertaken by me with disabled young people from Denmark in 2003 in order to reconsider its success [Photo 2.2]. What happens when we travel to the space of 'the Other'? How does dance allow a particular kind of tourism of the 'Othered' body? What can be

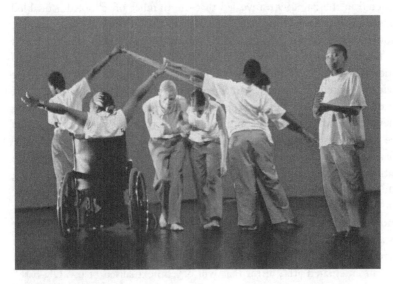

PHOTO 2.2 *Silent Love*
Photographer: Val Adamson

learnt from a reading of the politics of disabled dancing bodies and the politics of space? I maintain that the choreographic approach undertaken during *Who says, the ugly duckling?* applied a 'body-space' reading (Samuel, 2016) for disabled dancing bodies that is useful for understanding cultural exchanges.

The first section of this chapter will discuss some of the strategies and practices (workshops and classes) conducted at various schools, theatres and after-school day care centres and clubs in Denmark. I will share some of the practical challenges that I faced and the approaches I used to negotiate difficult terrain including cultural difference: language, race and religion. Section two will reflect my observations of the *performance processes* and is limited[2] to the specific performance of *Who says, the ugly duckling?*, which was performed in Albertslund, Copenhagen (2003), The Playhouse Company's Loft Theatre in Durban, South Africa (2004) and by invitation of the Danish Cultural Institute to Kecskemet, Hungary (2005).The chapter closes by clarifying a 'body-space' reading and arguing for its significance as a tool that enables insights into the embodied lives of children with disabilities and cultural exchange. How can we know more about the experience of 'the Other', like the disabled, that is made possible through dance? The notion of 'the Other' is also rooted in me given my socio-political heritage which under apartheid laws categorised me as non-white. Further, my cultural identity is linked to India, Mauritius and possibly the United Kingdom, which can place me as a foreigner in Africa. As a Catholic-raised gay man living in rural and patriarchal Zululand, and as one who chose ballet, such categorisation only partially describes my 'Othered' position. This conundrum continues to drive my research work in Performance and Cultural Theory and has instilled in me vigilance towards the multiple forces that underpin difference.

Strategies and practices in the dance classroom

The socio-political landscape of both Denmark and Europe itself has changed dramatically over the last twenty years. The influx of refugees and a need to grapple with the complex issues of multiculturalism surfacing in Danish society is something that I have embodied. I had noticed reactions by some learners to the fact that I was not a stereotypical black African man and how some learners with Muslim names seemed to gravitate towards me. Did I represent some sort of role model? My 'race/ethnic' antennae observed burka-clad young girls' attitudes shift positively towards me when presented with an 'Indian' dance teacher who was male. Was my gender or ethnicity an attraction? I also observed a gradual emergence of youth gang formation based on race and ethnicity, especially on urban trains and buses. These subtle societal shifts were evidenced over a decade (1995–2005). During this period I travelled in multiple social contexts and regions (from Holstebro to Falster, the Bornholm island to Gilleleje). How was a so-called homogenous space going to adapt to multicultural voices?

As a South African (outsider) I have been privileged to witness rapid cultural diversity in the Danish classroom. As a foreigner and black South African dance teacher, my entrance into a Danish school was always going to draw attention, more especially as I am of Indian heritage and acutely aware of the non-white status tattooed onto my identity by the apartheid regime. This becomes even more contentious when in my introductions I reveal my layered history as a classical ballet dancer and student of the Bournonville school (which is in fact rooted in the tradition of the Danish Royal Ballet). This issue of multiple identities, which I embrace, follows an anthropologic discourse. Loots (2006) writes that cultural identity "is in fact subject to a continuous interplay between culture and history and that these are themselves always discourses that negotiate power relations" (p. 89). The answer to the question as to how to find an entry point and connection with children with disabilities in a complex space such as a classroom for me lies in these notions of embodied identities.

Most of my engagements with young learners in Denmark began by dispensing with instruction and language *per se* (after all, I would be speaking in English to young people who were in all likelihood Danish speakers learning the complexities of their own written and spoken language). In my work I have attempted to create an atmosphere and sound-scape from an assortment of music that may be considered by many to be outside of the music/cultural frame of reference for a particular group. I first encountered an unapologetic emphasis on high quality music for school children at the Skovmoseskolen – a school serving the range of needs of children with learning difficulties. Danish composer Janne Aagaard's insistence on providing surround sound for not only her own *Zebra ze ze* compositions but all music was a welcome luxury which I later came to understand as a vital necessity. This attempt to divert children's attention from known to unfamiliar musical territory could neutralise a fear and permit the body to explore and indulge in the curiosity of its potential. Like so many teachers before me, I encourage refraining, and refrain myself, from using 'No!' and 'Do not...', rather suggesting 'Now go to somewhere else in the room or where you have not been to before'. This aspect of spatial experimentation forms a wellspring from which I am able to extract choreographic material (gestures, tones, dynamics of movement, relationships). I have noticed that inclusion of such expression of body is relished by the child with disabilities, especially when his/her special way of moving has been included in my movement phrases. Many teachers have been initially uncomfortable with my insistence on not knowing what kind of disability a child has been labelled with. This deliberate ignorance, I maintain, allows me to rather focus on the child's own choices of identities which I express through other questions such as 'Morten is the child that loves blue, correct? ...so, let's explore his sky blue dance'. This is not to suggest that questions of the health and safety of children should be ignored in relation to my pedagogic pursuit.

My teaching praxis includes a nonverbal contract with the learners to return weekly and to the same venue (where possible). This provides a notion of safe space. In my encounters with the many well-resourced (in general) schools in Denmark, this purposefully 'safe classroom' has resulted in children's gradual development and greater confidence. It has also provided me with an opportunity to strengthen my relationship as an outsider and foreign teacher with these learners. My teaching preference extends to leading from within – that is, without overshadowing the dance by the children for the teacher to join in an uninhibited manner. This view I expect has oppositional perspectives. My enthusiasm to dance and share a joyous celebration of music, with my body present and dancing my story, stems from my belief in a non-instructive approach when working in dance with children with disabilities. In as much as careful guidance is vital throughout the workshopping process, any performative aspect requires a freedom that sanctions *being* in the dance or accepting the act of *becoming* in the dance as an equally valued goal. In my experience, children are quick to fathom an instructive tone from pedagogues who are disengaged in their own bodies when only the children are expected to be the performers. Dances by, with and for children with disabilities, are in my opinion all the richer for the shared encounters with those of us who may consider ourselves able bodied and enablers of the experience of dance. The number of children in my classes in Denmark varied between eight and fourteen (whereas in South Africa I have worked with upwards of sixty children on one dance project) making this scenario feasible.

At the outset of my projects in dance with children with disabilities in Denmark (and in South Africa) was a firm insistence on the establishment of level playing fields – a space and attitude adopted by children and their teachers as co-participants, meaning no one is to be a mere spectator or bystander. This philosophy of inclusivity powerfully disrupts notions of normative bodies, and enhances a sharing of the embodied experience.

Who says, the ugly duckling?

The project *Who says, the ugly duckling?* was developed between the mid-1990s and the 2000s. The account hereafter attempts to re-awaken these events and performances from my viewpoint as the dance teacher, creative movement explorer and later the choreographer. H. C. Andersen's enduring tale *The Ugly Duckling* – an outsider duckling who becomes the epitome of beauty, the swan – was for me an ideal and suitably iconic cultural artefact from which to deconstruct the hegemony surrounding 'the Other'. The ubiquitous swan with her eternal struggle beneath the surface of the lake and her poised, sinewy neck and unruffled feathers above, invited the choreo-activist in me to play – to unpack the drama that is contained in the total creature. I noticed immediately that the head teacher, Lene Bang Larsen, used an inclusive and non-authoritarian approach by inviting all members of Klubvest to join in the dance theatre project. This made it all the more difficult for me to test my critical question: what does it feel like to be excluded because of one's disability? I began to explore these ideas of inclusion and exclusion, 'us' and 'them', 'self' and 'Other', with these untrained dancers' bodies, using movement, creative play and dance – dancing with and for one another. Teachers and caregivers joined in my sessions just as much as the young people and we began to interpret and build a confidence to share our unique stories. Smaller scenes relating to the larger theme of 'Othering' evolved.

In scene one, the mother duck, after tending her clutch of eggs, sees a happy birth of ducklings. She wanders off with her brood, rejecting the oddity they have discovered in their midst. The strangeling is alone. Scene two sees an overzealous swimming instructor and a not-so-eager young diver. Another rejected youngster. To compound matters, in each scene 'the Other' is played by a different actor. This was purposefully introduced to re-enforce the universal experience of people being placed as 'the Other', depending on various social and political contexts and therefore an equally universal need to combat prejudice and discrimination. The third, and perhaps the best-loved scene of the dancers, was set to pop and rock music by Queen and unfolds in a trendy cafe. A bunch of hoodlum teenagers, scoffing pizza and ogling the rock star with his red, shiny guitar, snub an unknown adolescent who tries to sidle up to the group. Rehearsing this section provided the most fun as movement was far less controlled, and included a kind of head-banging, bouncing and clapping range of movements. I realised the sensitivity of the young people to the overall theme of exclusion and their experience of exploring rejection in each of my dance workshops. The dancers, together with their teacher Lene, suggested that we could resolve the scene by singing *My Best Friend*, a popular Danish folk song. I agreed. A more abstract scene followed, in which the dancers played with pathways in space and the idea of mirroring (a hint of the problematic of conformity). The brief scene ended with a dancer staring into a mirror – testing the existential question, 'Who am I?', which in turn posed the open-ended philosophical thought, 'Who am I in relation to you?' The final scene contained the most complex movements, use of space, changes in dynamic and relationships to one another. The cast triumphantly return all dressed up as swans, or princes or princesses, each one no longer an ugly duckling but a celebration of self. Within the structure of the last dance scene, performed to Tchaikovsky's *Swan Lake* Op. 20 score, randomness was frequently associated with improvisation. I vividly recall that in the Durban performance there was a brief pause (perhaps disbelief) at the very end and then thunderous applause. The scenography introduced a further layer into my investigation in *Who says, the ugly duckling?* and was expressed via an oversized version of a pop-up book that announced scene changes as pages were slowly turned and lights came up to reveal a new scene.

The ugly duckling on tour

How did this performance create meaning? What were the responses from outside of the immediate cultural frames of the original cast? Christopher Bell, writing in 'Is disability studies actually White disability studies?', pointedly reminds us of the complexity that is the diversity of the disabled community. He strongly chastises Joseph Shapiro when he wrote, "[Shapiro's] insinuation that the disabled community is a monolithic one, struggling against the same oppressors, striving for identical degrees of dignity, recognition and cultural representation. Such characterisation is a limited one that does not consider or address the rich diversity within disability communities – racial, ethnic, diversity, for example" (Bell in Davis, 1997: 375). The first performances of *Who says, the ugly duckling?* took place in Copenhagen in 2003, and remarkably, toured to Hungary in 2004 and Durban, South Africa in 2005. The work has provided a working exemplar of disability arts conceived of initially in Denmark and later exported via the tours to foreign shores where new disability arts projects have emerged. It germinated certain impulses in South Africa which, I argue, may alter not only the recipients of the dance works (foreign audiences) but also the providers. According to Hall, "Diaspora identities are those which are constantly producing and reproducing themselves anew, through transformation and difference" (in Ashcroft, 1990: 438), which I maintain is germane to the lives of people with disabilities.

Similarly, whereas disabled bodies were formerly ostracised for their difference, the new spectacle of the disabled dancing body offers a re-imagining through performance to convey common human experiences. The encounter in the dance exchange between disabled and being in a foreign land develops a 'body memory' that becomes a shared and embodied experience of 'the Other'. Therefore, being a disabled, young Muslim girl from Denmark performing in South Africa can be compared to a prism radiating multiple and complex identities and agency. I have noticed that the notion of passive or docile bodies for the disabled can be rejected when these bodies become activated as provocateurs and agents in both Denmark and South Africa. As audiences embody such performances, the process awakens a curiosity to travel, to discover and thereby enliven the potentiality and imagination of 'the Other.' These readings must be welcomed not as specific forms of tourism of the 'Othered' body but rather as deeply sensory, cultural exchanges.

Notes

1 To compound this matter, I was awarded a paid-for study tour to the Federal Republic of Germany in 1980 and later, when I was a professional ballet dancer, joined student and civic protest on the very night of the historic collapse of the Berlin Wall, 9 November 1989. I am more than a little embarrassed to admit that apart from Hans Christian Andersen's stories and a town named Stavanger, which my father told me that Stanger in KwaZulu-Natal where I was born was named

after, I had scant knowledge of Denmark and other Nordic countries. Later, I learnt that Stavanger was in fact in Norway (!). Nevertheless, any opportunity to travel was welcomed, given the newly gained freedoms of the mid-1990s, as was a chance to learn and be exposed to how others lived.

2   I also created *The Pink Pearls* (2006), a disability arts project for children of the Skovmosesskolen, Copenhagen, in partnership with Janne Aagaard. Her music from *Zebra ze ze* was integral to both projects.

References

Bell, C. (1997) 'Is disability studies actually white disability studies?' In L. J. Davis (Ed.), *The Disability Studies Reader* (pp. 374–382). London: Routledge.

Bhabha, H. K. (1983a) 'Difference, discrimination and the discourse of colonialism, in the politics of theory'. *Essex Conference on the Sociology of Literature*. Colchester: University of Essex.

Foucault, M. (1991) *Discipline and Punish: The Birth of the Prison*. London: Penguin.

Gardner, H. (2011) *Frames of Mind: The Theory of Multiple Intelligences*. New York: Basic Books.

Hall, S. (2006) 'Cultural identity and diaspora'. In Ashcroft, B., G. Griffiths & H. Tiffin (Eds.), *The Post Colonial Reader* (2nd ed., pp. 435–438). London: Routledge.

Loots, L. (2006) 'Post-colonial visitations: a South African's dance and choreographic journey that faces up to the spectres of "development" and globalisation'. *Critical Arts*, 20(2), pp. 89–101.

Samuel, G. M. (2012) 'Left feet first – dancing disability'. In S. Friedman (Ed.), *Post-Apartheid Dance: Many Bodies Many Voices Many Stories* (pp. 127–145). Newcastle, UK: Cambridge Scholars Publishing.

Samuel, G. M. (2016) 'Dancing the Other in South Africa'. *PhD thesis (unpublished)*. Cape Town, South Africa: University of Cape Town.

2.3

DANCE, EDUCATION AND PARTICIPATION

The 'Planters' project in Girona, Spain

Gemma Carbo Ribugent

The ConArte Internacional 'Planters' projects are pilot schemes lasting two years in primary and secondary schools that have a high cultural diversity index and a proven track record of being open to educational innovation through dance and music. The project is based on the principles of UNESCO's (UNESCO 2006, 2010) Seoul Agenda for arts education, which recommends encouraging coordinated work between specialist schoolteachers and professional artists to boost the educational capacity of art, especially those schools in diverse and complex locations.

The educational value of the arts is amply demonstrated by numerous studies and works that show the existence of different types of intelligence not considered in education until recent decades (Gardner, 1983; Goleman, 1995). Other research places emphasis on the importance of engaging in all kinds of arts and music as a means of generating a need and liking for critical and responsible consumption of culture among children, who will one day become adults (National Art Education Association, 1995). However, in response to the basic cultural and educational challenges that countries face, there is still little emphasis given to artistic and cultural education. Dance in particular is absent in formal education in Spain.

The policies for constructing target audiences generally concentrate on marketing, advertising and support, all undoubtedly necessary for creation and production. In the field of education, Europe and international bodies such as UNESCO have, for some time, stressed the need to overcome fragmented and compartmentalised content disconnected from life experience and to work primarily on known, transferrable skills in order to be, to do and to live in harmony (European Parliament, 2006; Alsina-Giráldez-Abat, 2012). Within this framework, the body and movement play an important role.

The nineteenth-century Spanish education objective was to guarantee equal right of access through defining a national cultural model, and curricular content that was more or less homogeneous. Literacy, mathematics and science were proposed as neutral and essential subjects (Nussbaum, 2011; Giroux, 2001; Camps, 2011), while the humanities and the arts lost importance by being considered 'distracting subjects'.[1]

It is in the field of policies for cooperation and development on a global level that the central value of artistic and cultural diversity was first accepted in Spain, during the period

2004–2008, as a factor for sustainable growth. This directly related to the role of education as a fundamental system for the enactment of public policies by the Cultural and Development Spanish Strategy (AECID, 2006); education with the aim of supporting children and young people, with particular emphasis on artistic languages such as dance, music, theatre and visual arts. Artistic work is essential for intercultural dialogue, creativity and the protection and promotion of cultural expression (Cepal-UNESCO, 1992; UNESCO, 2005; UNESCO, 2009).

It is precisely the countries classified as the poorest in the Human Development Index (HDI) that are the richest in creativity and cultural diversity (UNESCO, 2001). Latin American and African countries supported by international organisations are increasingly promoting the education and training of their citizens through dance, music and artistic and cultural expression. Mexico and Colombia are leading examples in this respect with projects like ConArte Mexico and the IDARTES project (Bogotá); but it is also a challenge and a necessity that European countries have taken on board by signing the Roadmap for Arts Education leading to the creation of the 2010 UNESCO Seoul Agenda for arts education.

In Spain, the 'Planters' projects understand that if we do not work with the arts as a vector for change and for shaping free, creative and civic-spirited people, we run the risk of repeating the uses and abuses that have produced exactly the opposite situation, using differences and identities as a motive for confrontation and conflict leading to wars and the destruction of one of our primary assets: people and their creative capacity.

The 'Planters' project – *Ambar(t)* ConArte

In December 2013, an initiative was presented in Girona (Spain) called the 'ConArte Internacional' association. The concept came out of a connection with ConArte Mexico, a pioneering Latin American project integrating music and dance for the most disadvantaged state schools of Mexico City. Many people and a variety of institutions from the world of culture and education were at the presentation at the founding meeting of the association to explain what we had learnt from Mexico and what we wanted to attempt in Girona. Accompanying us was, amongst others, the dancer Cesc Gelabert, who after a brilliant artistic career now works tirelessly in communicating the educative possibilities of dance. As he said in a recent interview:

> One of my great frustrations is not having had more opportunity to work for including dance as part of education.[2]

What was presented was, perhaps, a utopian vision, a proposal that foresaw teachers and artists working together based on dance and music; children dancing with professional artists along with teachers in primary and secondary schools; young people from very diverse cultural, economic and social backgrounds in a state school participating in a process of discovering new expressive and creative languages that allow them to talk about what they feel, who they are and what they dream of, or fear. The idea of the project was to provide young people with tools for music and bodily expression and to inspire them to adopt an attitude towards the world shared by the best artists and teachers, allowing them to listen to others and themselves in order to learn and grow as creative and contented people and as increasingly discerning and committed citizens.

One could sense, on the other hand, that this mini-revolution in the classroom could generate, if properly managed, a multiplier effect in the teaching world, in schools, in families, in neighbourhoods and particularly also amongst the artistic groups, festivals and the cultural events that are proliferating throughout the Girona region. The project is all about testing how far the force of this impact could go and to analyse it in the most objective way possible to be able to explain it not only to future education professionals and arts students but also to politicians and decision-makers at domestic and international levels.

Explicit support was given from the outset, led by the UNESCO chair of the University of Girona, the Temporada Alta (High Season) Festival, the Catalan Government's Ministry of Education and, in particular, the Daniel and Nina Carasso Foundation,[3] one of the few cultural foundations that focuses on patronage and commitment based on very simple concepts: those that feed the body and those that feed the soul.

Thus, the ethereal and starry-eyed concept began to take shape in the form of the 'Planters' project which, in September 2014, was set up in five primary schools and three secondary schools in the region of Girona reaching close to 470 third-year primary children and secondary school adolescents, their families, twenty choreographers, musicians, actors and state school teachers, eight management teams, two major festivals featuring top artists, three city councils and a small management and coordination team supported by a board of directors and thirty partners in love with the idea.

Following the methodology tested by ConArte in Mexico, the structural axis was established as a joint teaching process between dancers, musicians and teachers of physical education or music for third-year primary school children and secondary school pupils in the proposed education centres. Teachers and artists create combined tandems at each centre to design new ways in which to teach classes and subjects based on shared expertise. The goal of this joint effort, which takes the form of a regular and continuous process of a weekly one-hour class over the course of two years, and a weekly one-hour coordination period for artists and teachers, is to build an innovative teaching approach based on dance, music and the theatre as strategies for learning and for personal and collective growth.

Principles and values of the 'Planters' project

The following are principles and values that have become important in the project:

- A break with the dominant view that culture, artistic education and the practice of the arts are activities suitable only for professionally creative people such as artists, or else the opinion that engaging in the arts is only an activity for occupying leisure time.
- Equally, we want to distance ourselves from the old assumption that arts education is a complementary but expendable part of basic education.
- We maintain that engaging in artistic education and practices is a fundamental human right, as well as a cultural right, for all, which is the very key to aesthetic literacy, enriching and expanding our expressive, communicative, emotional and social skills through very diverse media, languages and formats.
- We defend the power of art as a tool for transforming individual and collective reality, and as a generator of new forms of thinking, self-esteem and social relationships.
- We also understand the arts as a component of strategies that allow for diversification in economic activity and advances in design and the productive life of many countries that are taking care of the future of their economy by investing in creativity and social innovation.

The first edition of the 'Planters' project came to an end in June 2016 and starts a new cycle in October 2017. Outcomes for the first edition include the production of a short video of the artistic production, *Ambar(t)*, directed by Guillem Roma, Marta Roma and Santi Serratosa, and the presentation of a documentary film that gives an insight into the classes, the processes, the experiences and the results of this first edition. The last task being worked on is an impact study (led by the University of Girona) that will provide verifiable arguments that make an objective defence of strategies to deal with an assumed need: the renewal of education by considering the role of the arts.

Experiences to share

As the project is currently on-going we can at this point in time, before receiving fully quantifiable results, outline some preliminary thoughts about how we have advanced in relation to our goals:

In the creation of another important precedent

In Catalonia it is possible to work with professional artists in the context of formal education. This is not just based on residency agreements but rather is achieved in a coordinated manner over two school years. This has already been demonstrated by projects run by schools for music and visual arts but dance has thus far been somewhat neglected. What 'Planters' has introduced to the model is work by teachers and arts professionals to prepare joint sessions in the classroom one hour a week. They have set up a monthly working group recognised by the Ministry of Education that shares methods, learning, concerns and reflections. They have broken down invisible barriers between two worlds.

In raising awareness of the appropriateness and need

Over the course of these last two years more than twenty-five lectures, discussions, seminars and meetings have been held with students and artistic collectives to present the project and integrate the initiative with networks at local (Arts Observatory Applied to Education), European (European Network of Observatories in Arts and Cultural Learning linked to UNESCO) and international (INRAE, International Network of Research in Arts Education) levels that work in the field of artistic and cultural education.

In the proliferation of derivative projects

Projects such as: 'Arts Increase Motivation' (an ERASMUS project lead by one of our educational centres in the village of Salt); the training workshop for teaching staff in dance and emotional education in educational centres; joint initiatives with public orchestras and theatres; or other projects involving young people and music in Salt.[4]

In social participation

Participation by families in the community through more than thirty demonstrations of artistic processes in public and artistic venues, such as The Auditorium of Girona.

In the creation of an audience of young people

A demand for culture that has made it possible to go to over twenty-five dance and musical shows during non-school hours and in the context of festivals such as Temporada Alta (High Season) in Girona, amongst others.

What were the problems for the project?

Firstly, there was a lack of understanding of the complexity of the project and the arts and cultural education by some of the participants, which resulted in a lack of involvement and commitment. Some of the schools and local governments are not involved in the next edition of the 'Planters' project because they have not understood the deep sense of pedagogical innovation that the proposal implies. In that sense, the reluctance of some institutions and local government bodies was an obstacle which generated excessive bureaucracy, lost time and a great deal of frustration.

Secondly the project did not take into account the extremely difficult situation whereby the majority of the pupils required much more dedication from the mediator, which was planned for but not worked on sufficiently. The critical situation of poverty and exclusion for many families was not considered enough at the beginning of the process. In Spain the number of foreign people, most of them economic immigrants, is very high, especially in the schools where the project is taking place.

In terms of methodology, one of the main difficulties was in defining a shared method between artistic and educational processes adjusted to the different realities. There was always a lack of time and space in which to work together and a different understanding of the final goals. This is one of the most important challenges for artistic education. Aesthetics and ethics must go together but it is not easy to manage it with a group of thirty students that do not choose freely to be at school and to dance.

At the logistical level, the schools showed a lack of planning towards allocation of spaces for orchestras, dance and theatre, which generated the need for mobility. Some of the municipalities can offer an appropriate dance space in their context and that generates a positive connection between schools and cultural spaces, but also a need to move from the school with different groups and at different hours. The security protocols for schools make this kind of mobility more complex as they require the participation of parents and/or other teachers accompanying the groups.

Finally, we did not anticipate the different timings and rhythms of work in the worlds of education and culture that complicate the connection with the cultural offerings that are very concentrated in the summer time. In addition, and obviously, as ever, the project underestimated the structural operational costs.

What were we missing? In particular, time in which to explain more, give more support, listen more. Time to enjoy the music, theatre and dance more. Only time makes it possible to grasp and understand the slow processes of change that underpin education, but also a willingness to continue negotiating for more commitment from policy-makers and the education, artistic and cultural communities.

'Planters' defines itself as a pilot project that seeks, right from the beginning, a formula for continuity. This comes about, without a doubt, through shared responsibility between local authorities, cultural institutions (such as municipal schools for music, theatre and the arts), educational administration and artistic, cultural and social communities.

Equality, advocacy and policy: stand up for your rights

Given this overview, there is no other course of action but to continue trying. We are defending, at last, fundamental rights considered by the Universal Human Rights Declaration. The link between the "right to education" (article 26) and the "right to take part in cultural life" (article 27) is therefore evident. As for the right to education, positive state intervention is particularly important in guaranteeing the definition of the educational model and free primary education, as well as general access to secondary education. But it is important to point out that educational content is directly related, on the one hand, to fundamental cultural freedom and, on the other, to contemporary multicultural contexts; such content must also be a guarantee, from the standpoint of diversity, of the right of citizens to participate in cultural life.

The concept of cultural rights refers to the concept that encompasses both aspects (cultural freedom and multicultural contexts) by making education the instrument of participation in cultural life. It is a concept without precedent and with no specific legal expression; its interdependence and association with other rights – economic, social, civil and political – means it is a difficult concept to define. The Human Rights Council – through resolution 10/23 of 26 March 2009 – established a new special procedure entitled:

> independent expert in the field of cultural rights with the mandate, inter alia, to identify best practices and possible obstacles to the promotion and protection of cultural rights, and to study the relationship between cultural rights and cultural diversity. The legal debate is mired in theoretical conflict which appears to be insurmountable: the universality of human rights versus the right to cultural identity,

but in short, "All education worthy of the name should have as its goal and as its ideal, the traversing of borders and cultures, i.e. transculturalism, as opposed to confinement to one single tradition; it is within each individual where the notion of diversity becomes meaningful" (Augé, 2010: 45).

The right to education together with the right to participate in cultural life promotes the development of personality and identity. The Friburg Declaration on Cultural Rights[5] (2007) is very clear in this regard. It includes the right to education in its 'catalogue' of cultural rights. It is worth mentioning that such a right – as understood by the Friburg Declaration – goes beyond what we are referring to in this paper as 'culturally appropriate education' as it includes "the freedom to teach and to receive teaching of and in one's language and in other languages, as well as knowledge related to one's own culture and other cultures."[6] As definitively stated by Farida Shaheed, the UN Independent Expert on Cultural Rights, "the right to education … constitutes a cultural right" (Independent Expert of the Field of Cultural Rights, 2011).

Dance, music, theatre and visual arts are other languages and the way to get in touch with other cultures in intercultural dialogue, peer-to-peer. Thus, education must be culturally appropriate, include human rights education, enable children to develop their personality and cultural identity, and to learn and understand the cultural values and practices of the communities to which they belong, as well as those of other communities and societies. Education that does not consider music, theatre, visual arts or movement and dance, for example, cannot live up to these challenges.

As the American National Dance Education Organization (NDEO) states,

> Dance is a natural method for learning and a basic form of cultural expression. .... It is essential that education provides our children with the developmental benefits and unique learning opportunities that come from organizing movement into the aesthetic experience of dance.[7]

Since 2009, the task of the United Nations' special rapporteur in the field of cultural rights has been key to making steps forward in artistic and cultural education. In the right to freedom for artistic expression and creativity report (UN, 2013), for example, it is stated that there is a need to:

> Develop and enhance arts education in schools and communities, instilling respect for, appreciation and understanding of artistic creativity, including evolving concepts of acceptability, awakening the ability to be artistically creative. Arts education should give students a historical perspective of the constant evolution of mentalities on what is acceptable and what is controversial.

By the beginning of the twenty-first century, cultural rights formulated by the Universal Declaration of Human Rights, developed by the International Covenants and other human rights instruments, had obtained new importance. They are today 'empowering rights'. Without their recognition and observance, without implementation of the right to cultural identity, to education (in cultural diversity, cultural heritage and arts – aesthetics) or to information, human dignity cannot be guaranteed nor other human rights fully implemented. Without the recognition of cultural rights, cultural plurality and diversity, a creativity economy and fully democratic societies cannot function properly.

Notes

1   http://www.musicaantigua.com/la-educacion-artistica-distrae-de-las-demas-asignaturas/
2   https://www.dansacat.org/es/actualitat/8/1009/
3   http://www.fondationcarasso.org/es
4   https://arrelsurbanes.wordpress.com
5   http://hrlibrary.umn.edu/instree/Fribourg%20Declaration.pdf
6   Article 6. Emphasis added.
7   http://www.ndeo.org/content.aspx?page_id=22&club_id=893257&module_id=55419

References

AECID (Spanish agency for cooperation). (2006) *Spanish Strategy for Culture and Development Cooperation*. Madrid: AECID. Available at http://www.aecid.es/Centro-Documentacion/Documentos/Planificación%20estratégica%20por%20sectores/estrategia_cxdxenglishx.pdf

Alsina, P., A. Giráldez Hayes, & J. Abad. (2012) *La competencia cultural y artística: 7 ideas claves* [Artistic and Cultural Competence: 7 Key Ideas]. Barcelona: Graó.

Augé, M. (2010). *La comunidad Ilusioria* [The Illusory Community]. Barcelona: Gedisa.

Bauman, Z. (2008) *Múltiples culturas, una sola humanidad* [Multiple Cultures, One Single Humanity]. Buenos Aires: Katz Editores.

Camps, V. (2011) *El gobierno de las emociones* [The Government of Emotions]. Barcelona: Herder.

Cepal-UNESCO. (1992) *Educación y conocimiento. Eje de la transformación productiva con equidad* [Education and Knowledge. Axis of the Productive Transformation with Equity]. Santiago de Chile: Cepal-UNESCO.

Cepal-Oreal C., European Parliament. (2006) 'Recommendation 2006/962/EC of the European Parliament and of the Council of 18 December 2006 on Key Competences for Lifelong Learning' [Official Journal L 394, 30 December 2006].

Gardner, H. (1983) *Frames of Mind: The Theory of Multiple Intelligences.* New York: Basic Books.

Giroux, H. A. (2001) *Cultura, política y práctica educativa* [Culture, Policy and Educational Practice]. Barcelona: Graó.

Goleman, D. (1995) *Emotional Intelligence.* New York: Bantam Books.

Independent Expert of the Field of Cultural Rights. (2011) 'Report of the independent expert in the field of cultural rights', pp. 7–8.

Morin, E. (1999) *Seven Complex Lessons in Education for the Future.* Paris: UNESCO.

National Art Education Association (1995) *Aesthetics for Young People.* Chicago: University of Illinois Press.

Nussbaum, M. (2011) *Not for Profit: Why Democracy Needs the Humanities.* Princeton: Princeton University Press.

UN Human Rights Council. (2013) 'The right to freedom of artistic expression and creativity'. A/HRC/23/34.

UN. (1948) Universal Declaration of Human Rights.

UNESCO. (2005) Convention for the Protection and the Promotion of the Diversity of Cultural Expressions. Paris: UNESCO.

UNESCO. (2006) Roadmap for Arts Education. Paris: UNESCO.

UNESCO. (2009) Guidelines for Intercultural Education. Paris: UNESCO.

UNESCO. (2010) Art Education Seoul Agenda. Paris: UNESCO.

2.4

BUILDING IDENTITY THROUGH DANCE

Exploring the influence of dance for individuals with special needs

Nicole Reinders

Introduction

Roughly 4 per cent of individuals in Canada aged fifteen to twenty-four have some form of disability (Statistics Canada, 2015), which is about 550,000 individuals in Ontario, Canada. I searched for dance studios that offered inclusive dance programs (as advertised online) and found less than thirty in the entire province. Not only are there too few programs, many individuals are not in close enough proximity to attend the programs in existence. The narrative in this section explores the interaction between dance and self-identity experienced by four individuals with special needs, specifically focusing on three programs available in Ontario, Canada.

I am a dancer!

I have conducted qualitative research about recreational dance programs for individuals with special needs for four years, specifically regarding programs available in southern Ontario. My passion for this research is rooted in my history as a dancer and dance instructor, as well as my involvement with inclusive recreation programs. The theoretical orientation that has guided my research is phenomenology. In order to capture the lived experience of inclusive dance programs, I conducted interviews with dancers, parents, dance instructors, and volunteers. My goal was to provide individuals with a voice to share their experiences and what they meant to them. To enrich my data, I observed the dance classes and volunteered weekly in one of the programs. Over the course of this research, I noticed a trend that tied each of these studies together: the fostering of self-identity through participation in recreational dance. My work has focused mainly on Down Syndrome (DS) and Autism Spectrum Disorder (ASD), two very different diagnoses. DS is a chromosomal disorder occurring once in 800 Canadian births and affects intellectual and physical function (Canadian Down Syndrome Society, 2009). The cause of ASD is still unknown; however, it affects one in sixty-eight Canadians, and it primarily impairs social and behavioral function (Health Canada, 2013). While each individual was unique, they all benefited from dance in similar ways. All classes in the following studies were community-based, inclusive of dancers of all abilities, and offered a variety of dance techniques ranging from ballet to hip hop. Each class had at least one instructor and at least two volunteer helpers. Four stories about dancers and their self-identity are presented below.

Kayla

Kayla was ten years old when I interviewed her about her dance experiences. She was diagnosed with Pervasive Developmental Delay – Not Otherwise Specified (PDD-NOS, within the spectrum of ASD) and Attention Deficit Hyperactive Disorder (ADHD). When I met Kayla, she was beginning her second year of dance and attended two forty-five minute classes each week. Kayla told me about her tap class in our interview, saying "[my dance teacher] has been giving me harder moves because I already know some of the stuff and some of it's too easy for me." Kayla's mother, dance instructor, and assistant instructor all commented on the development of Kayla's self-esteem and confidence as well. For instance, her mother noticed that Kayla increasingly enjoyed regular physical activity, which she attributed to the dance program. Her instructor also noticed that Kayla was quick to answer questions and demonstrate the moves she learned from class to class. Her instructor said that Kayla even corrected her on choreography if she had forgotten something, indicating that she was confident in her memory of the moves.

Hannah

Hannah, aged fourteen, started her third year of dance when I volunteered in her class. She participated in one sixty-minute dance class each week as well as a three-hour performing arts program that included dance. Hannah was diagnosed with autism and had difficulties with verbal expression; therefore, we were not able to complete an interview. However, she was present when I interviewed her mother and she said "I like to dance" when we discussed her dance class. As stated in the introduction, dance provides opportunities for individuals to explore different roles. Hannah experienced a leadership role in the class, where she led the other dancers in a large circle from one formation to another. Regarding this experience, her instructor said, "I think that she really likes being the leader, I think that's been a really good thing for her." While her instructor and her mother did not comment on Hannah's self-identity directly, she was regularly provided with opportunities to express herself in the class. For example, one dance activity was to take turns 'melting' from a tall position into a small position. Initially, Hannah imitated another person's moves rather than creating her own. Progressively, however, Hannah created original movements and held her body in the end 'shape' for longer periods of time. These movements indicated that she was more confident in her abilities over time.

Luke

Luke was twenty-one and had danced for less than one year at the time he was interviewed (in 2010), but he has been dancing ever since. Luke had DS and primarily experienced difficulties with hearing and verbal communication. In our interview, I asked him if he was a dancer, to which he responded with a confident "yes!" I then asked if he was a good dancer, and his response was the same. Luke enjoyed being acknowledged by other people, as stated by his mother: "His dance moves have been acknowledged by people … even from the volunteers. I think I see them encouraging him. So I would say definitely his confidence was boosted." I asked Luke to show me the moves he had learned in dance class during our interview. He stood up from the couch in his parents' basement and performed roughly ten seconds of the choreographed dance without music or prompting. Clearly Luke self-identified as a dancer, and it seemed that he was proud of his abilities.

Megan

I recently mentored an undergraduate thesis student, who conducted a case study about a dance program in which she was involved (unpublished). Her study was about Megan, who was twenty-eight years old and had DS. Megan had been dancing for several years in the same program and said "I love to dance!" in her interview. She also said "If something is bugging me, I use my expression on the dance floor", when asked how dance makes her feel. Sarah, Megan's one-on-one dance volunteer, said the dance program positively influenced Megan's self-identity:

> When she dances she's really self-confident and she feels like she can do anything, like really. When she dances it's basically like she just lets it all go. You can tell that she's not thinking about anything else but like in that moment just dancing. Yeah it's awesome, so I think she really feels confident in herself.

Megan's dance instructor and mother also felt that her self-confidence was evident, not only in the dance class, but also in everyday life. Megan intended to continue participating in this dance program because she enjoyed making friends and learning new dance moves.

Instructors and volunteers

As illustrated above, young people with ASD and DS gained self-confidence and self-esteem from dance. These four individuals were not the only ones to benefit, however, as instructors and volunteers from the cases above discussed this outcome for all participants in their dance programs. Tricia, a dance instructor of over twenty years said that inclusive dance "… is developing some self-esteem and … a positive sense of body image and who they are." Furthermore, program creator and instructor Jaclyn said,

> I think it's that sense of achievement, you know. Coming to a dance studio, taking a dance class sort of changes your self-identity. Like you can now identify yourself as a dancer so you have something to be proud of and tell your friends about. You can show your family your recital, [show] your family the moves that you've learned. It just gives you sort of a sense of confidence, I think. You know I am no longer somebody with a disability; I am a dancer and that's what comes first.

Volunteers in these programs also noticed the far-reaching benefits of dance. For example, Cara, a high school volunteer who worked one-on-one with an eight-year-old boy with ASD said,

They learn different dance moves, which is important. But like, I don't know, they learn to be themselves [laughs]. Because it's just like, you go in and … you're with other people that like, everyone will accept you in that class. So it's like, I can be me, which is cool.

Cara felt that participants experienced a sense of freedom in the dance class to discover who they are and how they move. Finally, Katie, another instructor and program creator, discussed the influence of dance on other components of everyday life. When I asked her if there were psychological outcomes of dance, she said,

Definitely. Like I don't know if psychological is self-esteem and confidence building, but we've had parents say how much it's improved their ability … not necessarily just to perform, but even everyday activities of going up and talking to someone or their ability to raise their hand in class at school or that kind of thing.

Katie saw her dancers build confidence within the classes, but also heard about how this confidence contributed to other aspects of their lives, such as in the classroom at school.

Conclusion

Throughout my years as a dancer, dance instructor, and dance researcher, I have developed an appreciation for the benefits of dance. When I began my research four years ago, I hypothesized that instructors and parents would feel the same way. However, I did not anticipate that self-identity would be a common thread between all of the individuals mentioned above, throughout independent dance programs. While dance provides an opportunity to be physically active – a necessary component of a healthy lifestyle – it also overcomes barriers placed on individuals with special needs. I would argue that this is just as important, if not more so, than being physically active. Building a positive sense of self not only boosts psychological well-being, but also overall quality of life. Recreational dance supports the development of self-identity for individuals with special needs, both within and outside of a dance environment.

Acknowledgements

To my thesis supervisors Dr Pamela J. Bryden and Dr Paula C. Fletcher; Mallory and Jade Ryan at the Dance Ability Movement; Heidi Churchill at Carousel Dance Studio; my thesis mentee Jenna Auger.

Note

All names of individuals presented in this chapter are pseudonyms.

References

Canadian Down Syndrome Society. (2009) *What Is Down Syndrome?* Available at http://www.cdss.ca/information/general-information/what-is-down-syndrome.html [Accessed April 25, 2016].

Health Canada. (2013) *Autism*. Available at http://www.hc-sc.gc.ca/hc-ps/dc-ma/autism-eng.php [Accessed April 25, 2016].

Statistics Canada. (2015) *Disability in Canada: Initial Findings from the Canadian Survey on Disability*. Available at http://www.statcan.gc.ca/pub/89-654-x/89-654-x2013002-eng.htm [Accessed April 25, 2016].

2.5

ENCOUNTERING AND EMBODYING DIFFERENCE THROUGH DANCE

Reflections on a research project in a primary school in Finland

Liisa Jaakonaho

Introduction: entering the school

I open the door to the school and walk through the hallway, smelling the canteen food, hearing and sensing the stir of pupils' voices and movements. Suddenly I remember how it felt to be a primary school student, coming to school in the morning. Feelings that this memory brings back are mixed: I remember feeling safe and content, and at the same time uncertain and insecure. Do I fit in? Am I good enough, 'cool' enough? On the corridor wall I see a hand-painted poster with red letters on a black background: "Remember that bullying is absolutely forbidden in this school!" I walk towards the classroom, feeling affected by the environment, and optimistic about what is about to happen (Excerpt from my field notes in Martinlaakso school, Vantaa, September 2016).

Reflections at the beginning of the project

Children in Finland enter the school system the year they reach the age of seven. They come from different social and economic backgrounds, with different abilities, experiences, expectations and needs. Most of them have participated in some kind of formal early education, and all of them have had one year of pre-school education, provided by kindergartens and schools. Some of them have already had access to arts education as leisure activities, or in their kindergarten. Regardless of where they come from, all of them have had experiences of artistic activity – at the very least through playing. It is natural for children to explore their environment through their creativity, moving and interacting with each other, and with the world, in playful and experimental ways.

Children are likely to have ambivalent or difficult feelings about school: anxiety, excitement and insecurity about how they will fit in. In this sensitive phase, they need support and an empathetic presence from adults, both at home and in school. The change from kindergarten to school means less time for creative, free play and more sitting down in front of a desk; less physical, creative activity and more academic learning that involves discipline and concentration. However, physical activity and learning through the body is key to children's development (Anttila, 2015).

For children's learning, development and well-being, it is also important that the atmosphere in the classroom is open and supportive. Every child deserves to be accepted, seen and heard equally, as an individual. According to Tuula Gordon, Janet Holland and Elina Lahelma's research in secondary schools in Helsinki and London, the reason for teasing, bullying and cursing is often some kind of difference (Gordon, Holland & Lahelma, 2000: 131–132). Difference is potentially dangerous and the safe position is to be 'average' or 'same as others'. However, when students form groups and alliances, the constructions of sameness and difference become more fluid; some differences may be seen as positive and some negative.

In my work as a dance movement therapist and pedagogue, I have had the opportunity to encounter different individuals and groups whilst utilising the medium of dance. I have met people in care homes, day centres, hospitals, schools; people with a diagnosis of mental health problems, disabilities, special educational needs; people at different stages of their lives from the first years of their education to retirement. Through a creative approach to embodiment and movement, combined with a psychodynamic and pedagogic approach to verbal reflections, it has been possible to facilitate and foster positive change, integration and well-being. I have experienced that, through a sensitive and playful approach to contemporary dance pedagogy, it is possible to encourage awareness and acceptance of differences and support the development of self-awareness, social skills and confidence. Through creative movement and supported verbal reflections, children can become more aware, and able to acknowledge that difference is something we all share. This decreases the pressure to fit in, to be the same. Through performative play and movement, diversity can be acknowledged, celebrated and embraced.

Embodying (and making a) difference in the school

In ArtsEqual research initiative[1] I am involved in a research group called Arts@School. The group focuses on questions related to inclusion, participation and equality in Finnish schools from the viewpoint of arts education. In the project researchers design and carry out interventions in schools to develop institutional structures and teaching practices both in and through the arts.

My work in the group materialised into an ethnographic action research intervention, titled 'Embodying Difference through/in Dance'[2] in Martinlaakso primary school, Vantaa in Autumn 2016. In the intervention I facilitated small group creative movement sessions, together with a colleague, for groups of six to seven first and second grade pupils. Sessions lasted twenty minutes at a time. The pupils were from two classes; one basic education class and one SEN (Special Educational Needs) class. Pupils were mixed into small groups so that there were mixed-ability and mixed-gender groups, as well as single-gender groups, and one group with no SEN pupils. All together, there were five sessions per group, taking place once a week. Within the same intervention, during the same period, there was another researcher facilitating large group movement sessions for both classes together.

The small group sessions took place in an auditorium space of the school; a space with a stage and a large, rising audience area. We introduced various creative movement tasks and encouraged the pupils to come up with their own movement ideas. The small groups were also an opportunity for pupils to reflect and process their experiences from the large group.

My colleague and I also observed the large group sessions, so that we were able to repeat and develop further exercises that had been introduced there.

At the beginning of each session, one of us went to collect the pupils from their class-rooms and walked them to the auditorium. Entering the auditorium seemed to be exciting for pupils; they were running around the space and using their voices with high volume and energy. Before we managed to start, we witnessed, for instance, opera-style loud singing and cartwheels, amongst other spontaneous acts on the stage. When I reflected their excitement, they told us that they rarely have access to this space during school days. So, the first challenge was to get everyone's attention and gather them together.

While we were giving instructions and asking questions, many pupils were jumping up and down with arms in the air, asking to be the first one to answer a question or show move-ments, even before the instruction was given or the question asked. The sense of disappoint-ment when someone else was given the chance first was expressed clearly by loud objections, collapsing on the floor, moaning and even crying.

Obviously these behaviours could simply be seen as evidence of the pupils' enthusiasm to participate in the group. However, psychodynamically I see them as signs of the pupils' *need to be seen*. According to the psychodynamic view, early interactions between the baby and her mother are the foundation for one's sense of self. The baby starts to feel their own existence through the experience of being seen by the mother, looking at the face of her mother as the mother reflects to her with heightened affect (Winnicott, 1964, 1971).

Conclusion

The small group intervention gave the pupils an opportunity to receive individual atten-tion, beyond what is possible in normal classroom settings. Through performative, playful movement exercises, they had the opportunity to be 'seen' holistically as bodily and creative children, with their individual characteristics and needs.

As a researcher in the school, I also saw myself as one of the learners; I was (and still am) also on a journey to a better understanding and acceptance of differences between people. The project made me reflect on basic human questions about how to live with oneself and with others; how to respond to challenges, conflicts and differences; how to maintain open-ness whilst holding onto solid boundaries and values; how to 'see' and 'be seen' with open eyes and receptive bodies.

Notes

1   This research has been undertaken as part of the ArtsEqual project funded by the Academy of Finland's Strategic Research Council from its Equality in Society programme (project no. 293199). (See also www.artsequal.fi/en). ArtsEqual is a Finnish based multidisciplinary research project (2015–2020), coordinated by the University of the Arts Helsinki. ArtsEqual examines how art as public service could advance equality and well-being in society; what mechanisms in Finnish basic services in arts and arts education sustain unequal participation; and, assuming equality as the starting point, how practices in basic services in arts and arts education should be changed.
2   The intervention was a collaboration with post-doctoral researcher and dance pedagogue Isto Turpeinen, and dance teacher Pipsa Tuppela.

References

Anttila, E. (2015) 'Dance as embodied dialogue: insights from a school project in Finland'. In Svendler Nielsen, C. and S. Burridge (Eds.), *Dance Education Around the World: Perspectives on Dance, Young People and Change*, pp. 79–87. London: Routledge.

Gordon, T., J. Holland & E. Lahelma. (2000) *Making Spaces: Citizenship and Difference in Schools*. London: Macmillan Press Ltd.

Winnicott, D. W. (1964) *The Child, the Family and the Outside World*. Harmondsorth: Penguin; Reading, Mass.: Addison-Wesley.

Winnicott, D. W. (1971) *Playing and Reality*. London: Tavistock Publications Ltd.

2.6

NEW SPACES FOR CREATIVITY AND ACTION

Recent developments in the Applied Performing Arts in Catalonia

Jordi Baltà, Eva García and Raimon Àvila

Recent years have witnessed an increasing interest on the part of performing arts professionals in the region of Catalonia in Spain engaging in work in educational, health and community settings. It was in this context that, in 2014, the Barcelona-based Institut del Teatre (Theatre Institute) set up the Observatory of the Applied Performing Arts and later commissioned a report to map trends and needs in this area – addressing training, professional development, production, networking, policy and knowledge management. This article presents the main findings and recommendations emerging from the research, and illustrates them with local projects of inclusive dance practice.

Background

In 2014, Institut del Teatre (IT), a Barcelona-based public centre providing higher education in the performing arts, set up the 'Observatori de les Arts Escèniques Aplicades' [Observatory of the Applied Performing Arts, OAEA], with the aim of collecting, standardising, developing and disseminating specialised knowledge addressing the place of the performing arts in community, educational and health projects. OAEA was also the result of the perceived increase of activities in this area in Catalonia, as well as the acknowledgement that local professionals could take advantage of existing expertise in other countries.

In 2015, a report analysing the current state of this sector in Catalonia, as well as relevant developments in Spain and at the international level, was commissioned by OAEA, aimed at formulating recommendations for the future work of OAEA, IT and other relevant stakeholders (Baltà and García, 2016).

The resulting report addresses the notion of the Applied Performing Arts and examines trends, needs and recommendations. Its main findings, illustrated with some examples from the field of inclusive dance practice, are presented hereafter.

The Applied Performing Arts: defining the scope

The notion of 'Applied Performing Arts' adopted by OAEA draws on similar terms existing internationally such as 'applied drama' or 'applied dance'. However, this remains an emerging, rather than a well-established and universal concept, which coexists with a range of related notions, for instance, 'community arts', 'arts in prisons', 'arts and social inclusion' and 'art-therapy'. In this respect, the report opened with a section devoted to mapping relevant literature and defining the scope of the Applied Performing Arts.

Furthermore, a set of quality criteria which could allow for designing indicators and identifying good practices was also identified. The proposed criteria included the involvement of professionals from different areas of expertise, the contribution to the production of new aesthetics, the ability to integrate participants' demands, the observed effects or impacts in personal development as well as in terms of education, health or community, the sustainability of processes and the integration of a reflection on the ethical aspects of the process.

Evidence from the field

The core part of the report involved an analysis of developments, strengths, weaknesses, opportunities and examples in several thematic areas, as a basis to formulate recommendations, as summarised hereafter.

Training

While undergraduate education in the Applied Performing Arts has been non-existent in Spain thus far, some postgraduate courses have addressed the area. Non-formal education and training, in the form of workshops, courses and seminars, is often provided by practitioners and organisations with field experience, as well as umbrella organisations representing professionals.

In the context of the IT's increasing interest in the Applied Performing Arts, a new course on Applied Dance was added to the curriculum in 2015. The IT has also been involved in several other initiatives including:

- 'Tot Dansa' ['Everything Dances'], a partnership with Barcelona's Institut Municipal d'Educació (Municipal Institute of Education, IMEB) and theatre 'Mercat de les Flors' to foster access and participation in dance among secondary education students.
- 'Ballant amb l'Alzheimer' ['Dancing with Alzheimers'], a partnership with a local NGO representing relatives of Alzheimer's disease patients, which aims to provide patients, their relatives and carers with the benefits of practicing dance, by working with IT students.

In addition, measures have been adopted to adapt the IT's auditions to students with disabilities.

Creativity and production

While many professionals in the performing arts and in other areas increasingly express an interest in the Applied Performing Arts, the limited availability of funding for processes in this area (encompassing creativity, documentation, analysis, dissemination and more) limits methodology transfer and progress.

A relevant recent initiative is the collaboration between the 'integrated' dance company Liant la Troca and the IT's young dance company IT Dansa, who developed a joint production in the context of the 'Mercat de les Flors' 2015 programme 'Capacitats' ['Abilities']. The joint production process and subsequent presentation of a new piece was perceived as a very positive step towards mutual recognition among dancers with and without disabilities, and towards recognition among the broader public, fostering awareness-raising, education and understanding.

Similarly, the IT's dance conservatory and its group of musicians have recently collaborated with community youth orchestra Integra Sons, which provides opportunities for disadvantaged children and youth to develop music-playing skills. Since Integra Sons brings together young people from the Poble Sec area, where IT is based, this was also seen as a step enabling IT to reach out to its immediate environment and strengthen community connections.

Elsewhere, inclusive dance group Plataforma Marge Contemporani has explored the notion of (dis)ability, its relation with artistic practices and the promotion of community health. Its project 'Espais cecs' ['Blind Spaces'] involves participants with and without visual disabilities, who develop joint pieces exploring issues such as existence and absence, the visible and the unseen. Initially focusing on the experience of bodies and sight, the work goes on to explore imperceptible spaces in society, thus leading to a reflection on the issues that society prefers not to address.

Distribution

Recent years have witnessed the emergence of a set of specialised festivals in some areas of the Applied Performing Arts, for example art and disability, as well as the integration of Applied Performing Arts projects in mainstream festivals and venues. Rather than resulting from political leadership decisions or pressure from funding bodies, very often these developments have been the result of individual decisions by festival or venue directors.

One relevant example in this area is 'Barris en Dansa' ['Dancing Neighbourhoods'], one of the most visible projects in community dance in Barcelona. Led by choreographer Álvaro de la Peña and the Iliacán dance company, the project aims to strengthen community ties through the vehicle of dance. Initially conducted in small towns, the initiative was first established in Barcelona in 2012 and has been implemented in several neighbourhoods and towns since. Each new location involves a local venue and a wide range of participants including children, young people, adults, people with disabilities and artists who work in small groups over a year and later bring together their pieces in a final public presentation, reaching well-established venues in Barcelona.

Another significant project leading to a public presentation is 'PI(E)CE: Proyecto intergeneracional de creación escénica' ['Intergenerational Performing Arts Creativity Project'], launched in 2011 by choreographer Constanza Brncic and playwright Albert Tola alongside the independent theatre venue Tantarantana, and continuing to this day. 'PI(E)CE' involves secondary school students and elderly neighbours from the highly-diverse areas of Raval and Poble Sec in Barcelona, who jointly receive guidance from professional performing artists and develop a performing arts piece. One professional work, addressing personal, social and political issues, is produced and presented every year, the most recent one being part of the programme of the Barcelona International GREC Festival.

Networking

The Applied Performing Arts include a very diverse and fragmented range of initiatives – this leads to the segmentation of expertise and limits knowledge transfer, yet also makes it necessary to foster networking. Some networks in this area already exist and an increasing number of seminars and meetings, including the OAEA's own biennial forum, are held and enable networking. However, existing initiatives tend to mainly attract performing arts professionals rather than those active in education, health or community work.

Public policy

Public authorities have generally paid limited attention to the emergence of the Applied Performing Arts, even though a few exemplary initiatives exist. Public funding programmes and agreements with regularly-funded organisations rarely include criteria regarding the social and educational value of the arts. In addition, policy departments which could adopt 'enabling' measures for the Applied Performing Arts, for instance education and social affairs, appear to have a limited understanding of the relevance of this field. Transversal or 'joined-up' policy reflection and design mechanisms bringing together the arts, education, community and/or health are also absent in Catalonia.

Knowledge generation and transfer

Traditional research and training approaches in the performing arts in Catalonia and Spain have scarcely addressed their social value and relevant methodologies in this field. In addition, organisations active on the ground have limited resources to document, evaluate and disseminate knowledge generated, while networks and umbrella organisations facilitating the systematisation and transfer of experiences are also missing.

References

Baltà, J., & E. García. (2016). *Nous entorns de creació i intervenció: Informe-diagnòstic de les arts escèniques aplicades [New Environments for Creation and Invention: Diagnostic Information of the Applied Scenic Arts]*. Barcelona: Institut del Teatre. Available at http://oaea.institutdelteatre.cat/wp-content/uploads/2016/04/Nous-entorns-de-creaci%C3%B3-i-intervenci%C3%B3_-Informe-Diagn%C3%B2stic-de-les-Arts-Esc%C3%A8niques-Aplicades.pdf [Accessed 17 September 2016].

Institut del Teatre. (2014) *Fòrum d'Arts Escèniques i Inclusió Social. Informe final* [Forum on Performing Arts and Social Inclusion. Final Report]. Barcelona: Institut del Teatre. Available at http://oaea.institutdelteatre.cat/wp-content/uploads/2014/11/informe_observatori_novembre14.pdf [Accessed 17 September 2016].

PART III

Changing practice for dance education

PHOTO Freefall Dance Company UK
Photographer: Alex Griffiths

3.1

SUPPORTING CHANGE

The identification and development of talented young dancers with disabilities

Imogen Aujla, Emma Redding and Veronica Jobbins

Introduction

In 2013, Trinity Laban Conservatoire of Music and Dance partnered with Dance4, a national dance agency in the UK, to conduct research into the identification and development of talented young dancers with physical disabilities. Broadly, the aims of this research were to: assess the applicability of existing criteria used to identify individuals with potential to identifying talented dancers with disabilities, and explore the barriers to opportunities in dance faced by disabled dancers. In doing so, recommendations were made for greater access and provision. This research culminated in two published peer reviewed journal articles and a symposium with key policy makers and teachers working with and supporting young dancers with disabilities.

This chapter will provide context to the Trinity Laban research by acknowledging the general concerns within UK education and the arts and dance sector as to the relatively few disabled dance artists. The research will then be discussed with an example of how the findings of the research have since been implemented by a very well regarded, inclusive dance company, Stopgap.

Context

For many years, the UK community dance sector has played an important role in widening access to dance for people with disabilities. A large variety of recreational opportunities for participation now exist in the UK, which range from regular classes to one-off workshops and projects for people of all ages. At the other end of the scale, several professional inclusive dance companies produce high-quality performance work, touring nationally and internationally; notably Candoco Dance Company, formed in 1991 as a dance company for both disabled and non-disabled dancers [Photo 3.1]. However, there has been a perceived gap between community dance participation, especially with young people and the training opportunities and routes for progression that could lead to performing in a professional company (Charnley, 2011; Verrent, 2003). This suggests either that young disabled people are

PHOTO 3.1 *The Show Must Go On*
Candoco Dance Company,
Choreography: Jerome Bel
Photographer: Pedro Machado (2015)

not accessing dance training, or that they are excluded from participating. As a result, professional disabled dancers often 'learn on the job' rather than follow an established progression
route (Verrent, 2003).

These issues have become more prominent in recent years in the UK as disabled dance
artists themselves have become more vocal, and dance sector organisations and individual
dance practitioners have become more aware of the need for change across participatory
practice as well as at a professional level. The research outlined within this chapter is just
one initiative among many in the UK that seeks to combat the barriers that exist for young
disabled dancers in first accessing dance and in developing their dance skills, and in their
potential progression into a professional dance career. Strategically, a number of dance and
disability organisations have been working together to identify and raise awareness of the
issues that prevent full participation and progression for disabled dancers, forming networks
such as those led by People Dancing and Dance for Change. The Arts Council for England
has equally made a commitment to promoting and embedding diversity throughout their
work through their Creative Case for Diversity.

Activity across the dance sector that has attempted to address these issues has included a
range of approaches. These include: broadening opportunities for children and young people

to first encounter dance, both in the informal youth dance sector as well as in schools; developing training courses and programmes to enable dance artists and teachers to understand better how to provide inclusive dance experiences for young disabled dancers and build their confidence to do so; developing resources and digital platforms to disseminate opportunities and practice; promoting positive role models; and supporting disabled dance artists to develop a professional career.

Research project: the identification and development of talented young dancers with disabilities

Introduction

There is general recognition of the dearth of progression routes for dancers with disabilities who wish to undertake advanced training for a professional performing career. Alongside the many concerns from the dance sector as to how best to train disabled dancers, there is a lack of understanding of how to identify talent among dancers with disabilities in the first place. This issue was highlighted in 2013 by Dance4, a national dance agency in Nottingham, as they were establishing their Centre for Advanced Training (CAT) in Dance. The ten national dance CATs, supported in England by the Department for Education, aim to identify and train young people aged ten to eighteen years with exceptional potential in dance by offering non-residential intensive dance training programmes. "Whilst establishing our Centre for Advanced Training in the east Midlands, it became apparent that disabled young people were not presenting themselves as potential students" (Paul Russ, Chief Executive/Artistic Director, Dance4).

Thus, Dance4 worked with Trinity Laban to undertake a research project which aimed to investigate the criteria that might be appropriately applied at audition, and then explore practical considerations for talent identification and development.

Dance talent is complex and multidisciplinary, comprising at the least physical and technical skills, but also psychological characteristics and artistic abilities (Walker, Nordin-Bates & Redding, 2010). Importantly, weaknesses in one area (e.g. technique) may be compensated by strengths in another area (e.g. creative potential), and indeed no one factor alone can indicate talent or predict future success (Walker et al., 2010). Furthermore, many of the physical characteristics associated with talent, such as flexibility and balance, can be improved with training (Redding, Nordin-Bates & Walker, 2011), indicating that the talent development environment is as important as the talent selection process. However, to date very little research has been conducted addressing notions of talent identification and development among young dancers with disabilities.

Method

This study adopted a qualitative methodology and included a series of in-depth semi-structured interviews and focus groups with eighteen expert dance practitioners who had at least ten years of prior experience in the inclusive dance sector. Three of the participants had a disability although the majority were non-disabled. An interview guide was created, which included questions around talent identification and talent development. In addition, the talent identification criteria used by four of the existing gifted and talented inclusive youth groups and training programmes were collected, and observations of four dance groups' technique classes took place.

The data were content analysed according to guidelines for qualitative analysis, trustworthiness (Patton, 2002) and data triangulation (Moran-Ellis et al., 2006). Quotations from the interviews are included in the results so that readers can independently assess the appropriateness of interpretations (Sparkes, 1998).

Results and discussion

Talent identification criteria

The results from the analysis of the talent identification criteria shared by four known inclusive dance companies are shown in Table 3.1. The criteria fall into four broad categories: physical and performance skills; creative potential; psychological characteristics; and approach to working in dance. A fifth potential category emerged, which was around support. Importantly, it was not being suggested that each dancer should exhibit every criterion at audition; rather, it seems a combination of some of these factors could indicate talent or potential in a young dancer with disabilities.

TABLE 3.1 Talent identification criteria as identified by four known inclusive dance companies

Category	Criteria	Notes
Physical and performance skills	• Physical potential/raw talent • Dynamic range • Control • Spatial awareness • Movement memory • Working to optimum • Performance quality • Embodiment	 Can be affected by dyspraxia Can be difficult for SEN students
Creative potential	• Creative response • Improvisation • Problem-solving ability • Effective communication of ideas	
Psychological characteristics	• Passion and enthusiasm • Interest in all aspects of dance • Commitment	

Approach to working	• Able to work as a group
	
	• Focus and concentration
	
	• Able to use feedback
	• Able to evaluate and reflect
	• Openness
	• Task persistence
		Can be difficult if on autistic
		  spectrum
		May fluctuate but can be
		  trained
		Can be difficult for SEN
		  students
		Can be difficult if on autistic
		  spectrum

Support system	• Parents/carers/PAs • Transport needs	

A small number of the interviewees who took part in this study mentioned the importance of specific physical factors traditionally associated with dance, such as flexibility and strength, as talent criteria. Most practitioners recognised that if such skills are trainable then they are not essential to assess at audition, particularly among young disabled dancers whose access to prior dance training may be limited. These findings are in line with new thinking around the physical characteristics of dance talent, many of which improve over time with quality training, and thus need not be honed to a great extent at the point of audition (Redding et al., 2011). Rather, movement quality, creative potential, passion and the young person's approach to working emerged as being far more important.

The interviewees shared that they look for "an exquisite movement quality" (p. 10) or "something innately interesting in their movement" (p. 6). Embodiment was also mentioned indicating a preference towards individuals who explore, positively, their own unique bodies. This, combined with creative potential, passion and the dancers' work ethic, appeared to form the cornerstones of talent identification. Psychological characteristics and approach to working in dance included passion, commitment, openness, concentration and task persistence.

It was felt by the interviewees that educators conducting auditions should be open-minded when applying audition selection criteria to different dancing bodies. The practitioners interviewed recommended that auditions are multi-modal, including a practical session with a creative element, some collaborative or group work, and an informal interview. The interviews could assess the dancers' interest and passion for dance, and would provide an opportunity to find out more about their specific needs, and the level of support they already have in place and would need. Ideally, multiple sessions rather than one-off auditions should be conducted, because:"... a good day for you or me is a great day – a bad day, you can get through it. Good days and bad days for young disabled people can fluctuate so enormously" (p. 1). By giving young people the opportunity to work on skills across several audition sessions, educators can further assess a dancer's potential, enthusiasm and ability to work with others, while the dancers themselves can gain insight into the level of work and commitment involved.

Talent development and training

Three key themes pertinent to talent development emerged from the interviews with practitioners: mechanisms that should be in place prior to commencement of training; the approach of the educator; and practical considerations.

Mechanisms that should be in place prior to commencement of training

It is important to get to know the dancer and his or her physical and communication needs before training starts so that support thereafter can be optimised. Prior knowledge of the student should include not only physical factors but also "movement memory and ability to deal with change" (p. 2), and could be gleaned from physiotherapy screening, doctor's reports and conversations with students, their parents and/or personal assistants (PAs). This information can be used to plan training, including whether or not support assistants will be needed in the studio.

An understanding of the dancer's physical range and limitations could ensure that teachers challenge dancers appropriately and that intensive dance training would not be detrimental to their physical health. Skilled dance assistants can provide valuable support to individual dancers for adaptation of exercises and detailed feedback. This may be particularly important given that disabled dancers without significant prior training may lack confidence and knowledge about the structure, expectations, pace and discipline of a technique class (Whatley, 2007). Additionally, parental support, and/or support from personal assistants, is crucial. One of the interviewees explained: "As a young person you absolutely need the support and encouragement of people at home" (p. 3). In fact, parental support is so important that, as noted in Table 3.1, it may represent a secondary talent criterion during selection processes.

Approach of the educator

The practitioners interviewed felt that teachers should be skilled, reflective and flexible, and willing to adapt and develop their own teaching style to suit the needs of the students. This could be achieved through an open-minded, problem-solving approach and an investment in reflecting on one's own practice.

Several practitioners stated that communication was a critical consideration for training young disabled dancers. The importance of building a partnership was discussed whereby students can feel confident in discussing their strengths and limitations with a teacher, and where the teacher does not feel pressured to 'know everything'. Indeed, teachers should recognise that disabled dancers themselves can bring much to the educational and training process: "they probably know their body really well, they have to manage physical challenges in their daily lives, and that's how you learn precision and control" (p. 14). The use of inclusive language was also deemed important, alongside a willingness to try several different methods of communication in order to connect with students. Effective means of communication may include verbal instruction, visual prompts such as pictures and symbols, and shadowing (Block & Johnson, 2011).

Teachers often lack confidence and report anxiety with regard to inclusive work and adapting the curriculum, which can result in them being reticent to challenge students with disabilities (Verrent, 2003; Whatley, 2008). However, it was noted in both the interviews and observations that practitioners had high expectations of their students. Setting high standards presumably not only pushes students to develop their talents, but also enhances their confidence. Additionally, the notion of encouraging or expecting a level of professionalism emerged, so that students are engendered with an understanding of the etiquette of class and performance, and the hard work that is necessary in order to improve.

Overall, an approach which emphasises mutual respect and reflective practice will facilitate open communication, confidence and talent development. The creation of a task-involving motivational climate (Ames, 1992) may encompass these suggestions, through an emphasis on self-referenced learning, effort and hard work, peer collaboration and acceptance of mistakes as part of the learning process. A task-involving motivational climate can encourage young people to remain committed to training, even when such training is technically difficult and physically tiring (Redding et al., 2011).

Practical considerations

All of the interviewees recognised that dancers with disabilities typically need more time to learn and embody skills: training programmes should be of longer duration than those for non-disabled dancers, which may have resource implications for both the provider and the student. Repetition is also crucial for learning skills. However, while more time and repetition may be necessary to work on technical skills, the pace of the class is still important. Maintaining pace while meeting varied student needs can be challenging (Darbyshire & Nilsen, 2001), but it could be that the focus of the class changes over time to a deeper understanding of technique once the young person is accustomed to the nature of the class. Furthermore, rest breaks might be needed, at least initially, to prevent discomfort, overuse injuries and 'information overload' (Darbyshire & Nilsen, 2001; Whatley, 2007). Balancing repetition with opportunities for students to make autonomous choices will help to maintain their interest and promote self-confidence.

A second key practical consideration was adaptation of class material. Successful adaptation relies upon setting clear expectations and identifying the essence or aim of the movement (e.g. rotation) rather than a particular aesthetic. Importantly, adaptation represents a means for teachers to develop their own practice: "it means that we can't be lazy about these terms [e.g. elevation] … we have always to interrogate and make sense of those ideas, and that's great because everybody has to do it" (p. 13). Indeed, participants felt that an ethos of adaptation for all is valuable "to always encourage participation and adaptation and translation for everybody so that becomes the norm" (p. 13). In terms of responsibility for adapting material, it could be that initially the teacher and dance assistant set the adaptations and then, as his or her confidence increases, the dancer can work with the dance assistant, or independently, to adapt material (Whatley, 2008).

Conclusion

The results of this study suggest that movement quality, creative potential, passion and a strong work ethic are the most important and appropriate criteria with which to assess a young disabled dancer's talent and potential for further training. Regarding talent development, teachers should aim to know the dancer and his or her particular support needs before training commences and should adopt an open, flexible approach to teaching. Allowing more time and using effective adaptation are important aspects of classes, in addition to ensuring that high standards are set. By adopting the recommendations reported here, teachers may be well placed to support and develop their students' talents optimally.

Case study: Stopgap progression and training model for young dancers with disabilities

Since the publication of this research in 2014, the professional company Stopgap has been developing a progression route for talented young dancers with disabilities as part of their youth work.

Stopgap Dance Company has been training disabled dancers since its establishment in 1995, and it has successfully nurtured a number of disabled dancers in the community to become renowned professionals. Stopgap creates dance productions with these disabled dancers and their non-disabled peers and tours nationally and internationally.

The Stopgap dancers generally take several years of intensive and focused training to gain sufficient skills and professional experience to cope at the highest level, and this has been apparent to the company from early on in its history. If non-disabled dancers require rigorous dance training spanning several years, then disabled ones also require at least the same level of educational investment. The disabled dancers, however, lack the opportunity to receive remotely the same level of investment as their non-disabled peers because the existing training is highly inaccessible. The company therefore recognised that it had to develop alternative training within the organisation to develop adequately trained disabled dancers.

Stopgap's training was largely developed through trial and error because the company had no prior knowledge to use as a reference. Until the early 2000s, most inclusive dance sessions were largely improvisation based with emphasis on creativity and enjoyment. However, Stopgap had wanted to develop classes that instilled more rounded dance skills in all its participants.

The company was fortunate to receive funding from Arts Council England while developing its methodology. This enabled the company to employ two disabled and two non-disabled dancers on full-time contracts, which allowed the company to retain a core team to devise and run the training on themselves. Without having the Arts Council funding over a long period, Stopgap would not have succeeded in keeping its dancers to devise and deliver its innovative training methodology.

Stopgap has since refined its training and has become more efficient at developing disabled dancers. It has created several training tiers within its organisational framework, which is modelled on academy systems used by professional football clubs. It consists of outreach workshops that identify talent in the community, which feeds its youth companies, and they in turn feed the emerging artists and professional companies higher up the chain. In effect, Stopgap has built an inclusive pathway to profession within its own framework.

All the training is designed to serve the artistic vision of the company, but the level of rigour is made appropriate to each tier. The company piloted its inclusive dance syllabus called IRIS at the Youth Company in 2016. In developing IRIS, Stopgap focused on two barriers identified by the research reported above. The first barrier is the codified techniques, created on a certain type of body, on which dance training is typically based. Existing dance education tends to be led by a traditional set of aesthetic values, and these are manifested in syllabi that many young people follow. These traditional views dictate that technically advanced dancers are able to move in certain ways, and this acts as the major barrier to grassroots dance training for disabled people. However, Stopgap knew from experience that contemporary dancers who are considered to be 'exceptional' are not necessarily bound by these traditional values. Rather, many contemporary choreographers appreciate diversity and they judge dancers on whether they know how to use their physique for non-verbal expression. Stopgap therefore decided to create an alternative syllabus that values diversity and enables disabled people to succeed and progress. This discovery has progressed further up Stopgap's development pathway, and the company is currently reviewing how they judge dancers at emerging and professional levels.

The other barrier that the company has focused on is the fact that dance provision for disabled people from the UK varies from region to region. The company realised that the role of a syllabus is to bring consistency to the training and assessment of a group of people, and its distribution to different regions can act as a widening of this consistency. It will require continuous teacher training to sustain such consistency, but IRIS allows Stopgap to share its systematic training for disabled people in the UK and worldwide.

Summary

Young disabled people wishing to access dance face several barriers, including aesthetic, attitudinal, training-related, logistic and access barriers. Further, they appear not to have access to information about dance provision. One of the most effective means of overcoming barriers to dance training appears to be the establishment of local and national networks in the inclusive dance sector in order to build progression routes to increase the visibility of inclusive dance, signpost activities to young people and provide enrichment opportunities such as shadowing and mentoring. The more that communication is facilitated between providers, the greater the chance that young disabled people will be encouraged to engage in dance at a range of levels, be it for enjoyment or talent development.

There is shared agreement in the UK that there are still intractable barriers for many young disabled people in dance, including the perception among the young people themselves as well as their families, teachers and many in society around them, that dance is not for them.

In the introduction to the publication *Changing Perceptions* (Dance4) Caroline Bowditch, a Scotland-based independent disabled performance maker and choreographer, highlighted that while many more opportunities for young disabled dancers are opening up there is still much work to be done: "One of the greatest sticking points that remains is convincing disabled people, of any age, that they DO belong in dance studios, that dance IS for them and that they CAN dance!"

Acknowledgements

This research was commissioned by Dance4 with funds from the Department for Education (DfE).We gratefully acknowledge the contribution of Stopgap Dance Company to this chapter.

References

Ames, C. (1992) 'Achievement goals and the classroom motivational climate', in *Students' Perceptions in the Classroom: Causes and Consequences*, edited by J. Meece & D. Schunk. Hillsdale, NJ: Erlbaum, pp. 327–348.

Aujla, I. & E. Redding. (2013) 'Barriers to dance training for young people with disabilities'. *British Journal of Special Education*, 40(2). Wiley & Sons Ltd, partially reprinted by permission of the publisher.

Aujla, I. J. & E. Redding. (2014) 'The identification and development of talented young dancers with disabilities'. *Research in Dance Education*, 15(1). Taylor & Francis Ltd. Available at http://www.tandfonline.com, partially reprinted by permission of the publisher.

Aujla, I. J. & E. Redding. (2013) 'Barriers to dance training for young people with disabilities', *British Journal of Special Education*, 40(2), pp. 80–85.

Aujla, I. J. & E. Redding. (2014) 'The identification and development of young talented dancers with disabilities', *Research in Dance Education*, 15(1), pp. 54–70.

Block, B. A. & P. V. Johnson. (2011) 'The adapted dance process: Planning, partnering and performing', *Journal of Physical Education, Recreation and Dance*, 82(2), pp. 16–23.

Charnley, E. (2011) 'Towards a new vision of dance', *Animated*, Winter, pp. 25–27.

Dance4. (2013) 'Changing Perceptions', publicity publication.

Darbyshire, C. & S. Nilsen. (2001) *Investigating Inclusive Teaching Practice*. London: Independent Dance.

Moran-Ellis, J., V. D. Alexander, A. Cronin, M. Dickinson, J. Fielding, J. Sleney & H. Thomas. (2006) 'Triangulation and integration: processes, claims and implications', *Qualitative Research*, 6(1), pp. 45–49.

Patton, M. Q. (2002) *Qualitative evaluation and research methods*. Thousand Oaks, CA: Sage.

Redding, E., S. M. Nordin-Bates & I. J. Walker. (2011) *Passion, Pathways and Potential in Dance: An Interdisciplinary Longitudinal Study into Dance Talent Development*. London: Trinity Laban.

Sparkes, A. C. (1998) 'Validity in qualitative inquiry and the problem of criteria: implications for sport psychology', *Sport Psychologist*, 12, pp. 363–386.

Verrent, J. (2003) *Disability and the Dance and Drama Awards Report*. Sheffield: DfES.

Walker, I. J., S. M. Nordin-Bates & E. Redding. (2010) 'Talent identification and development in dance: a review of the literature', *Research in Dance Education*, 11(3), pp. 167–191.

Whatley, S. (2007) 'Dance and disability: the dancer, the viewer and the presumption of difference', *Research in Dance Education*, 8(1), pp. 5–25.

Whatley, S. (2008) *Moving Matters: Supporting Disabled Students in Higher Education*. Coventry: CeMAP/ Palatine.

3.2

REFLECTIONS FROM A/R/TOGRAPHY

Perspectives to review creative activities with special needs children

Shu-hwa Jung and Chung-shiuan Chang

Introduction

Working with fifteen special-needs children the researchers highlight participants' experiences and objective thoughts on, for example, the spatiality and motility of the body to investigate how these children are facilitated to develop and learn in their own way. Through the methodology of a/r/tography and the theoretical concept of Merleau-Ponty's 'Phenomenology of Perception' (2002), this chapter shares arts-based action research processes and reflections that were incorporated in an arts integration teaching programme.

This research was undertaken within a three-year curriculum reform project under the framework of a 'Society, Humanity, Science' infrastructure sponsored by the Ministry of Education in Taiwan. The purpose of the project is to encourage, in higher education, inter-disciplinary curriculum design and co-teaching with more practice-oriented as well as action research-based methods.

This chapter shares the process and outcomes initiated in the arts curriculum in an elementary school in Taipei. The two researchers cooperated with twelve postgraduates to deliver arts courses weekly from February to June of 2014. By integrating various creative arts activities, the participants formed a cooperative-learning team to guide fifteen special-needs children (ten boys and five girls), to help them develop longer concentration time in learning, and greater awareness of themselves, as well as their environment.

Research methodology

The class is our research field, and the place for creativity and practice. A/r/tography is a research methodology (Irwin, 2004) that comprehends both arts-based and practice-based life inquiry educational research; the methods can be applied to an exploration of life, dance, drama, autobiography, narrative and more. A/r/t stands for 'artist, researcher, teacher', a person who can adopt these three roles in their professional life or in a research/teaching community that is composed of a multi-disciplinary group. Irwin (2004) describes a/r/tography as a metonymic métissage: "artist-researcher-teacher accounts of their work as they attempt to integrate theoria, praxis, and poesis, or theory/research, teaching/learning, and art/making" (p. 28).

Irwin likens this structure to the social and cultural development that occurs when a new language enters a culture which, over time, would create a third new culture and identity.

Methods

Based on action research, there are three research purposes as follows:

1. To develop a learning community of a/r/tographers in which each member gradually crosses the boundaries normally found between the artist, teacher and researcher, therefore providing different models or paradigms of identity through this learning community of.
2. Link and deepen Merleau-Ponty's theory to integrated arts teaching and learning (creative activities).
3. Special-needs children are facilitated to learn and express in their own ways through various arts activities, named 'arts-integration teaching methods' (AITM).

Learning community

This community consists of all participants including professors and postgraduates from the university, Kun-du Elementary School teachers and elementary students. We university professors proposed a course-based programme within which twelve postgraduates designed arts-integration activities for fifteen special-needs children to develop their social and language skills. The twelve postgraduates are majors in theatre, dance, fine art, music, interactive arts and social work.

Course setting

For the programme for teaching and learning, we used an 'arts-integration teaching method' (AITM), in which all participants were working together.[1] The courses lasted ten weeks and consisted of 150-minute-long sessions. The teaching targets were:

1. learner centred
2. arts-based activities
3. learning through aesthetic experience
4. inquiry-based learning
5. discovery learning

The course was divided into four parts:

1. 45-minute arts-integration activities for elementary students; these had three sections: warm-up for 8 minutes, main activity for 25 minutes, ending review for 12 minutes
2. discussion, dialogue, idea exchange, experience sharing and reflection-on-action (this part did not apply to elementary students)

3. reading of relevant literature and articles by postgraduates, who also mentored other students to encourage questioning and discussion
4. response to, and summary of, the various points by professors, in the context of the whole process

Inter-disciplinary cooperation

Postgraduates from different fields made good use of their expertise to contribute to the teaching; for example, a fine art major would introduce an art work as a main contribution; a dance major might use body movement as a focus; and a drama major could use improvisation in dialogue. Subsequently, they would focus on different professional perspectives in discussion, question the framework of ideas and innovate new thinking within the project.

Trans-disciplinary view points

In this project we hoped to view arts education from the perspective of the phenomenology of the body and the development of children; we did not want to be trapped within a single framework or point of view. Therefore, we invited two professors who specialise in Merleau-Ponty's notion of 'Phenomenology of Perception' and who gave the postgraduates four keynote lectures on the phenomenology of the body, to rethink what is the subjectivity of the body, and to think of the connection between experience and memory. We reflected on these ideas that inspired all of us to modify our understanding of knowledge in relation to special-needs children, making us examine, consider and observe the body from a changed perspective. For example, one professor was from the field of child psychotherapy and could inform us of relevant points related to psychological counselling during the process.

Data collection

Before we started the courses, we included the postgraduates to observe students' behaviour in the class, and discussed issues that arose with their teachers. Following this, the ten-week course began (see Table 3.2).

Data was collected during the ten-week period from all participants' work, including postgraduate's reflective diaries, professor's observation charts, children's art work and interviews, elementary school teacher's reflective thoughts and interviews, video tapes and photos. There was an inter-weaving and exchange of thoughts among artists, researchers, teachers and students in the manner of A/R/T as a research methodology and its processes of reflective, recursive, reflexive and responsive practice [Figure 3.2].

Data analysis

The research data was analysed according to the qualitative methods outlined by Creswell (2009). The research aimed at those special-needs children, so data was classified according to desirable qualities they might acquire or develop, such as social skills, communication skills, cooperation with others, expression, language skills, DIY skills and more.

TABLE 3.2 Course plan

Week	Course Content	Notes
1 2 3	Arts integration activities for the whole group	Getting to know each other through the group activities 1st to the 3rd week were whole group work Activities focused on improvisation involving body sculpture, movement, drawing and painting
4 5 6 7 8 9	4 small group followed with four themes: (1) water, (2) fire, (3) wind, (4) earth Postgraduates designed arts-integration activities related to the different themes Children rotate each week among the activities for experience of different themes and postgraduate personnel	The 4th week to 9th week, we divided students into four small groups, each group had one theme
10	In the last week, according to the four themes, postgraduates dramatised a story which they named 'Seeds Travelling'	

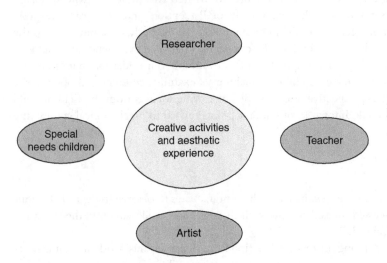

FIGURE 3.2   Four roles inter- and intra-influence

Each postgraduate was asked to write a reflective journal using an 'objective-reflective-interpretive-decisional' method (ORID) (Hogan, 2003). They described objectively what they saw, for example:

- the original status of a child when they joined the course
- what they observed in each child, such as behaviour and character
- whether they had any reflection-in-action during activity-leading
- how they interpret these children's learning conditions
- why and how these children feed back from their experience

The final step was reflection-on-action which led to decisions on how to modify arts-integration activities. These reflective journal entries formed essential data. We spent time in repeated viewings of these videos and readings of the interview manuscripts and reflective journal entries to ensure that the important issues were captured.

Findings: learning and development

Learning community of a/r/tographers

Each member of the 'learning community' played together; we 'played in the arts' and 'education through the arts' was the core of the teaching. We used various artistic media to stimulate the children's sense of body, thus exploring their ability to touch, to feel, to move and to play a role in the space.

Through the process of arts activities, children were becoming more concentrated and committed [Photo 3.2a, 3.2b]. Effective arts' teaching and learning involves all participants in the creative process. The following quotations from journal writings demonstrate some key issues:

> A learning community provides dialogic communication between teachers and students in an interactive relationship in which students' ideas ought to be accepted, given a considerate response, and leads to helping students to have confidence to face reality...
>
> *(PG G journal writing 1 May 2014)*

> In this week, I am guiding to read and discuss the paper on a/r/togrophy written by Rita Irwin. This paper reminds me that the three roles – artist, researcher, teacher – have different functions; how to intermingle with different thoughts from these three roles and also keep in-between is the most difficult and challenging work.
>
> *(PG E journal writing, 24 April, 2014)*

PHOTO 3.2A Hand-made puppets by the children
Photographer: Shu-hwa Jung

PHOTO 3.2B Exploration with elastic bands
Photographer: Shu-hwa Jung

Action through the body

Merleau-Ponty stated that "I do so in so far as my body, always present for me" and "My body, it was said, is recognized by this power to give me 'double sensations' … in passing one role to the other" (2002: 106), which indicates the importance of body awareness. All courses we delivered were designed to cover diverse artforms, and conceived the body as an axis. Multiple activities such as painting, sound design, drama, dance and crafts gave space and opportunities for students to express themselves in a variety of ways. Through the process of arts activities, space, time and other essential elements, and the characteristics of the body, interrelate. The body connects with the outside world directly and space exists there for this to happen. Physical contact with the outside world is the basis of relations between humans and the world, which echoes the concept of Merleau-Ponty's phenomenology. A human being uses the body to see, to hear, to sense, to feel, and it is the basis for how he or she embodies aesthetics and the aesthetics of experience; reflecting on this, we may understand children's physical and emotional changes during the learning process.

These special-needs children had their own characteristics, and they understood the world through their experiences and interaction with others, with the revelation of meanings. The following quotation is from a postgraduate journal and concerns a boy, 'A-ming'. On the day of the journal entry, all participants were attracted by A-ming's words and actions; he gave new metaphors and meanings.

> At the beginning of introduction, A-ming asked: "Can I use a fake name?" The facilitator tried to ask him why he wanted to use a nickname. Afterwards, A-ming began to share many of his nicknames. But he mentioned one nickname "Angel" several times. He said that when he helped a friend who had been bullied by classmates, he was given

the nickname "Angel" that day. He said "This is a secret", and made a body movement of Angel wings flying.

(PG D 27 March 2014)

Visible and invisible

The potential of these children fails to appear in the general classroom; but during the period of arts integration teaching, we saw some very good performances and it became clear that they possessed talents that their teachers were unaware of. They had not previously understood that the children had a variety of potentials. They understood finally that the arts have the features of openness, freedom and passion and that adults should give students space and opportunities to vent their emotions and energy, and also that they should provide a stage for the display of this.

In the course of the artistic creation, everyone was given a variety of possibilities to use different materials and everyone was encouraged to do something and take action. Gradually, we saw the transformation and development of the children.

The group of four children had experienced collaboration for the first time – at the

> beginning they had done everything alone. Several weeks later, my observation is that children can mount activities, they employ their creative thinking to discover more, and the atmosphere of the practice was more relaxed. They were willing to cooperate with others.

(PG D 15 May 2014)

Conclusion

This achievement does not mark the end of the journey; the process should be continued to:

Create a learning community

Neither inter-disciplinarity nor intra-disciplinarity are easy to achieve as each field has its own speciality. It is necessary therefore to create a learning community which offers opportunities for people from different fields to work and study together.

The arts have a potential integrative and therapeutic function, as we can see from the changes that occurred in those children in Kun-du Elementary School. We have begun to create a learning community in which we studied, read, discussed and exchanged thoughts on various topics, such as the a/r/t conception, special-needs education and integrated arts teaching methods, plus phenomenology as a research approach. This procedure allows people from different professional areas, who come together to investigate the topic, to share ideas and outcomes as perceived form the perspectives of their different fields, to seek the opportunity for cooperation and coexistence. This interweaving process can lead to the establishment and exploration of a new point of view.

Promote the arts-integration teaching method, AITM

To promote the 'arts-integration teaching method' (AITM) needs long-term planning.

Education processes usually require hard work over a long period to deliver worthwhile results and need time to take root and nourish people during the process of becoming empowered.

Through the strength and quality of arts education, everyone can learn from her/his own ability, so that differences can exist, as Merleau-Ponty says: between seeing and being seen, between touching and being touched, between the eye and the other eye, and the inclusive difference happening in everyone (Merleau-Ponty 2002).

In the process of these courses, we seek every possibility of constructing and blending various media so that children can learn from their own ability. The course will continue to cooperate with Kun-du Elementary School, and continue to explore and discover more about the uses of the arts in teaching.

Government agencies and schools should have the intention to engage in educational reform and be willing to promote school teachers' teaching and learning innovations. In-service training programmes should be mounted to increase teachers' perspectives on teaching and learning and to improve their educational response skills. In addition to the complement of specialist arts teachers, every teacher could become a teaching artist, employing a range of creative approaches to learning. The training system for special-needs teachers should have a profound and rigorous planning programme, which would involve the integration of the arts and AITM into the cultivation of a special education system for teaching and learning. With these capabilities, teachers can help the development of special-needs children and, through early intervention with those children, achieve enhanced learning outcomes.

Note

1   AITM: Arts integrations teaching methods has two parts to explain. The first part is 'arts integration'. That term is from the John F. Kennedy Center for the Performing Arts, who define arts integration as 'an approach to teaching in which students construct and demonstrate understanding through an art form. Students engage in a creative process which connects an art form and another subject and meets evolving objectives in both' (written by Lynne B. Silverstein and Sean Layne for Arts Edge program © 2010).

 The second part is 'teaching methods', which means we use the idea of arts integration when designing our course plan, for example using improvisational drama skill to learn about the conflict in communication and cooperation with others, and in oral as well. Then, we have named it 'arts integration teaching methods' and used the initials AITM. We are continuing to develop various arts integration activities for those special children.

References

Creswell, J. W. (2009) *Research Design: Qualitative, Quantitative, and Mixed Methods Approaches* (3rd ed.) Thousand Oaks, CA: Sage.

Hogan, C. (2003) *Practical Facilitation: A Toolkit of Techniques*. London: Kogan Page.

Hong, Yongshan. (2013) *Art for Teachers' Professional Development*. New Taipei: National Institute for Education.

Irwin, Rita L. & Alex de Cosson (Eds.) (2004) *A/r/tography: Rendering Self Through Arts-Based Inquiry*. Vancouver, BC: Pacific Educational Press.

Irwin, Rita L. (2004) 'A/r/tography: A Metonymic Métissage'. In Irwin, Rita L. & Alex de Cosson (Eds.), *A/r/tography: Rendering Self Through Arts-Based Inquiry*. Vancouver, BC: Pacific Educational Press.

Merleau-Ponty, Maurice. (2002) *Phenomenology of Perception*. Translated by Colin Smith. London and New York: Routledge Classics, Routledge.

Zheng, Jinchuan. (1993) *Merleau-Ponty Aesthetics*. Taipei: Yuan-Liou.

3.3

LEARNING IN ACTION

Intersecting approaches to teaching dance in Timor-Leste and Australia

Kym Stevens and Avril Huddy

> The Timorese communities empowered us … their willingness to learn and acceptance of us into their lives had an impact on us all … I have never felt so connected and I have never performed or taught with such passion and purpose. But it was not until we arrived in Timor that we understood the true meaning of what 'community practice' is, and what working together can achieve.
>
> *(Pre-service teacher, Timor-Leste project)*

Introduction

Dance teachers in twenty-first-century classrooms must be able to adapt their pedagogy to respond to the diverse needs of their students, using reflexive skills often associated with experienced teachers who have been part of a wide range of community collaborative projects. This descriptive case study research examines nine pre-service tertiary dance teachers' pedagogy, developed in a Special Needs school in Australia, as a part of a university project, and how it was then adapted to teach English as an additional language in Timor-Leste (Yin, 2003). This project identified, through group reflective critical analysis, points of intersection in these teaching approaches.

Dance teachers working in community contexts need to be able to adapt to the dynamic and changing nature of their work environment. The ability to acclimatize to changing contexts and to draw from a teaching skills 'toolbox', through self-evaluation and reflective critical analysis, empowers the dance teacher to meet the demands of a changing work environment. As a result of a longitudinal research project into curriculum development in an undergraduate dance course at the Queensland University of Technology, a creative teaching pedagogy that embraces dance teaching and learning in diverse contexts, the Performance in Context Model (PCM) was developed (Stevens and Huddy, 2016). This chapter looks at the findings of a descriptive case study that explored the interrelationship of teaching approaches between one of these Performance in Context units and a Creative Industries project, a unit developed in response to the findings of the PCM research. It identifies the transferable dance teaching skills of the pre-service dance teachers between two projects of diverse contexts: a special needs school in

Brisbane, Australia and an immersive English school in Maliana, Timor-Leste, focusing on the ways in which the pre-service dance teachers implemented these teaching approaches in Timor-Leste as a way of teaching English as an additional language through dance.

By observing the teaching journeys of the pre-service teachers, illuminated through reflective writing (journaling and online), questionnaires, observations and discussions recorded across both projects, the development of their personal teaching practice was documented. This valued the pre-service teachers' previous teaching experiences and also sought to reveal what may be universal in practice as well as identifying what is unique to these particular contexts. In this learning environment, the pre-service teachers take this individual body of previous experience, both pedagogical and cultural, and apply it to a wide variation of authentic learning experiences.

Often the development of a dance teacher's pedagogy is based around their personal learning and teaching experience and a deep knowledge of the students with which they engage. In the case of community dance educators this may involve a long gestation as the artist comes to better know and understand the people with which they will teach and create dance. The innate teaching skills they bring to the community may be a result of many years of trial and error enacted in a range of classroom situations. For pre-service dance teachers training to be a part of these arts communities, this lengthy creative process is often not logistically possible in a university setting and their engagement with communities may be brief and, at times, unrewarding. This highlights the need to duplicate these kinds of experiences for the pre-service dance teacher, within environments that are closely related to those in which they may work in the future.

This accelerated kind of learning experience can be somewhat disjointed, as the changing contexts demand a fluidity in lesson design and implementation. The establishment of a constant within these learning teaching experiences, that articulates commonalities and connections in each of the dance classrooms, enables the beginning dance teacher to consolidate their teaching skills. Conversely, voicing what is already known empowers them to continue to evolve and renew, as both teacher and artist, through recursive teaching experiences. This is not about the homogenization of teaching skills but is rather concerned with the finding of connections between pedagogies that enlighten both student and teacher in a range of teaching contexts. Avoiding a disconnection between theory and practice, and valuing the tacit while articulating a deeper understanding of teaching grounded in tangible life experiences, are central to the training of dance teachers who will work in diverse communities.

Dance scholar Ralph Buck (2015) raises the "need to identify and articulate the values that drive their (dance teachers') practice" (2015: 162), recognizing that teaching dance is about more than teaching steps and embracing the view of dance as an agent of change. Key to the learning experiences of the pre-service teachers are projects that result in some attitudinal change but also develop core dance teaching skills appropriate and adaptable to a range of teaching and learning contexts. In intercultural inquiry with pre-service teachers, Guo, Arthur and Lund identify the importance of teachers being able to negotiate a range of cultural identities and having a view of culture as "dimensions of identity that shift across contexts and over time" (2009: 566). This demands that the pre-service teacher first develops their view of their own culture and how they interpret and relate to their own immediate community, as well as in a broader global sense.

The complexity of these requirements acknowledges the difficulties of training dance teachers who have an acceptance of diversity, with pro-social behaviors, who are altruistic and empathic but above all resilient. For the nine pre-service teachers who were a part of this research, this sense of the complexities of teaching were to be highlighted through the Brisbane project, and then reflected on, as they further developed their teaching skill set in Timor-Leste during the Timor-Leste Dance Teaching project.

The context

Brisbane special needs teaching project

The nine pre-service dance teachers, in their third year of study as a part of an undergraduate dance degree program, initially engaged with Brisbane Special Needs students in a creative collaborative performance and teaching project. The Special Needs students, aged twelve to eighteen years, had a broad range of physical and/or intellectual impairments. This project encompassed a multifaceted collaboration between the pre-service teachers, the school students, teachers and support staff from the school, an experienced community dance artist and two tertiary dance lecturers. The culmination of the project was a performance involving the pre-service teachers and the school students.

This project aimed to immerse the pre-service teachers in collaborative community based arts learning contexts that acknowledged the diverse role of the dance teacher-artist. These experiences assisted in developing high level problem solving skills that supported teacher adaptability through reflective decision making processes. It served to develop links between the pre-service teachers' cultural understandings and to develop a more humanistic teaching approach that supports the view of their students as individuals within their specific context. This moved their learning beyond teaching competency towards a conscious awareness of teaching and learning approaches that acknowledges the complexity of the dance classroom within a community context. Activating both creativity and empathy among these beginning teachers served the purpose not only of teaching, but also reinforcing purpose and building community within the learning environment. "Before this project I was more sympathetic rather than empathetic as I had never really been in a situation where empathy was such a crucial part of the success of the project," commented a pre-service teacher. The sympathetic approach often problematizes students' history and experiences, impeding growth and learning. A more empathetic approach not only acknowledges but also understands students' experiences, facilitating relevant learning activities for each individual.

Timor-Leste English through dance project

The 2016 Timor-Leste Dance project included creating, facilitating and performing dance works and workshops through a collaboration between a teaching team of the nine pre-service dance teachers from Brisbane, supported by a dance lecturer, in Maliana, Timor-Leste. This transcultural dance workshop experience included professional development and shared teaching and learning opportunities, with a focus on exploring teaching English as an additional language through dance.

This multidimensional project aimed to expand and progress the teaching and learning skills and cultural understandings of all teacher participants, Australian and Timorese, while benefiting the students in the Timorese schools. Within this community dance teaching context, with no prescriptive curriculum to adhere to, the pre-service teachers actively created learning activities specifically for the needs of a range of Timorese communities; three to five year old and seventeen to twenty-one year old students. The three to five year old students, who had the choice to attend and leave when they pleased, required lessons designed to engage and entertain, whilst simultaneously embedding English language skills. In the Timor English school context, the young adult students (seventeen to twenty-one years old) were part of a full-time immersive English program which demanded engaging lessons that presented complex interpretation of language as it related to movement. The other dimension of the project involved few moments of explicit instruction, but instead, saw collaborative planning and reflection between the pre-service teachers and Timorese teachers to explore pedagogy. The project served to not only identify the differences that are a result of cultural contrast around language and cultural practices, but the dance specific practices that may shape the pre-service teachers' ideas of what dance, movement and art are. A pre-service teacher after the Timor-Leste project reflected, "I see myself as a communicator and teacher but more importantly I can now envisage my role in a global community to create positive change. I see teaching as a way of using my skills as an artist."

Identifying points of intersection

Reflection on not only teaching approaches, but also on personal responses to changing teaching and learning contexts, informed the identification of points of intersection in teaching approaches implemented in both projects. The development of clear objectives for both projects supported focused reflective activities and allowed the pre-service dance teachers to identify thought-through teaching strategies rather than just tacit dance teaching pedagogies. These reflective activities included observations of their own and others teaching through personal journals, small group focused discussion, small group written reflections, whole group oral presentations, recalls, procedural information and online written reflection in response to specific questions. Reflective activities were ongoing throughout both projects and enabled the pre-service dance teachers' new perspectives through seeing others work in the communities and then developing their own approaches. These developing teaching skills were enhanced through feedback from peers, participants and community stakeholders who were an essential part of this reflective process.

There was a need to identify, through critical reflection, what was valuable and what could be used and why. This questioning enabled the pre-service teachers to not only reflect on their response to teaching situations in the Brisbane school project but to explore what may be fundamental to their practice as teachers. These reflections were then categorized by the researchers into community engagement skills and general teaching skills.

Community engagement skills

The importance of creating relationships with the community as a whole as well as the organizations involved with the community, and the identification of individual community leaders both prior to and during the project, was noted. In the Brisbane project, prior to the pre-service teachers entering the school a relationship had been developed between the tertiary lecturers and the staff of the school, brokered by Life Stream Australia, an organization working to provide opportunities for people with disabilities in the community. This relationship had further been supported by the community dance artist beginning dance classes before the pre-service teachers began their workshops. The community artist began movement exploration that developed fine and gross motor skills through creative activities that looked at home, place and personal narratives to introduce students to the themes of the project. This relationship acted to establish the requirements of the project, to orientate the project participants to the scope of the project and to ensure that the young students were comfortable with the kinds of activities that were planned. The overarching thematic approach was postcards from home which facilitated connections with specific school curriculum requirements i.e. numeracy, literacy, science and life skills.

Transferring this pre-planned community relationship approach to the Timor-Leste project was more difficult as the pre-service teachers had limited access to the Timorese learning communities. Therefore, a number of learning experiences were implemented, prior to leaving for Timor-Leste, to assist the pre-service teachers in orientating themselves to the context; for example, research about the culture and history of Timor-Leste and the existing relationship with Australia provided background to this new country's turbulent past and the resilience of its people.[1] This initial research served to make the pre-service teachers more curious about a country that, although geographically close, was largely unknown to them.

A series of discussions and workshops with a community dance artist who had been working in Timor-Leste provided links to the language and bridged some of the contextual unknowns in the project. The community artist highlighted the importance of engaging with the language and facilitated workshops with visiting Timorese artists who included musicians, dancers, actors and visual artists. The workshops with the Timorese artists enabled the pre-service teachers to trial their teaching strategies, identified through the Brisbane project, and, in a collaborative environment, to experience the challenges of working with a language other than English. It provided a link with the Timorese arts culture as well as raising the awareness of the dilemmas that may arise as a matter of course when communicating in a language other than your own.

Prior to the commencement of the project, a cultural liaison representative established the initial contact with the learning community in Maliana. This link to the community, via a highly regarded friend of the community, resulted in the project starting from a position of trust. This trust acted to build a sense of confidence in the Timorese communities and also enabled the pre-service teachers to have confidence that the project would be supported by these communities. More importantly, it meant that the pre-service teachers had insights into the learning needs of the community, which enabled them to design individual learning experiences for the diverse contexts within Timor-Leste.

The collaborative activities that were designed for the Timor-Leste project mirrored those of the Brisbane project in that they acknowledged the need for co-creation, privileging participation over product creation. The Timor-Leste activities also had strong links to place and individual narratives, although they used purposeful integration of English language skills such as vocabulary, comprehension and pronunciation. Phrasings, emphasis, double meanings for words, synonyms and vocabulary to do with body parts and local geography were used as the basis for movement creation. The unique aspect to both projects was the deliberate and strategic engagement of community members as an embedded part of the project structure. The result was twofold: there was an immediate impact on the pre-service teachers whilst delivering the project, the residue of which, through discussion, facilitated rich ongoing classroom practice.

General teaching skills

Although the learning objectives for each project were different (the Brisbane project was focused on aesthetic movement outcomes and the Timor-Leste project encouraged interaction with spoken English language), many of the general dance teaching skills were transferable. In both contexts, it was essential that the pre-service teachers were self-identifying as both teacher and artist. This privileged dance as a living language and not just as a physical artifact, through its ability to express thoughts and articulate possibilities for the future. In both contexts this resulted in reaching beyond verbal communication and sharing the students' deeply felt beliefs about 'place', using dance as a medium of creation and communication. The pre-service teachers used their artistic knowledge and practices through the physical to lead their students to a more sophisticated use of kinesthetic, oral and written communication.

Use of language

In both of the contexts, the explicit language demands fostered in the pre-service teachers a new inquisitiveness about language and its connection to the kinesthetic. They recognized the need to learn about the learners so they could adapt their linguistic approaches as much as the physical aspects of both projects. With this knowledge following the Brisbane project, the pre-service teachers were more 'ethnographic' in their approach to the learners in Timor-Leste, taking note of personal aspects of the learners' interactions both in and outside of class. They observed the importance of dance and music as a means of communicating historical, social and cultural information in everyday life to the Timorese students. They then used this information to explore the connection between the needs of the learners and developed their linguistic and kinesthetic teaching approaches to establish a new kind of clarity and specificity in communication. "Having knowledge about the students I am teaching will enable me to refine lessons, class discussions, and activities so that they are more effective learning experiences and make the class seem more personal and the material more accessible" said one pre-service teacher (post Timor-Leste project).

The Brisbane project demanded clear modeling of instruction as well as language clarity and constant changes to questioning in line with the variety of abilities within the class. The pre-service teachers identified this teaching approach in reflection prior to the Timor-Leste project but acknowledged the need for an additional focus on error correction when teaching English as an additional language. These oral corrections were often reinforced by physical and written expression as a range of purposeful and meaningful activities were developed to balance linguistic skill development with artistic meaning-making.

Lesson structure

Lesson structures, although similar in both contexts in that they would begin with discussion, a warm-up, exploration of a movement idea and development of choreography, did differ in how they were expressed. In the orientating phase of the lesson Brisbane students would often engage in socially oriented speech interactions, if voice was available to them, using these discussion topics as a starting point for physical explorations. The Timor-Leste pre-service students began class with a shared discussion that compared the pre-service teachers' life and experiences in Australia with that of the Timorese experience as a way of developing interactional language function; these discussions were supported by photos brought by the pre-service teachers, of family, hobbies and other community activities in Australia. This was followed by a physical warm-up that was linked to the use of language for transactional purposes: moving and naming body parts, breaking words into syllables with movement, or movement greeting phrases.

Teaching approaches

The pre-service teachers identified the need for greater flexibility in many aspects of their teaching in response to the diverse needs of their students during the Brisbane project. This was particularly noticeable with instructional wait time when leading activities. Giving time for the students to think and react, either verbally or physically, was directly transferable to the Timor-Leste context. Both student groups required the teachers to pause and give the participants space to gather their thoughts, devise answers and to choose appropriate ways to communicate ideas. This was also transferable to the physical explorations for both groups as they explored and devised ways to communicate ideas through their bodies.

As a part of this flexibility in teaching approach the pre-service teachers used greater reflection 'in action' as they responded to the students within the dance environment (Thompson & Pascal, 2012). After the Brisbane project the pre-service teachers automatically built in reflection, for the students and for themselves as teachers, as a part of the lesson and overall project design, identifying the importance of an awareness of past experience. It also resulted in the design of the teaching and learning approach supporting more focus on goal setting and being more student centered.

> Throughout the lessons I had to search for alternatives if something wasn't going right, to experiment and to be consistently conscious of my environment and the individuals in that space. Ideally, my thinking is that I can plan and prepare all I want but I will only get that fullest capacity of expanding myself through an authentic and engaged experience.
>
> *(Pre-service teacher, post Brisbane project)*

Conclusion

> I learnt that much of teaching is not reciting words and information to students but encouraging them to ask questions, explore theories and create without fear of being judged and simply to guide.
>
> *(Pre-service teacher, Timor-Leste project)*

In an era of teacher accountability, the kinds of critical self-reflection that were an integral part of both these projects helped to develop dance teaching artists who had a clear vision of what they were working to accomplish. By identifying these intersecting teaching approaches across both projects, they were conscious of the learning needs of their students and were able to advocate for an environment within the dance classroom to achieve these learning outcomes. Just as we expect our learners not to 'wait' for knowledge to come to them, these pre-service teachers took whatever conditions were offered to them and used them to create an innovative dance teaching practice, taking at times confronting first person experience and pairing it with external knowledge to explore a range of teaching approaches.

This encouraged an open minded and confident approach to their practice that helped to grow each teacher's individual teaching identity.

Both projects highlighted dance teaching approaches that honored varied ways of communicating with students. This served as a reminder of the importance of observing oral interactions in addition to non-verbal signals as a way of determining progress and comprehension in the dance classroom. Training of dance teachers in university settings should place even greater emphasis on teacher and student use of language, and literacy skills. However, further research into measuring the effectiveness, particularly in the English classroom as an additional language context, of these dance teaching strategies is required. Future action research that focuses on specific dance pedagogies used in the language classroom, in a range of teaching contexts, will help to develop a systematic approach to grappling with the challenges of language teaching and learning through dance.

Acclimatizing teachers to the nature of the communities in which they will practice ensures that learners do not feel marginalized and that they have the necessary support from within their own community. The nurturing of community relationships in association with dance teaching practice ensures that transcultural perspectives are incorporated into all aspects of the dance classroom's social and learning environment. The knowledge from local community leaders and those with specialist knowledge from within these contexts broadens the social and cultural understandings of both teachers and students.

Further examination of intersecting teaching approaches will support the development of the dance teachers of the future who will practice across the breadth of the learning landscape, discovering unexplored ways to engage with dance in community settings. The dance teacher training offered in tertiary settings has developed beyond the formulation of career plans to promote an ethical perspective on teaching an art form through challenging tasks and the use of critical reflective practice. This enables our dance teachers to accept change in themselves and others in this changing global environment and to articulate their challenges and illuminate their own growth as dance teaching professionals.

Note

1   The movement, from the colonial governance of the Portuguese to the conflicts of the Indonesian invasion and subsequent occupation, leading to Timor-Leste's independence in 2002, has resulted in a nation with very little infrastructure and a whole generation of people who have died as a result of this conflict.

References

Buck, R. (2015) 'Stepping back to step forward'. In Svendler Nielsen, C. and S. Burridge (Eds.), *Dance Education Around the World: Perspectives on Dance, Young People and Change* (pp. 182–188). New York: Routledge.

Guo, Y., N. Arthur and D. Lund. (2009) 'Intercultural inquiry with pre-service teachers', *Intercultural Education*, 20(6), pp. 565–577.

Stevens, K. and A. Huddy. (2016) 'The performance in context model: a 21st century tertiary dance teaching pedagogy'. *Research in Dance Education*, 17(2), pp. 1–19.

Thompson, N and J. Pascal. (2012) 'Developing critically reflective practice'. *Reflective Practice: International and Multi-Disciplinary Perspectives*, 13(2): p. 311–325. DOI: 10.1080/14623943.2012.657795 [Accessed 10 January 2014].

Yin, R. K. (2003) *Case Study Research Design and Methods*. Thousand Oaks, CA: Sage Publications.

3.4

EXPLORING DISABILITY AND DANCE

A Papua New Guinean experience

Naomi Faik-Simet

Agnes Aimo comes from the East Sepik province in Papua New Guinea and is forty-one years old. She took a deeper interest in dance after leaving school and joined a small theatre company called 'Raun Isi Travelling Theatre Group' which was an active group in the province and which promoted the performance of contemporary and traditional forms of dance. In 2006 Agnes started working at the Papua New Guinea Red Cross Special Education Center with hearing- and speech-impaired students. This case narrative focuses on her journey as a dance artist who dedicated her passion and time as a teacher to hearing- and speech-impaired students where she saw that the students were very talented and eager to learn – this led her to focus on the students' abilities to learn and perform dance rather than on their disabilities.

Developing hearing and speech through dance

Ms Aimo's undivided commitment has seen many of these special children develop their hearing and speech through certain dance techniques that combine indigenous and modern methods [Photo 3.4]. Using various aspects of Papua New Guinea's traditional dance techniques, Ms Aimo extends the basic techniques to include creativity for easy learning. Firstly, she identifies students' strengths in each of these areas: speech, hearing and their response to movement, music and vocals. Following this initial assessment, she works with the students according to their forte.

The kinds of methods used by Ms Aimo are sign language to communicate mathematics, numbers and dialogue, and speech development for understanding movement and expression. Recorded music and traditional musical instruments such as rattles (made from plant seeds), *kundu* (traditional hand drums) and *garamut* (slit-drums) are fused together and choreographed by Ms Aimo, who calls this Papua New Guinea contemporary performance. Since the introduction of this technique as a process for teaching dance to the disabled, Agnes has seen marked transformation in their cognitive development. Dancers were able to identify with movements that were mimetic of animals and birds. Using these mimetic dances, students could relate to creation as they were familiar with the movements. Ms Aimo consistently developed these techniques with the use of facial expression for the hearing- and speech-impaired dancers.

PHOTO 3.4   Ms Aimo (in front) dance performance with two of her hearing- and speech-impaired dancers
Port Moresby Arts Theatre
Photographer: Naomi Faik-Simet

Mimetic dance movements portraying Papua New Guinea's vast traditions and way of life are extensively used, such as the actions of fishing, flying like a bird, or swimming like a crocodile. These are some of the main dance techniques taught by Agnes. Others are symbolic relating to spiritual mask dancing from her place of origin in Kanduanum village in the East Sepik Province. She uses masks to design costumes and create story lines in the movements, which are easily followed by her students. While dancing and moving, the students develop their hearing and speech ability to respond to the messages in each movement. After each performance, they communicate through sign language and verbal gestures about the story depicted in the dance. She has successfully used this method to develop pedagogy to teach dance to these hearing- and speech-impaired children who have overcome their disability with the power of creative intelligence.

High-Speed Outreach Performing Troupe

An emotional Ms Aimo is always thrilled to discover the talent and ability of her students, and to be able to relate creative dance movement to cognitive learning. Through numerous dance activities, the level of cognitive learning increased in her students who were able to concentrate and perform better in other subject areas. The approach she has taken has led her to establish a performing dance troupe consisting of hearing- and speech-impaired dancers, called the High-Speed Outreach Performing Troupe. The exposure of the group began in 2008 when they were invited by the Institute of Papua New Guinea Studies and the Theatre Arts Strand, University of Papua New Guinea to perform at the celebrations for International

Dance Day. This event showcased their talent to the public and other students, who were encouraged to learn of their ability to dance despite their disability. Following this, the High-Speed Outreach Performing Troupe toured to various places and performed at functions and on special occasions.

Conclusion

In her efforts to deliver the appropriate pedagogy to the students, Agnes has connected her mental, spiritual, and physical strength to ensure the students receive and produce the best. One of the virtues that endured throughout was patience, which was shared as a tool for teaching. She had exhausted all avenues to gain recognition for the role of dance as therapy for these special children who she regards as her own.

As a result of her perseverance, many of her students succeeded in their learning and have graduated from the Papua New Guinea Red Cross Special Education Centre to take on employment with various organisations and companies.

Agnes moved on to teach in a formal school – the decision to leave was hard as she was connected to the special children with disabilities. Although Agnes left the centre, she is still very much involved with the students who are part of her High-Speed Performing Arts Troupe. In 2016, they toured Australia and met on the weekends for rehearsals and organizing fundraising drives.

Agnes has set a benchmark for Papua New Guinea using dance as a tool for developing cognitive learning amongst disabled children. Her efforts have gained recognition and some progress has been made at the community and national levels to support disability programs in the country, using dance as the medium for promoting education and self-care.

3.5

ASEAN PARA GAMES 2015

Dancing for inclusivity

Filomar Cortezano Tariao

> To build a human, you need 3 billion of that [DNA base pairs] … Every one of you—
> what make me, me, and you, you, is just about 5 million of this … for the rest we are
> all absolutely identical …
>
> *(Sabatini, 2016)*

The opening dance for the 8th ASEAN Para Games 2015 empowered Luo Mang, a fifteen-year-old with moderate autism, to perform to an international audience.[1] Autism, one of the most common neurological disorders affecting children, impairs normal motor and cognitive development. This piece allowed Luo Mang to express herself truthfully, revealing her condition without prejudice. Instead of hindering us from exploring artistic possibilities, her dance became a validating tool in the path to wellness. Both the physically agile and the specially abled connected and integrated with each other through this work.

This optimism in diversity and assimilation is the reason I took on the challenge of choreographing the opening of the 8th ASEAN Para Games. It was a wonderful opportunity to present the work of the dance diploma students from Singapore's Nanyang Academy of Fine Arts (NAFA) and at the same time, inculcate the values of teamwork in them. By July 2015, the creative team had met and fleshed out ideas for the piece. After passionate negotiations, we agreed to incorporate elastic bands into the dance. Alwin Nikolai's *Tensile Involvement* (1953) was an inspiration for the choreography, with pictures an inspiration for the piece (albeit counter to the alleged principles with which Alwin Nikolai conceived his work) (Gitelman and Martin, 2007, 111, pp. 70–71, 112). These bands symbolised the suppleness of our connections in the community. I understood it would not be easy to manipulate them, while simultaneously showcasing our dancers, but I also knew we had time to experiment with the material. I selected twenty dancers, seven of whom had a dance movement therapy (DMT) background. They had a critical role in assisting the cast to interact with our special-needs partner in the choreography. Little did I know this decision would prove to be the best one I would ever make in the creation of this work.

Rehearsals commenced and Luo Mang was assigned to us as our partner for the piece. Her coach, Pua Jing Wen, had previously rehearsed the Chinese fan-dance movements with her, which she would use as a solo before the NAFA dancers came in with the bands.

The ensemble choreography was designed to complement these Asian gestures. We planned for the dancers to rehearse from 10 am to 2 pm while Luo Mang joined them from 3–5 pm twice a week. This arrangement permitted Luo Mang to practise her steps in the space and in the same sequence determined in the programme. To make the process easier and less complicated, we decided to have her variation unaccompanied by any of the dancers, reducing the interaction between her and the rest of the cast to almost nil. This process ran for the first week before we had a run with the parts where Luo Mang had to enter.

That first run was an utter disaster. Not only were the dancers' combinations significantly separate from Luo Mang's, the composition of the piece did not reflect the convictions that made me sign up to this project! I was so preoccupied with technical exhibition that I missed the entire point of the activity. Consequently, I asked Jing Wen if we could rehearse with Luo Mang more often (daily, or at least four times a week) so that we could incorporate her into the piece more cohesively. Jing Wen acceded, noticing the same thing I observed. This is when all the DMT techniques our students had learned became invaluable.

Whereas previously, we had allowed Luo Mang to warm-up alone with her coach, in the succeeding days we started rehearsals with her, in a circle with our hands linked. We increased the frequency and time of the integrative warm-ups we tackled in DMT. We marched, jumped and turned together. The dancers played and ate with Luo Mang during the breaks. The goal was to create a safe and nurturing environment for Luo Mang within the group. Process and purpose became equals. These let the performers root their skills to sound and safe technique, while allowing the dancers to be more comfortable working with Luo Mang, and vice-versa. It was obvious that we had developed a deeper rapport with each other, so that Luo Mang was able to do more with the dancers and with the dance. By the third week, Luo Mang was giving and taking verbal cues to and from the dancers. She would call out the names of the dancers who would interact with her in the dance. Her opening solo developed into an interaction between two dancers in a *pas des deux* between virtuosity and special ability.

The piece, entitled *Elastomere: Stretching the Boundaries*, used the bands as figurative connections [Photo 3.5]. We stretched and manipulated them, sometimes causing conflict; but more meaningful than any problem is its resolution – discovering opportunities in difficulties. We navigated through perceived boundaries around individuals with special needs, and broke them. We paid tribute to the Games through abstract movements borrowed from the fifteen sports in the Games. What started as an exploration between dancers of different abilities had grown to a homage to the inclusivity heralded by the Para Games. The opening night of the Para Games could not have been more spectacular, not just in pageantry, but also in the camaraderie that developed amongst the participants. Pictures of our performance flooded social media, with the Times of London posting "beautiful performance...".[2] Choreographing for the event was an honour I will always treasure.

One of the most valuable gifts the Para Games has given any programme that aims to establish a unified community is the prospect of continuity. It was a serendipitous moment when, at the closing dinner with the Prime Minister, I was seated beside Michelle Lee, CEO of I'm Soul Inc.[3] As a social enterprise, I'm Soul Inc. was involved in bringing music, through the use of sound beams, to those with special needs. From this meeting, another collaboration between music and dance was born. *Letters* is a performance involving the NAFA dancers with several new partners with special needs; Marilyn, a septuagenarian, Jaspreet, a person with Down Syndrome, and Ryan, a boy with moderate autism.

Everything is a metaphor. In *Elastomere,* the bands represented the relationships amongst humanity, in all its diversity, not unlike the strands of our genetic heredity, unravelling to spark

PHOTO 3.5 *Elastomere*
Choreographer: Filomar Cortezano Tariao
Dancer: Luo Mang
Photographer: Collection of Ministry of Culture, Community and Youth (Singapore)

new life. The human genome shows that we are all identical, save for 0.18 per cent of these 3 billion base-pair sequences. This means we have every justification for inclusivity. Any argument against that is less than a percentage of the code of life. To dismiss this small fraction of uniqueness, however, is foolhardy. This same minuscule proportion has given rise to an array of cultures, all of which have been a complex response to the environment that is as varied as our genes. Our lives and the organised chaos that we call our world are a microcosm of the greater entropy of this universe. No individual organism can lay claim to any singular supremacy. Science has taught us that diversity is the hallmark of evolution. Embracing this principle is key to progress. In a multiracial country like Singapore, this concept of equality, beyond beliefs or abilities, cannot be more applicable. The poetry of acceptance and understanding is encoded in our cells. We try to decipher this code daily. Through dance, we have proclaimed this benevolent truth and continue to practice it in the spirit of the Para Games.

Notes

1 The Para Games video link is available at https://vimeo.com/154862901.
2 https://www.instagram.com/p/-1YckfL-wl/?taken-by=thetimes.
3 http://imsoulinc.com/.

References

Gitelman, C., R. Martin (Eds.). (2007) *The Returns of Alwin Nikolais: Bodies, Boundaries and The Dance Canon* (pp. 66–75). Middletown, CT: Wesleyan University Press.
Sabatini, Ricardo. (2016) 'How to Read the Genome and Build a Human Being'. Available at https://www.ted.com/talks/riccardo_sabatini_how_to_read_the_genome_and_build_a_human_being?language=en [Accessed February 23, 2016].

3.6

DANCING PARTNERS/DANCING PEERS

A wheelchair dance collaborative

Miriam Giguere and Rachel Federman-Morales

Neighbors can be geographically close, but socially quite separated. Such was the case with two groups, the HMS School for Children with Cerebral Palsy and the Dance Program at Drexel University, both located in Philadelphia, Pennsylvania, USA, until a dance collaborative was established in the fall of 2008; it is still ongoing at the time of writing. Located only blocks away from each other, the two groups of dancers—half in wheelchairs as residents of the HMS School and half from a dance major program at a private four-year university—would have no way of meeting if it weren't for the collaborative weekly class. The residential students at the HMS School are typically middle school aged to twenty-one and dance in wheelchairs. Their partners are able-bodied dancers from Drexel University's Dance Program who volunteer to be a part of the project.

The project, referred to as the Wheelchair Dance Collaborative, consists of a one-hour weekly class that meets from early October through May of each year [Photo 3.6]. The class is led by Rachel Federman-Morales, a board-certified dance/movement therapist, employed by the HMS School. The program culminates in three performances: an assembly for the other students at HMS, an evening performance for parents and volunteers at the HMS School, and a matinee for Philadelphia public school students at Drexel University's Mandell Theater. This project has had a positive impact on both its respective groups. Certainly, the university students, interviewed about their HMS experiences for a research study on the impact of community-based learning, see this project as making an impact on their understanding of dance, of themselves, and on their potential career choices. For example, one participant remarks, "I learned a lot about myself, but I think the most important thing I've learned is that I have the ability to touch people and share so much through the art of dance."

Project structure

There are three key features of this project that make it so successful: its structure, having mutual goals for both groups, and the creation of an environment that is free from judgment and committed to making connections.

PHOTO 3.6   Wheelchair Dance Collaborative
Photographer: Joel Schwartz

Each week the students come together in one-on-one partnership. This structure, where partnerships are consistent over a long period of time, allows the students to build relationships with each other and develop an understanding of how to communicate with their partners. Each partnership has a unique profile for communicating, which is developed through extensive contact. The project continues for eight months of weekly lessons, allowing ample time for real relationships to develop. The project culminates in several performances, both for the HMS community and for Philadelphia public school students. The goal of performing drives the participants to stay committed and to work together on a common goal. This in turn leads to deeper connections and increased socialization between differently abled dancers of similar ages, which is an empowering paradigm.

The structure of the dance class starts in a circle with breathing and focusing on a drum. The group breathes with the drum rising and sinking. This exercise is a ritual opening to help the dancers relax, focus, and become more present in the space. Body warm-up consists of body tapping, utilizing cross lateral movements activating different parts of the brain, and actively listening and following songs with movement instruction in the lyrics.

The next portion of the class utilizes props. This is beneficial, gaining all participants' focus and maintaining their attention for longer periods of time. A buddy band, octaband, balls, and scarves are utilized during the warm-up exercises. The Efforts from Laban Movement Analysis are always incorporated, embodying Time, Weight, Space, and Flow. Presence is encouraged throughout the dance class. Staying present reinforces for the Drexel dancers the importance of embodying their partner's posture, gesture, shape, feeling tone, facial expressions, and body language. By mirroring movements, the dancers can reflect on how their partner might be experiencing the dance class, and learn an individual's movement repertoire, style of expression, and communication, thereby practicing empathetic listening.

Rhythm, repetition, and structured improvisation exercises are used next in the class structure to support themes that emerge and lead to building movement phrases developed from the dancers' movement repertoire and self-expression. Themes vary each year and have included the art and dance of Isadora Duncan, story books, nursery rhymes associating text and movement, nature and the elements (earth, air, water, and fire), and music selections that can rouse ideas for traveling patterns, shapes, emotion, and imagery.

The efforts phrase is used as a cool-down and closure for class. The instructor recites each time, "Up with lightness, down with strength, across with directness, open with indirectness, retreat with quickness, and move forward with sustainment." As the movement phrase is practiced repeatedly, the dancers embody the phrase giving them a vocabulary to practice and build skills for retaining information, which can lead to better body memory.

Mutual goals

The structure also supports the goals of the project to tap into each dancer's strengths and see beyond their limitations, so that partners can communicate and relate. The project offers the participants an opportunity in decision making, creative thinking, motivation, imagination, increased body awareness, expanded movement repertoire, and emotional well-being. The environment encourages them to assert themselves and socialize, and promotes self-expression. As a group, the members work toward involving everyone to fully engage in the class. For the Drexel Dancers, this means paying attention to their partner's rhythm of exertion and recuperation, offering hands-on support and guidance, and willingness to take an active role when dancing with a person whose needs are different from your own. The collaborative dance project provides the dancers with a therapeutic outlet where they can interact with people their own age, thereby enriching the lives of the group members, inspiring each other, having fun, and sharing their joy for dance.

For the university students, another goal is to broaden their understanding of dance as an art form, and to see its connective power. Participating dancers were asked to define dance at the beginning of the project. One of the students said, "It's a movement, it's an art in the form of movement used to either perform or strengthen the body." The same student, at the conclusion of her dancing at HMS, defined dance somewhat differently as, "To me a dance is more than just about the movement it is about the community of relationships that you build with the people you dance with and how you improve yourself and get to be a better dancer."

Another important goal for the university students is to find their own capacity to develop therapeutic relationships. Many of the dance majors are planning to undertake a Master's program in Dance/Movement Therapy at Drexel when they complete their current undergraduate experience in dance and consider this community-based learning opportunity to be one of the most pivotal in their self-discovery process.

Environment

Creating the right environment for severely disabled children and their partners gives them a sense of belonging where everyone involved can be him- or herself, take risks, and contribute to the creative process. Participating in a repetitive and consistent movement structure allows group members to become alive and vibrant. They can discover themselves as people able to participate, dance, socialize, express, and feel confident despite any differences. The set goals for the project allow the therapist/leader to design a dance experience that supports the participants' learning and efforts through a consistent and repetitive design, which has therapeutic value for the participants. It also gives them a sense of belonging where everyone can be him- or herself, take risks, and contribute to the creative process. Patterns of connections develop. This method supports the dancers to experience feelings of empowerment upon accomplishing the tasks. The environment becomes one where both the university dancers and the HMS dancers feel safe to take risks with one another. The structure of consistency and repetition allows the therapist to chart progress and celebrate achievements. It also supports the progression of positive experiences and a movement dialogue, which develops from each participant's form of communication.

Conclusion

The Wheelchair Dance Collaborative, which brings together differently abled peer dancers in a long-term collaborative project, is a powerful experience for all involved. Both sets of dancers get a chance to socialize with their seemingly distant neighbors. As one Drexel dancer remarks, "with the HMS dancers it's not so much guidance as it is collaboration between the two people." By creating one-on-one partnerships over an extended period of time, developing mutual goals for both groups participating, and creating an environment of safety through repetition and consistency, this project has empowered dancers to find their own voices and the voices of their partners in the process.

Note

Student quotations through the article are taken from data gathered in a 2014–2015 study, 'The Development of Identity in Teenage Dancers through Community Engagement', undertaken by the first author through the consent of the Institutional Review Board of Drexel University.

PART IV

Community dance initiatives

PHOTO 2016 project for Companhia Limitada (Portugal)
Choreographer: Madalena Victorino
Photographer: Jen Brown

4.1

DANCE AND AFFECT

Re-connecting minds to bodies of young adult survivors of violence in India

Urmimala Sarkar Munsi

A group of girls pour out into the courtyard of a rehabilitation home for women on the fringes of south Kolkata. They are to attend a dance class with a young trainer in the court-yard. The differences among the residents are striking. The shapes and sizes and the personalities are varied. Some girls are barely in their teens, and the oldest might be in her 40s. The rest are in between. Some are fit and smiling, while others are frowning and definitely show-ing signs of resistance to this forcible invasion into their time. Many of the women stand in clusters—with tell-tale signs of excitement or at least readiness to start with the activities that are planned into their weekly routine. Some stand aloof, resigned, and not really part of the group. One teenager sits down on a raised platform and looks unwell.

> The instructor starts her class formally with an instruction for all of the girls to hold hands and stand in a circle. That is the point where I am drawn into their circle, tem-porarily becoming a part of it, preparing to share their world at least symbolically, for a while. The instructor, introduces me formally, as a guest who is a dancer and who will be joining the group as a facilitator/participant for the next two days.

Some hands extend and hold those of their neighbours rather tentatively, while other hands stretch eagerly—apparently ready to start with the day's exercise without hesitation. The class starts with a song that is sung together with hand gestures. The preliminary and tentative navigation of recovery starts for the day.

Such dance classes were introduced in shelter homes for young female survivors rescued from situations of sex trafficking and subsequent exploitation, in the hope that dance would bring happiness and relaxation to their lives. This particular class was organized by Sohini Chakraborty, who later founded Kolkata Sanved in 2004, an organization which currently works with Dance and Movement Therapy as a tool for creating spaces, principally for work-ing with groups of young women with diverse histories of trauma, and at different stages of adjustment and recovery, following rescue by police from situations of trafficking or bond-age. This work described above slowly became more organized and structured as Kolkata Sanved became more and more organized through years of experience.

The young women in such shelter homes are usually rescued from different exploitative situations of bondage, such as organized brothels or sexual slavery. Some of the women rescued are daughters of sex workers, having grown up in or around the work space of the mother. Memories are diverse for all of them. While some have direct understanding of, and trauma from, actual physical and sexual violence inflicted on them on a daily basis, others have memories of their mother's 'work' and clients, while also having a sense of belonging in the mother's community, as that is the only family they have known. A few have attended school for a few years. Some young women remember being sold off by parents to traffickers, or the situation that led them to being trafficked, and are glad to be away from the deeply exploitative and often violent bondage that such unequal exploitative power relations perpetrate. Some others are resentful and scared at being forcefully taken away from the only space that they knew as their own. Such a range of reactions makes these women different subjects as well as differently receptive to any external motivational, educational, or therapeutic intervention.

Trauma survivors have several different physical and psycho-social manifestations due to Post Traumatic Stress Disorder (PTSD), which is an anxiety disorder that is classified as a neurotic stress-related and somato-form disorder according to the *Diagnostic and Statistical Manual of Mental Disorders* (DSM). H. Javidi and M. Yadollahie in their article on Post Traumatic Stress Disorder (2012: 12) say that PTSD may appear at any age and is a very common symptom noticed in young adults, as they are more likely to be exposed to situations that lead to deep scars arising from trauma-related stress (Javidi and Yadollahie, 2012: 12–13).

Dance and Movement Therapy aims to address the problems arising out of PTSD, resulting in different psycho-social symptoms in women survivors:

- low and fluctuating levels of self-esteem
- withdrawal from social spaces and social interaction
- vulnerability resulting often in re-traumatization
- hyper-sexuality
- bouts of anxiety, violent anger, depressive disorder, and self-harm

This chapter focuses on four principal conceptual strands behind the Dance and Movement Therapy (DMT) initiated recovery processes for survivors of sex trafficking, and resultant abuse and violence. These survivors are often survivors of PTSD:

1. The somatic perceptions are the bodily sensed, socially informed ideas that a vulnerable survivor has about her own body and its image. Somatic movement therapist Martha Eddy refers to Thomas Hanna as the father of somatics and quotes him while discussing the use of somatics within Dance Movement Therapy. She talks about living organisms (somas) as "integral and ordered processes of embodied elements which cannot be separated from their evolved past or their adaptive future" (Eddy, 2002: 46). According to her, a soma is an "embodiment of a process – constantly adapting and enduring the changing patterns of embodiment through time."

In this context, one of the most important works using all the above-mentioned concepts is that of dancer/choreographer Anna Halprin, whose use of dance and expressive grammars of the body together with the specific use of touch for integrative therapeutic well-being of the mind and body, remains a primary example of work that can initiate a process of healing for survivors of sex trafficking, sexual abuse, and violence. Eddy sees the focus on body, movement, and the expressive arts as a "healing approach" that builds on the premise that the body stores all imprints of life events within it. She adds,

> When remaining at the unconscious level, these imprints may lead to imbalance and conflict; when explored and expressed consciously and creatively, the connection between body, mind and emotion makes a vital contribution to the artful development of the self.
>
> *(Eddy, 2002: 49)*

The survivors of sexual violence and abuse generally show lack of self-confidence and low self-esteem, with a sense of guilt about their own body. This condition is often enhanced by the views of the society that they often return to following their rescue from situations of oppressive and exploitative trafficking. The healing processes in DMT often depend heavily on the understanding of the somatic contour of the individual patients to begin the process of addressing mind-body issues of specific patients of PTSD.

2. Kinesics and the survivor—According to Jinni Harrigan (2005), the field of kinesics (body movement research) focuses on positions, movements and actions of the body, head, and limbs. In the context of DMT, somatics becomes important as a subject that includes the conscious and unconscious moving patterns of the body, which are at the same time reflective of and reactive to past experiences of the body, i.e. violence, exploitation, or abuse.

The connections between socialization and the projection of the socialized body through movements are often discussed in dance. In my previous research (Sarkar Munsi, 2016), I have concentrated on the body image that becomes intrinsically linked to the grammar of dances that are often structured as the genre reflective of a particular culture. Bharatanatyam grammar is one such very important example where any projection of the bust and the hips is intentionally subdued and an over-emphasis of the facial expressions and hand gestures is encouraged instead of expressions through the use of lower body parts.

All cultures create an image of the perfect woman, and for the survivor of sexual violence her own guilt over the past about which she may not have had choice, creates a sense of understanding of the defiled and, therefore, imperfect body, which she now has to carry on living in and move with. Addressing the experience of trauma through the relationship of the mind of the survivor with the different body parts is thus one of the important methods in what I see as the core pedagogical tool in working with Dance and Movement Therapy.

To substantiate the understanding of kinesics, Harrigan says that the principal focal point of attention has been,

> ... on the hands and head, two areas with the greatest overall movement frequency. For body movements in general, and for the head and hands specifically, researchers' coding methods are varied, rarely well-defined, and, with few exceptions, are not often organized conceptually or theoretically.
>
> *(Harrigan, 2005: 149)*

Kinesic research still remains in its embryonic stage. For this chapter however, kinesics becomes an important phase in between somatic and proxemic understanding and processing of trauma.

3. Proxemics and gaze behavior are indicators of the way in which people share spaces with other human beings. In terms of reactions to and acknowledgement of other bodies in the surroundings, it involves coded behavioral structures that become indicators of trauma and PTSD in survivors of sexual violence. Jinni Harrigan's work on "relevant variables for operationalizing gaze behaviour and spatial parameters in social settings with respect to territoriality, intimacy, personal space, public behaviour, and cultural differences" (Harrigan, Rosenthal, Scherer, 2005: 4) helps in locating the strength of understanding the above-mentioned connections while working on a structure for group therapeutic exercises for PTSD patients among survivors of sexual abuse and violence.

Within this category, the interpersonal communication that a survivor is able to have, or is ready to allow through visual communication, remains an important territory. Often, it is seen that the survivor of severe and prolonged sexual violence is unable to shut her eyes, even while in class with a number of others. Even when asked to relax by lying down on the ground, they tend to keep their eyes open. This is the result of a fear of unpreparedness for any sudden violence. DMT, through its process of using physical tools, can recreate and renew a sense of self-reliance and confidence in being in control of the surroundings through a painstaking but structured process.

4. Significance of touch: Touch studies is a comparatively under-explored area, especially in the Indian context of DMT. While Indian classical dance vocabularies have restrictive and specific grammatical usages for touch, in most of the community dances among the large tribal population in India one of the most common formats of group dancing is to hold hands and link bodies somatically and visibly. The movements, often repeated and appearing simple in their structure, generate a common kinetic thread through the linking of hands, bodies, and the uniform steps that create and regenerate the sense of togetherness and community bonding in psycho-somatic ways. As touch is understood in different cultures in completely different ways, it is important to know that touch gestures are understood and interpreted very differently in India. General gestures of familiarity such as hugging between members of the opposite sex, holding hands, and public displays of affection are viewed according to culturally prescribed value systems. Socialization also plays a very important role in this structure of understanding. The hyper-isolative shunning of any touch, shrinking away from other bodies, and reacting to any sudden movement and touch with aggression in anticipatory caution against violence are a few of the complications that are seen in the PTSD cases among the survivors of sexual violence. The other extreme is the hyper-sensuality that generates an exaggerated need for touching, either of sexual or non-sexual nature. DMT focuses on the building of communicative skills based on general sensory perceptions of touch and specific reactions of survivors. According to Harrigan, "social conventions—'display rules' (Ekman 1972)—guide our behavior by the exercise of culturally learned rules that govern 'when it is appropriate to express an emotion and to whom one can reveal one's feelings' (Ekman & Rosenberg 1997: 10)." Harrigan also observes that "behaviours that are exhibited outside the expected presentation of oneself usually are so atypical as to be diagnostic with respect to mental or emotional stability or level of intellectual functioning" (Harrigan, 2005: 138).

As can be understood from the above section, much of the four specific orientations—somatic perception of self, the mind-body dynamics that control and pattern moving and movement quality (kinesic ability), the proxemic behaviour and gaze through which any survivor connects to the world, and the sense and reaction to touch—are heavily dependent on social conventions, that are deeply ingrained into the minds of a particular society.

The work of Kolkata Sanved: towards specific pedagogies of DMT for survivors of sexual abuse in India

Until very recently, there were no diploma courses in Dance and Movement Therapy in India, nor were there trained therapists specifically working on methods of DMT for the different requirements of patients. Dance has been a tool for developing cognitive processes and therapeutic recovery for a long time. As earlier stated, this chapter investigates certain concepts that link the educational elements within dance to the therapeutic ones in order to understand the ways in which it is being used as a tool for recovery and regeneration of self-image in young adult women survivors of sexual violence and trafficking.

Kolkata Sanved—a non-governmental organization working with DMT as a tool—currently runs one of the few certification/diploma courses in India, in collaboration with one of the premiere social science research institutes in the country, and has its own structure for the theoretical as well as practical training for DMT. In its twelve-year-long work with survivors of trafficking and sexual exploitation, Kolkata Sanved has developed specific DMT tools for a pedagogy that may be used for working with the PTSD of survivors. In my association with Kolkata Sanved since its inception, I have been a facilitator of/trainer on the DMT training program, an evaluator for the same program, and an advisor for its curriculum development program. My analysis of the DMT program thus uses personal experience and observations, as well as interviews and conversations with the Director of Kolkata, Sanved Sohini Chakraborty, since 2006, the latest of which was a prolonged interview with her at her office in Kolkata.

The next section of this chapter deals with the structure of the DMT process developed by Kolkata Sanved in the state of West Bengal in India, and the work of its Founder Director Sohini Chakraborty, to understand the applicability of the four processes specifically mentioned as the basic conceptual structure that can help us clarify connections between the theoretical structure and the practice of DMT. By doing so, this chapter hopes to facilitate the ongoing process of strengthening the pedagogical frame for the DMT course "Sampoornata" that has been a creation of Chakraborty's prolonged engagement with dance as a therapeutic tool.

In a 2016 interview with Chakraborty she emphasized the importance of using the words "free movement" instead of "dance" in connection to DMT. She highlighted the need to emphasize the freedom to move, with or without specific training as a dancer, and pushed for a non-judgmental stance that is very difficult for trained dancers to have regarding movements that are called dance. As is commonly emphasized by DMT specialists the world over, Chakraborty's insistence is on use of movements as tools for creating or restructuring the patient's mental or physical scape for therapeutic process, which is an entirely different function for movements than the aesthetic expressions that movements are used for in the specific genres of dance. In Chakraborty's words, "dance for therapy can never be judged as good or bad, it is for the subjective pleasure, satisfaction and expression."[1]

According to Chakraborty,[2] the DMT process developed by Kolkata Sanved relies on the cultural specificity of the survivors on the Indian subcontinent, and more specifically within India. It uses understanding of the cultural constructs as well as social norms that the survivors are deeply connected to. Apart from this, it trains what Chakraborty calls a batch of new "young advocates" from the survivor community itself, for spreading the message against trafficking and building resistance from within the community against this prevalent evil.

As mentioned already, many female survivors of sex trafficking and sexual abuse become victims of PTSD. Visible effects of PTSD are depression (e.g. sitting in isolation or listless gait), a closed bodily expression, an inability to relax or smile, a lack of physical confidence, inability to make eye contact, restlessness, and issues of anger management, among many others.

According to Chakraborty, Kolkata Sanved has started using a Trauma Symptom Checklist.[3] This checklist is a survey through a series of questionnaires given to survivors of trauma in order to assess the depth, type, and reasons for trauma and post-traumatic stress, and is analyzed by professionally trained experts. Symptoms of PTSD may vary from person to person, and may sometimes be very obvious like extreme issues with anger management and self-destructive tendencies. At other times symptoms can be less explicit, like negative sexuality, depression, and problems with self-image. Chakraborty underlines the principal goals of Kolkata Sanved's therapeutic work using DMT as:

- to instil somatic skills;
- to equip PTSD patients to ward off negativity that could push the person towards re-traumatization;
- to help survivors to develop ability and skill to relax and help others to do the same
- to help them improve image of self, self-esteem, self-acceptance and confidence in self and own body;
- to improve social communicative skills and abilities to adjust to altered social settings
- to help identify depression and deal with anxiety and stress, by introducing survivors to easily usable "tools" from DMT;
- to help the survivors to acknowledge emotions and to deal with restlessness and hyper-arousal;
- to create a regime of trust building exercises;
- to extend the capacity to move and enjoy communicating through movements and dance.

The following examples of a few selected techniques by Kolkata Sanved are helpful in understanding the use of Somatics, Kinesics, Proximics – Gaze, and Touch as the four basic conceptual tools explained at the beginning of the chapter. Though these therapeutic exercises were not developed on the basis of the frameworks of Somatic, Kinesics, Proximics – Gaze, and Touch initially, the frameworks can and do actually lend a logical structure to the DMT exercises used commonly.

Expression of anger: Encouraging a participant to recognize anger as one of the driving emotions may then be taken to the stage of kinesthetic expression by generating movements to express that anger, to the accompaniment of rhythm. One of the common tools is to use the rapid Kathak footsteps or even unstructured stamping of feet to rhythm to express anger.

Construction of a comfortable/comforting situation: A group exercise commonly used is to encourage the participants to imagine themselves in a happy place/comfortable situation and then ask them to use fellow participants from the workshop to construct and choreograph a happy situation—encouraging the use of touch and working in close proximity between the participants during the workshop session, ultimately leading to opening of the mind to collaborative process and the creation of positivity. Actual physical problems like sexually transmitted diseases, suicidal tendencies, and often long lasting ailments from malnourishment, self-abuse/harming tendencies, and excessive smoking and drinking are some of those physical results. Grounding the beginning of some of the exercises in the physical bodily activity thus helps to establish or re-structure the body's connections to the mind. Some physical exercises such as holding oneself lovingly in a self-embrace, or holding hands with fellow participants in a circle and moving together to rhythm, are facilitated to yield visible and fruitful psycho-social results.

Mirroring movements: A common exercise is to encourage participants to form a partnership with another participant, and do exercises like mirroring each other's movements, or moving together while holding two ends of the same thread between their teeth. This involves each gazing at the other constantly and intently to be able to follow their movements. Such forced coordinations also push participants into kinesthetic understandings of sharing space and helps them in restructuring their social uneasiness around other bodies.

The healing touch: The healing touch technique is an exercise that is often used by the DMT facilitator to create a soothing experience for the participants. The process is generated and circulated so that the participants experience the healing touch and in turn provide the same to others in the class. Besides being tremendously popular as a relaxing tool, the experience of calming touches and being able to provide that experience to others, create a feeling of belonging and communion among survivors, helping them to cope with the sense of disrespect most trauma survivors experience from society [Photo 4.1].

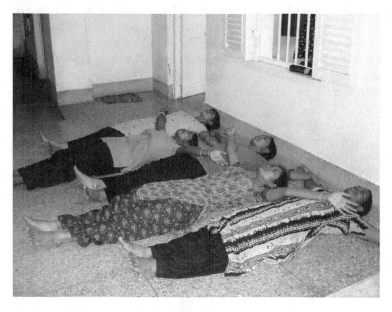

PHOTO 4.1   Kolkata Sanved participants
Photographer: Urmimala Sakar Munsi

Conclusion

The work of DMT is based on creating processes through which mental impulses and reactions, along with body movements and dance, alter socially prompted "display rules" (as explained by Harrigan's quote on "social convention" above) adopted by the survivors of sex trafficking, and eventually also the relationship of the PTSD-affected survivors with their bodies.

Acknowledging the influence of the work of the American Dance Therapy Association (ADTA) in her early days of establishing Kolkata Sanved, Chakraborty in her interview talked about Kolkata Sanved and its principal area of work around movement practises from Asia which have in their turn influenced many of the first generation DMT experts from around the world, who developed their own signature techniques of somatic movement practices. While the principal dedication of Kolkata Sanved remained that of restoring a smile and positive self-image to the survivors, using dance as a tool, more and more importance is given to creating a practice/theory combination model of DMT pedagogy. Chakraborty says, "we understand the need to start addressing the problem as a psycho-somatic one, with disorder of both mental as well as the physical nature that may recur time and again. The recovery programme, as a result is made up of physical as well as mental nature. Some of the exercises start with challenging the mental scape of the PTSD patient, focusing on concentration, memory, nostalgia, or imagination and then push for physical outcomes such as expressive movements or coordinated group exercises".[4]

Over the last ten years, DMT tools have developed in India. Their origins may be traced to the personal understanding of dancers who became interested in the therapeutic use of dance and movement and explored these experientially in India. As the therapeutic structure has matured and consolidated over the last ten years, it is now important to create a conceptual understanding of method, especially to create a logical understanding of the pedagogy for teaching the DMT technique in a professional manner. Keeping in mind the theoretical underpinnings of the practice of DMT, this chapter has tried to highlight and analyze the basic mind-body requirements that are ideally addressed through DMT. The four basic conceptual frameworks of Somatics, Kinesics, Proxemics – Gaze, and finally Touch, can be understood as the four focal needs that are to be addressed in survivors of sexual violence and PTSD.

Notes

1   Interview with Sohini Chakraborty on Dance and Movement Therapy and the Curriculum of DMT named 'Sampoornata', developed by Kolkata Sanved; Kolkata Sanved office, Kolkata, 14 May 2016.
2   The interview with Chakraborty, dated 14 May 2016, covered a conversation about Kolkata Sanved's therapeutic programs and its training programs for young women survivors of trafficking, who are interested to continue working within their own communities—to build public opinion against and resistance to trafficking, along with being trained as DMT practitioners.
3   Trauma Symptom Checklist is a method of checking PTSD symptoms.
4   Interview with Chakraborty, dated 14 May 2016.

References

Eddy, Martha. (2002) "Somatic Practices and Dance: Global Influences," *Dance Research Journal*, 34(2), pp. 46–62.

Elliot, D. M. & J. Briere. (1992) "Sexual abuse trauma among professional women: Validating the Trauma Symptom Checklist – 40 (TSC-40)," *Child Abuse & Neglect*, 16, pp. 391–398.

Harrigan, Jinni. (2005) *Proxemics, Kinesics, and Gaze: The New Handbook of Methods in Nonverbal Behavior Research*. New York and Oxford: Oxford University Press (pp. 137–198).

Javidi, H. & M. Yadollahie. (2012) "Post-traumatic stress disorder," *International Journal of Occupational and Environmental Medicine*, 3(1), 2–9.

Sarkar Munsi, U. (2016) "Mediations around an alternative concept of 'work': re-imagining the bodies of survivors of trafficking," *Lateral: Journal of Cultural Studies Association*, 5(2). Available at http://csalateral.org/issue/5-2/mediations-work-bodies-survivors-trafficking-sarkar-munsi/ [Accessed 18 January 2017].

4.2

DIGITAL STORIES

Three young people's experience in a community dance class

Sue Cheesman and Elaine Bliss

Touch Compass Dance Company, based in Auckland, describes itself as an inclusive dance company comprising both disabled and non-disabled dancers who view "diverse physicality as a creative springboard, rather than a wall that needs to be overcome." They run an integrated community dance class weekly, which attracts male and female participants with a range of embodiments. The specific aim of these classes is to enable dancers to discover their own creativity, expression and self-confidence. This, we argue, is strongly connected to identity.

In this chapter, the authors analyse the making of digital stories, from the perspectives of young people, about why they dance. Ariel, Alex and Annalise, three youth members of the Touch Compass integrated community dance class, accepted our invitation to be involved in a digital storytelling project around their dancing and why they like to do it. They all attend courses in higher education institutes and are in their early twenties.

Context: why digital storytelling?

Bliss and Fisher (2014) describe digital storytelling as "a person-driven, self-created ethnographic narrative process ... produced through a combination of first person, narrated voiceovers, digital still and/or moving images and music" (Altrutz, 2015: 3). Digital stories that result from this process are short, three to five minute, personal audio-visual vignettes. The digital storytelling process used for this research project was adapted from a practice developed at the Center for Digital Storytelling (CDS) in Berkeley, California. Lambert (2009) asserts that digital storytelling is a process for freedom of expression: most importantly, it is participant-centred and individuals are encouraged to find their own path in their story.

Bliss (2015) points to the work of Murakami (2008) who identifies three distinctive characteristics of digital storytelling that contribute to fostering and nurturing identities. First, digital storytelling utilises a multi-modal approach that likely appeals to young people with learning difficulties; secondly, digital storytelling provides a performative space for participants; and thirdly, digital storytelling has the ability to transform cultural and social environments. Nicholson (2005: 65) defines identity as "a continual process of becoming, rather than a pre-given expression of being." Rather than fixed, identity is viewed as fluid and constantly shifting. Benmayor (2008) claims that both product and process in digital storytelling empower participants to find their voice and to speak out, especially those marginalised by racism, educational disadvantage or language. The emotional imperative in digital storytelling is pivotal when incorporated creatively as it allows the storyteller to communicate a personally powerful positionality that creates a convincing 'situated truth' for the audience (Bliss & Fisher, 2014). This, we argue, is strongly aligned with principles of social justice through embracing new perspectives on different forms of embodiment and opening up spaces for a range of representations that disrupt outdated constructs of youth and difference (Cheesman, 2011).

Context: the participants

Digital storytelling in this research is used as a tool to empower three young people to tell their personal dance stories. The participants were: Ariel, Annalise and Alex (two females and one male), who are all youth members from Touch Compass community class; and the facilitators, who are both teachers at the University of Waikato [Photo 4.2a]—Sue in Dance

PHOTO 4.2A Annalise, Ariel and Alex strike a pose outside the Faculty of Education in the University of Waikato
Photographer: Sue Cheesman

Education and Elaine in Geography and Digital Storytelling. The three young people were invited to take part because they had been regular attendees of this class for at least two years prior to the project. They are very different individuals. Annalise has a larger-than-life personality, whereas Alex is introspective and more serious and Ariel is quiet and thoughtful. They each bring a variety of skills, interests and discipline-specific knowledge to the class. All are very caring and responsive to each other's needs as they negotiate their various physical and cognitive learning challenges in this dance class. They have the ability to work very closely with each other in a physical way, in the generosity of spirit exhibited in how they work, in their acceptance of other class members, and in their level of expressivity and their general ability to launch into higher-order problem-solving. The Saturday community dance class is taught through a problem solving improvisational approach with various scores and tasks having a close connection to contact improvisation in which the participants are constantly making decisions in the moment. 'Follow the leader' and 'call and response' are two frequently used teaching strategies. Participants work in solo, duet and class groupings and are given open-ended questions/problems to explore and solve in multiple ways. Scaffolding the learning is important and often tasks are revisited each week from a slightly different perspective (Cheesman, 2011: 31). Benjamin points out that "Borrowing and reintroducing movement material, echoing and developing it through a course of improvisation is one way of adding texture and depth to improvisations and giving coherent structure to choreographed works" (Benjamin, 2002: 58). In this class we celebrate and embrace diversity of movement responses.

Our digital storytelling process

The digital storytelling workshop took place over two consecutive days. From an ethical perspective, all participants were fully informed of the project aims and requirements and provided their consent to share their stories and the process of making them.

The seven steps of digital storytelling are point of view, dramatic question, emotional content, image, sound, pacing and voice (Lambert, 2009). There is, however, considerable flexibility to improvise and adapt the process to the needs of participants. Our process evolved as we went along with participants being coached in how to use the elements of digital storytelling in crafting their stories. We adapted the process to allow for fluidity and flexibility as challenges arose, drawing on extensive past experience in facilitating digital storytelling workshops to guide this creative process.

Sue collected many photos and video footage of Ariel, Annalise and Alex dancing in a contemporary dance genre as part of the Touch Compass programme in a variety of settings, including community dance classes, a youth dance work and a male duet performed as part of Tempo Dance festival, photo shoots and short dance film stills from Touch Compass's short film DanceBox series. Collected over the last two and half years, these include stills and video of all three dancing as part of the regular community dance class, and Ariel and Annalise in a youth dance performance that was the culmination of a five-day dance intensive in which material was generated and structured to form the piece through choreographic tasks. Alex is featured in one of Touch Compass's DanceBox collections of short films, portraying a significant moment in his life. The collection of works are choreographed and devised by Touch Compass and its community and all filmed within the confines of a 2 x 2 x 2 m plywood box. In conjunction with the making of these short films, photo shoots were executed to capture images of Alex and Annalise. All of this visual material from over the last two and half years was collected to use as data prior to the workshop.

Day One

The adventure for Ariel, Annalise and Alex began with a road trip from Auckland to Hamilton. On arriving at the Faculty of Education in the University of Waikato they instantly noticed a building with the initials T. C. on it, which of course meant Touch Compass to them. This gave them a connection and there was laughter and the taking of photos that were uploaded to a social media page immediately.

We began the first process by viewing the collected data and considering a variety of images of Ariel, Annalise and Alex dancing. They selected photos based on ones they liked and thought represented their dancing. In addition, they were asked to select one or two photos that they could talk about in the story circle in the afternoon. At this point in time they seemed to make these selections easily. For example, Alex liked to see his face and Annalise was adamant she wanted three photos to talk about.

In the afternoon, the story circle consisted of each one being interviewed, which opened up possibilities for reflection and shared learning. They were encouraged to speak to their chosen images with the help of prompt questions: who they are as a dancer; why they chose these particular photos; what they can tell us about themselves and dance and how it makes them feel. They engaged with this task fully either as an active listener to others or a teller of their own story around the chosen photos. All were attentive and mutually supportive of each other's stories.

Subsequently each participant had a chance to ask the others questions at the end of their time. These three-story circles were audio recorded to capture the participants' spoken thoughts. This allowed for both facilitators to be fully present, fostering, prompting and engaging with the emerging narratives. We listened to each recording together, during which the participants analysed, discarded and selected audio text they liked and wished to keep for the next step. Each selected audio text was transcribed at that time. The transcription notes were read back to participants to check that all their choices had been documented correctly.

This was a productive process with much hilarity plus a strong sense of trust, commitment and honesty. Dinner out that evening added to our sense of community and knowledge of each other.

Day Two

The selected transcribed snippets of audio were printed out and cut up into strips of text and the pre-selected photos were colour photocopied. The next step was to consider how they wanted to re-envision their narrative by deciding how the photos and text related to one another. Several possibilities were given to support the decision making, for example photos with no text. Together we stuck these on to giant post-it notes, thereby creating a storyboard for each individual [Photo 4.2b]. During this process they were given the opportunity to work together and question one another on their decisions.

Each dancer was audio recorded narrating their text as they followed along their storyboard. When Ariel's turn came, she asked if we had "got that." The answer was audio only,

PHOTO 4.2B Ariel and Annalise working, reflecting on their storyboard
Photographer: Sue Cheesman

to which she replied she would do it again for us to record her on video. She was insistent, determined and implied that the audio was not enough. We were very aware of her sense of authority and ownership at this point. Her narration of her story was an expressive and powerful performance. Subsequently this video recording became the foundation of her digital dance story.

In summary, at the end of day two we had created three giant storyboards consisting of photos and text plus audio recordings with three different stories evolving from the three different young people. These storyboards were pivotal for the next step of making the digital story for each one at a later date. Throughout the two-day process, we were all curious, attentive and sustained our focus for each individual's story. Analysing, thinking, deciding and reconceptualising were active in this digital storytelling creative process. It had been a magical two days: connected, respectful, exciting and human.

Analysis of the process

Digital storytelling workshops are performed, therapeutic and transformative spaces for 'doing' emotion and affect. 'Voicing' personal stories in digital storytelling workshops can be transformative and affective experiences for storytellers. Individuals make sense of emotions in the context of particular places, and 'feel' place in order to make sense of it (Bliss, 2015).

One key area of interest for us in the digital storytelling workshop was whether digital storytelling would be an appropriate method for exploring issues of empowerment, identity and community development. The emotional intimacy of the workshop spaces enabled the participants to perform their identities in a way that created affective meaning for them and for us.

The participants throughout the process had to grapple with complex thinking and embrace "theory and practice through a dynamic interchange of action and reflection that together constitute a creative practice" (Alrutz, 2015: 3). Divergent and convergent thinking were present with the latter particularly in the selection part of the process. The participants were required to assess the viability of the ideas, by analysing, narrowing down and selecting the best option. We would

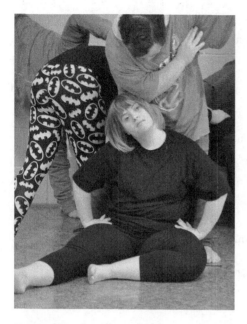

PHOTO 4.2C   Annalise and Jesse participating in Touch Compass integrated community dance class
Photographer: Sue Cheesman

contend that Carr and Claxton's (2002: 15) disposition of reciprocity was seen throughout this
process, for expressive and receptive, and verbal and non-verbal dimensions were present as participants used imitation, empathy and listening, collaboration and interdependence. Fostering of
interdependence was seen when the participants stood their ground in debate and were resilient
to challenges from the group about the reasons why they made their decisions in creating their
storyboard. Molm (2010: 129) argues that reciprocity promotes positive feelings and perceptions
of relationships that counter the negative effects of power inequality. Unpacking some of the
dialogue produced in the process gives clues to what these young people thought.

Annalise selected the following text to accompany this photo [4.2c]:

> He has contact with me, he is nice and funny good dancer
> I am flipping my legs away

She describes how they are relating physically and acknowledges the other dancer's ability
and character traits. The photo of her striking a pose, leg extended, had this text:

> I was being ballerina
> Looks funny and my toes look really cute
> Comes up pinky

Her description captures her unconventional and quirky character. She often radically juxta-
poses ideas against one another. In the following she revels in her capacity to take a leadership
role in the dance class:

I love leading
They loved following me doing the stomp move
My moves give other people ideas

And below clearly expresses her sense of self-confidence, favourite moves and agency around dancing:

It is a funky shape it really nice I love dancing I say ye ha dancing
I like floor work doing splits, mermaids, rolls diving
I can do a solo on myself
It's really really good cause I
I'm not afraid actually

Alex selected the text below in relation to learning a handstand:

Something for me to learn to do and try to stay up longer
My handstand special move
I have seen others do it Adus – Helene
Strong arms to keep body steady
Good and achieved new moves
Covered in sweat for the hard work concentration and focus

He elaborates further:

Twister tangled up like being trapped
Shape connecting combining and working in groups
In dance I like to sweat, concentrate and impress people showing how talented we are

Alex speaks about challenging himself through physical feats and acknowledges his achievement through the physical exertion dance offers him. He is open to learning from others in the class by way of imitation.

Performing at Interact I feel proud and it is something exciting to look forward to and we can see how good we are by the comments from family and friends
Show audience good dance moves you like and enjoy your self
I come back each week to be with people and learn new things

He describes his emotions in regard to performing and his sense of affirmation from family and friends seeing him perform.

Ariel's storyboard begins with the following text:

Different drops and different partners try new friends each time, happy
And we do it again
I like doing movement and dancing
Everyone enjoys their time together
It is really fun

Ariel refers to her positive attitude to dance, enjoyment and the importance of relationship to others and the use of repetition. In answer to the question "How do you know you have improved?" she states:

> People show me small steps and I did better each time
> Improves my body
> Be flexible really good for me and my muscles

She articulates how she learns step by step and comments positively on the physical changes dancing brings about.

There were commonalities between the three stories. They described particular dance moves they liked to perform with enthusiasm, clearly signalling each individual's preferences and ownership of their dancing. This quote from Alex captures a sentiment present in all three stories in relation to them coming to this community dance class, which clearly alluded to the importance all three place on relationships. "Good meeting different interesting people and I come back each week to be with people performing differently."

All acknowledged the worth of imitation by learning and copying skills from others, especially the tutors in the class. They placed value on enjoyment, being engaged and challenged, and the opportunity to embrace multiple roles. These include being a leader, a follower, a supporter of others, a dancer and a performer. We would agree with Ehrich (2010: 246) that "empowerment as a construct … values relationships with others and sees individuals as unique persons who can give and receive." This was a productive process underpinned by a strong sense of trust, commitment and honesty. All of us seemed to be swept up, moved by the workshop experience. Bliss (2015: 188) describes this sensation as affect, a "relational mobility and movement of human experience that may not achieve a material end point but something more fluid and active." Being 'swept up' indicates a transformation, a personal sense of being activated, moved or altered that we all experienced in the workshop.

Expectation, tensions and limitations

Digital storytelling is about the creative journey and not necessarily the end product. The aim was not an excellent, product-driven process that made artistic video dance. It was important that these digital stories show the dancers at their best and that it is not an even playing field when it comes to society and difference. This initially created a tension for Sue between product versus process. Facilitators needed to support and enable but leave room for the participants to have the power of decision making. Bliss (2015) argues that emotional bonds are created in the performance of digital storytelling that fosters a sense of faith and intimacy between workshop participants. As this powerful process evolved, Sue's understanding of digital storytelling increased, enabling her to let go of these concerns. It may be argued that she stepped back from control and power to trust the process, and its affective richness took over and enveloped us.

There were several limitations. One was the short time frame available. The workshop process is usually three days but this one was conducted over two, meaning that the editing was done post-workshop. A consequence of this was that the editing process was not entirely driven by the participants. During the workshop we produced giant storyboards for each individual and during the editing Sue adhered to these to keep the decision making process as much as possible in the hands of the participants.

Due to limited time a video editor was employed and worked in conjunction with Sue to complete the process one story at a time, with Ariel's being first. Another crucial step in the process once the draft digital story was edited was to gain feedback from a variety of people, in particular Ariel, Alex and Annalise, and the Artistic Director of Touch Compass. This feedback was reflected upon and subsequent changes were made to the draft.

Responses to the draft of Ariel's digital dance story

Sue showed the draft to Ariel at the beginning of the Saturday community class. The class clustered around with Ariel sitting directly in front of the laptop and everyone watching intently. Ariel looked around to see how others were responding. She smiled, laughed and looked down slightly embarrassed with her head in her hands on one occasion. At the end, when asked what she thought, she replied, "Pretty good" followed by two thumbs up in the air. Alex sitting beside her said, "It was fantastic." Others in the group echoed that reaction with their thumbs up. When asked if she would like anything changed she indicated no. However, Sue wondered whether if the video had been shown to her separately initially, her response would have been different.

Another response to the draft was thought-provoking. It was suggested that the whole digital story be subtitled or edited where it was difficult to understand what she was saying. This raised considerable debate. Did we need to hear everything? Was she being compromised by subtitling all her spoken words or vice versa. After much deliberation it was decided that it was crucial not to edit or transcribe any of Ariel's speech for the following reasons: this visual narrative of her performing her storyboard provided the foundation for her digital story, her choices, her voice, her dance and her identity; it was important to let the dance, text, still images, video footage and spoken word build up a complex web of interactions that include engagement with different embodiments to celebrate who she is and why she dances; this opened up the possibility for this digital story to be read in multiple inter-textual ways, thus resisting a single reading. However, the addition of more visual text in the parts where the dialogue was more difficult to understand did provide more clarity. Both facilitators agreed that having her voice throughout makes her story very powerful.

Another response from an outsider to this process in relation to viewing the digital story draft was, "You did not tell me she was disabled." It is interesting to note that in declaring one of the participants as 'disabled' the viewer saw the disability first. This response calls into question the following: can we move beyond labels or a sympathy vote or is the disability so hyper visible that nothing else is seen (Kuppers, 2011)? The debates within the disability culture around labels and definitions are difficult. As Cheesman (2011: 323) asserts, "The notion of a label that puts a box around people, often the marginalised, confining them into a set of expected behaviours is simplistic and hugely problematic." In contrast, we saw vibrant strong young people making digital stories on their dancing and what it meant to them. They all gained further understanding of themselves through active engagement in this process through embodied experiences [Photo 4.2c].

Conclusion

We all agreed that an ineffable sense of community and connection was generated over the two-day process. Digital story making enhanced their agency and empowerment by giving these young people a voice about their dancing, maximising the learning throughout the creative process. This opened up shifts in personal understanding and challenged dominant narratives and power structures that limit and disempower young people's identities – especially those with different embodiments. We would contend from these digital stories that identity in these young people is not fixed and singular but far more complex and existent on multiple levels. In documenting our experience of the process, we hope this might encourage others to use the digital storytelling process to empower other youth in order for a spectrum of voices to be heard.

References

Alrutz, M. (2015) 'Digital storytelling and youth: toward critically engaged praxis.' *Youth Theatre Journal*, 29(1), pp.1–14.

Benjamin, A. (2002) *Making an Entrance: Theory and Practice for Disabled and Non-disabled Dancers*. London: Routledge.

Benmayor, R. (2008) 'Digital storytelling as a signature pedagogy for the new humanities.' *Arts and Humanities in Higher Education*, 7(2), pp. 188–204.

Bliss, E. (2015) *Performative Methodologies: Geographies of Emotion and Affect in Digital Storytelling Workshops* (Doctoral Thesis, Waikato Hamilton, New Zealand). Available at http://hdl.handle.net/10289/9354 [Accessed 20 March 2016].

Bliss, E. & J. Fisher. (2014) 'The journey to a good life: exploring personal and organisational transformation through digital storytelling.' In R. E. Rinehart, K. N. Barbour & C. C. Pope (Eds.), *Ethnographic Worldviews. Transformations and Social Justice* (pp. 93–109). Dordrecht, The Netherlands: Springer.

Carr, M. & G. Claxton. (2002) 'Tracking the development of learning dispositions.' *Assessment in Education: Principles, Policy & Practice*, 9(37), pp. 9–37.

Cheesman, S. (2011) 'A dance teacher's dialogue on working within disabled/non-disabled engagement in dance.' *The International Journal of the Arts in Society*, 6(3), pp. 321–330.

Cheesman, S. (2011) 'Facilitating dance making from a teacher's perspective within a community integrated dance class.' *Research in Dance Education*, 12(1), pp 29–40.

Ehrich, L. C. (2010) 'Shall we dance? The story of The Radiance Dance Project.' *Australian Journal of Adult Learning*, 50(2), pp. 239–259. Accessed from Education Research Complete.

Kuppers, P. (2011) *Disability Culture and Community Performance: Find a Strange and Twisted Shape*. New York: Palgrave.

Lambert, J. (2009) *Digital Storytelling: Capturing Lives, Creating Community* (3rd ed.). Berkeley, CA: Digital Diner Press.

Manning, C. (2009) 'Inclusive learning disability research using ethics, oral history and digital storytelling.' *British Journal of Disabilities*, 38(3), pp. 160–167.

Molm, L. (2010) 'The structure of reciprocity.' *Social Psychology Quarterly*, 73(2), pp. 119–131.

Murakami, K. (2008) 'Re-imagining the future: young people's construction of identities through digital storytelling.' In *Beyond Current Horizons* (pp. 1–14). Bath, England: Department of Education. Available at https://issuu.com/gfbertini/docs/re-imagining_the_future_-_young_people_s_construct/1 [Accessed 13 May 2016].

Nicolson, M. (2005) *Applied Drama: The Gift of Theatre*. New York, NY: Palgrave.

Touch Compass Dance Company. (n.d.) *Vision*. Available at http://www.touchcompass.org.nz/about/vision [Accessed 25 May 2016].

4.3

COMMUNITY INITIATIVES FOR SPECIAL NEEDS DANCERS

An evolving ecology in Singapore

Stephanie Burridge

Introduction

Enabling initiatives that promote access and inclusion in dance classes and performances for Singapore's young people with diverse abilities are featured in this chapter through case study examples. The ecology involves communities, peak organisations and professional arts projects that have a commitment to offering opportunities for social engagement, personal expression and development through dance. The approaches to open the space for inclusivity to give more access to dance are various; they may evolve from ground up awareness of a need led by individuals, while others respond to government directives in the education sector, or their aims and objectives may be reflective of larger directional influences from other countries. Although some inclusive dance performance projects by local companies have been staged locally, professional companies that exist in many overseas countries (such as Candoco in the UK and Restless Dance Theatre in Australia) for professional artists currently do not exist in Singapore. Programmes for the performing arts (not specifically dance) are included across the school system and community opportunities for young people with special needs are evolving; however, the dance scene for young people with diverse abilities remains fragmented.

Pedagogy

The pedagogy generally adopted in teaching and learning for dancers with special needs in Singapore, and perhaps in much of the Asian region, mirrors established cultural traditions and protocols whereby local dance forms (Indian, Chinese, Malay) follow a master teacher/ guru centred approach (Burridge, 2010: 127). The students not only expect to follow the teacher for most of the class but are comfortable doing so; this is coupled with an expectation and desire to perform that is potent and underpins much of the activity and direction of programmes in this sector. Alternatively, teachers might be trained in Western classical ballet or follow a jazz/street dance path where similar teacher/student hierarchies are in place. Few teachers are trained in Laban-based creative dance education so both the teaching and learning in many dance programmes is mimetically-focused. Lomas (1998: 157) identifies these polarities as teachers trained through the 'dance education' route (creatively based) or "via a craft and theatrical emphasis." Locally, this mimesis (Dowling, 2011: 3) occurs, with some small variants, in classes for dancers with disabilities. It corresponds in part to Foster's (1997: 253) notion of the 'hired body' whereby an eclectic range of pre-existing techniques are taught and physically embodied; however, this occurs in combination with some investigative, 'inside out' strategies to develop individual movement phrases and self-expression, particularly in performance projects. This might be termed 'structured creativity' and is aligned to French scholar Paul Ricoeur's notion of triple mimesis (in Dowling, 2011) whereby personal expression is arrived at over time through imitation, reconfiguration and transformation.

Context

Although all Singapore schools are required to be resourced with a team of teachers trained to work with students with special needs, their skills are necessarily diverse as they transit curriculum areas and are rarely specific to the arts. In 2005 the Ministry of Education implemented an Allied Educators programme (Learning and Behavioural Support) to support students with mild special educational needs such as dyslexia, Autism Spectrum Disorder (ASD) and Attention Deficit Hyperactivity Disorder (ADHD) in mainstream schools.[1] It also provides a list of schools that cater specifically for groups such as hearing or visually impaired students. Several pre-schools, and primary and secondary schools include dance as a core learning area in their programmes for what is termed 'special needs' education in Singapore. For instance, the Pathlight School is designated for children with autism[2] and other disabilities offering a blend of academic curriculum and developing 'life readiness' skills to promote independent living as well as access to a varied arts curriculum including Dance Movement and Creative Dance electives.

This exclusive, or 'separative,' approach, also reflects the education system in Singapore that streams all students after sitting the Primary School Leaving Examination (PSLE) into selected schools and learning areas; these are titled Normal (Academic) and Normal (Technical). Normal (Academic) leads to O Level exams or an Integrated Programme leading to either an International Baccalaureate or A level exams. Although new initiatives to incorporate a wider breadth of curriculum subjects and diverse learning experiences are in place, movement within a restrictive system rather than one that is "flexible, varied, provide [ing] multiple pathways" (Zongyi, Gopinathan and Lee, 2013: 23) becomes even more complex and limited for special needs learners.

The National Arts Council (NAC) is also involved through strategies to support artists-in-residence working in schools with special needs[3] students via a collaborative approach between the classroom teacher and the artist. Schools can apply to the NAC for a grant to bring a teacher to their school. Training teachers in dance to cater for schools that would like a programme is currently limited by the number of dance teachers and above all, those interested in training and moving into the sector. Essentially dance for all students through an inclusive, open access approach remains an ideal.

Special arts community organisations

Rainbow Centre and Very Special Arts (VSA)[4] offer both visual and performing arts to children with special needs. The first operates two special education schools and two early intervention centres,[5] plus Rainbow Centre Training and Consultancy provides training for professional artists wishing to work in their schools. Embracing a holistic curriculum including the arts they have trained teachers to work in dance but music remains a major focus. VSA is the case example in this section as dance is an integral part of their programming.

Very Special Arts

VSA is an organisation that provides recreational dance therapy classes and performance opportunities to young people with disabilities aged six to eighteen years old. Social integration underpins all activities presenting the chance to come together, learn and share. While access is the key, the dancers work with others of similar disabilities with the exception of their teachers and volunteers, who assist with the classes.

In April 2016 the Creative Dance students were practising a new routine with their teacher for an annual charity gala 'Care and Share.' The VSA dance group performed with a young singer to the song 'You raise me up.' Most of the performers were autistic, with a greater number of boys than girls in the group. The choreography was a creative dance piece utilising the lyrics of the song to guide the movement. For example, with the lyrics "You raise me up," they all raised their arms; to "I feel strong," they made muscle man poses; for "Stand on shoulders," they touched their shoulders. The performance had a lot of repetition (like the song) with some creative variations that allowed freer movement with the bodies curved in and then opening out. The dancers obviously enjoyed the experience of being on stage. More than that, the combination of the song lyrics and movement left them with an embodied experience that was shared by the young singer and a couple of dance volunteers in an integrated performance. There was empathy, collaboration, trust and confidence among the performers and the choreographer. With a packed house of 4,000 people, the experience could have been overwhelming. Speaking to the dance teacher after the show she shared, "I know the feeling of performing and I want them to experience it authentically."[6] She conceded that the lyrics certainly helped the dancers to remember the movements – it is her experience that it takes them seven lessons to learn a new routine. Her methods incorporate a mix of set movements and task-based explorations where the dancers extend their movement vocabulary through some improvisation and exploration. This is linked together in their performances on stage.

A week after the show I met the dancers, their two teachers and the VSA arts organiser. Seven ASD boys and one girl comprised an advanced level class and two regular volunteers assisted the dances and teacher by demonstrating the moves and helping individual students. The students were practising movement to the beat of the music followed immediately by a free section whereby they took turns to do their own 'signature move' before repeating the whole phrase like a chorus. A teaching point for this group was to combine some stylised set phrases with some natural free movement (like jumping) then an individual free expression part that combined into set counts so the students could remember when to perform each section. The attention was intense and they responded to the teacher, following instructions. He noticed their spatial awareness was improving over time while he was also learning how to communicate more effectively with the students. The exchange back and forth between teacher, the volunteers and students was evident and built through trust, collaboration and cooperation within the group. The volunteers are 'crucial' to the programme as the dancers need others to follow and help them. In this class, after every try at the routine there were high fives all around and congratulations to everyone. The atmosphere was fun and committed – everyone joined in, remembered the sequence and 'grooved' to the music on the individual sections while awaiting their turn.

The dance studio had ballet bars and mirrors and the teacher ran the hip hop based class in the format common for any genre-specific dance technique class with a warm-up and short sequences danced behind the teacher while he faced the mirror; then extending into longer phrases and routines. This method was intentional and the experienced dance teacher commented on this approach, "I want to make it like a typical dance class with no 'concessions' … they learn like a regular class … the etiquette of performing and doing a mainstream class, how it operates, stage directions, what to do in a theatre when performing."[7] Continuing, he felt they should be challenged, "It is great to see what they have achieved when they perform on stage." He also wants them to experience different genres of dance so each term there is a new style introduced – jazz, lyrical jazz, hip hop, contemporary, Bollywood, K pop: "Experimentation is important." He also noted some of the challenges in teaching ADS dancers such as it was important for the teachers to know participants' 'triggers' (loud noises, responses to things like scolding or not allowing certain behaviours in the class). Both teachers spoke about some unpredictability with teaching autistic children including elements of spontaneity and surprise. Having detailed information (medical and behavioural) about the participants allows them to handle incidents better; for instance, one young dancer was deaf and autistic and responded much better to visual cues.

Reflecting the way most dance is taught in Singapore (and much of Asia) through following the teacher, the instructors noted that creativity *per se* did not work for their students and that they were "happier following instructions." They learnt to move together, respond to the music, feel the rhythm and coordinate simple shapes in unison in a positive environment with the teacher supporting and reinforcing their progress in accomplishing short phrases that lead to longer routines for performances – they loved these and this approach is an essential component, and aim, of the VSA programme. Although there were regular performances the main focus was for the dancers to grow in confidence, develop social skills, coordination and above all express their love of dance.

Towards inclusivity in dance performance projects

Two local companies that have performed projects created via an inclusive process are Maya Dance Theatre and Flamenco Sin Fronteras (FSF). Maya combines contemporary techniques with Indian classical Bharatanatyam while the other is a flamenco based company working with contemporary expression in an intercultural context. A common thread is that both artistic directors are not only dancers but have training in the health sector; Kavitha Krishnan from Maya is an occupational therapist while Daphne Huang Vargas from FSF is a medical practitioner.

Maya Dance Theatre

Over the past decade, Kavitha has been working with the Down Syndrome Association, Singapore (DSA). Assisted by company dancer Shahrin Johry, the DAS dance group now involves a multi-tiered structure whereby some of the dancers have moved into a new performance orientated group called STAR. Krishnan commented, "Involvement of the arts has

PHOTO 4.3 World Dance Alliance Asia Pacific Dance Bridge 2015: Connectivity through Dance conference
Dancers: Down Syndrome Association Singapore
National Library Singapore
Photographer: Stephanie Burridge

not only benefitted their personal well-being and development ... [but created] an awareness of the abilities beyond the disability and an opportunity of a possible career in the arts: to also enable a place for their expression along with the other dance artists and arts professionals" (Burridge & Carino, 2014: 109).

In October 2015, at a community showcase at the National Library for the 'World Dance Alliance Asia Pacific Dance Bridge 2015: Connectivity through Dance' conference, Shahrin Johry, principal dancer of Maya Dance Theatre, performed with the Down Syndrome Association dancers in an integrated collaboration [Photo 4.3]. It was a Bollywood/pop number that had the crowds cheering. This collaboration reflects a long association with the dancers who gave an early glimpse of their love of dance and willingness to work with the company in 2013 when they appeared in *Release 2013* with Maya Dance Theatre at the Substation as part of *Small Steps*, created by Shahrin Johry and Hafeez Hassan for Maya and Down Syndrome Association (DSA) dancers.[8] Maya is committed to access and empowerment for the DSA dancers (who also have their own performances) and on occasion present inclusive dance choreography.

Flamenco Sin Fronteras

Artistic directors of Singapore dance group Flamenco Sin Fronteras (FSF), Dr Daphne Huang Vargas and Antonio Vargas began working with mental health institute (MHI) patients in October 2014. Since then they have met once a week and sometimes twice if there is a forthcoming collaborative performance project. Each session is one and a half hours.

It is an intergenerational group with members ranging in age from teens to thirties. They live independently in a cluster of six homes. It has an Activity Hub that offers various art therapy activities – this is where the weekly classes are conducted. To facilitate the movement sessions Daphne believes her medical training is extremely important in recognising and predicting issues regarding the health (and attitudes) of participants in the session; for instance, many participants in dance/arts programmes are on medication that might affect their energy levels and concentration throughout an activity. Flamenco is the core activity: "flamenco can be used as a therapeutic form of emotional release and expression while improving co-ordination, movement and musicality in disadvantaged communities."[9] Daphne spoke about the power of the rhythms of flamenco (*bulerias* and *jaleos*), clapping, body percussion and drumming, to unite the group and develop confidence. As the rhythms build different people can enter the circle to do a variation and express themselves in their own way. Drumming is also universal and an easy entry point for everyone no matter what their cultural background. "It engages them and evolves and changes so it can be a combination of old and new." The drumming and rhythms take people out of their comfort zones and they become freer and more spontaneous. Being open to where the class wants to go is important rather than restricting it to just movement – personal creativity is the goal and the teachers "encourage spontaneity in the process for them to become engaged and make their own movements." The focus for FSF is on the regular class sessions although some of the teenagers combined with the general community to create a flash mob at a local shopping mall in 2015. Performances have gradually become a part of the programme but are arrived at through careful work-shopping and consensus amongst the group.

Local influences merge with the flamenco material in interesting ways to create an east/ west sensibility. Each session begins with Qi Gong and breathing while working in a circle is essential to the structure of the class. Gradually they introduce texts and storytelling. Sometimes it is a combination of both and as participants move in and out of the circle local language references in Hokien, Malay or Singlish (local Singapore 'slang') might be included, becoming a powerful means of self-expression. The company asserts the sharing of stories is key to FSF integrated projects with the group; for instance, they introduced a ten-week pilot co-creation, multi-disciplinary workshop project, called 'Heroes' Stories.' These tell about overcoming challenges and MHI participants have responded to this theme very well. It enables them to externalise their thoughts and feelings; however, in the early stages, most were happy with just a combination of a pose and some verbal comments to denote characters. The development of this project was performed in June 2016 as *Drama Flamencas: The Hero's Journey*.

Another performance work, *Breaking Silence* (2014), was a multidisciplinary theatre production directed and choreographed by Antonio Vargas in collaboration with the Singapore Association of Mental Health. Identifying four types of mental illness – schizophrenia, obsessive compulsive disorder, bi-polar disorder and depression – the dance theatre choreography used material from interviews conducted with Singapore Association of Mental Health clients and the public regarding perceptions of, and social stigmas around, mental illness. It was performed by the dancers of FSF with an additional performance by the clients of the Singapore Association of Mental Health developed from an eight-week workshop conducted by Flamenco Sin Fronteras.

Like Maya Dance Theatre, Flamenco Sin Fronteras is not an inclusive dance company and their work with the MHI is part of their outreach activity that they are firmly committed to as part of their vision.[10]

Audience development – a sensory friendly initiative

In 2016 the premier performance venue in Singapore, Esplanade Theatres by the Bay, introduced sensory-friendly children's shows for special needs audiences. Through focus group discussions with autism experts, teachers and parents, Esplanade has incorporated appropriate strategies and made technical adjustments to the performances. The shows are advertised as such and usually comprise three performances selected from a run of up to twelve. *Bunny Finds the Right Stuff*, a children's theatre production recommended for two to four years olds and written by local author Emily Lim trialled the concept.

The shows are brightly lit with no total blackouts and no sudden loud noises that autistic children can often be hypersensitive to; for example, a loud dinosaur sound was mellowed. The costumes and props are colourful and often tactile and the shows are interactive with catchy tunes that the children can dance to in a multi-disciplinary experience. The relaxation of usual theatre rules and protocols has the biggest impact; children can move around the theatre, make a noise and even leave to go to a quiet place next door known as Pip's Playroom where they can play or view a TV monitor projection of the show. Teachers and therapists were fully engaged in the consultative process and the fact that the series occurred at all was already 'a win' according to some. Among the many advantages for families that parents enthused about, one was, "the opportunity for the whole family to go out together for an outing to a performance and feel comfortable."[11] Esplanade works with the schools to prepare the children to come to the performance through providing an attractive kit of the story with photos and, most importantly, the use of 'social story' to reduce anxiety – a step by step guide about what to expect when going to the theatre.

The theatre staff are also briefed and encouraged to promote the inclusive atmosphere where everyone felt "it was OK to be different." The initiative is in line with Esplanade's vision of community engagement and 'social responsibility' across all sectors to offer access to inclusive arts experiences.

Concluding remarks

The directions of the dance classes discussed corresponded to the skills and expertise of the individual teachers. More than that, they parallel how dance is typically taught in education settings in Singapore where it is not a separate subject in schools but is popular throughout the school years in what are termed co-curricular activity elective courses (CCAs) that are usually orientated towards perfecting a routine in a dance genre for performance.

The teachers interviewed felt the need for training workshops, opportunities to upgrade their skills to enhance knowledge about the different needs of groups. While acknowledging that accreditation of teachers could be appropriate they believed passion is the main driver that makes their classes work. They noted that practitioners become 'isolated' with few opportunities to work with people of various disabilities in order to experience the needs of each. Typically, classes in dance are for one focus group only – for instance Down Syndrome, autism or hearing and/or sight impaired. A network for sharing and meeting other dance teachers would be useful and provide support. In every community there are children missing out on the chance to dance and it is clear a wider network should be established with many more dance teachers trained to work in this sector. At present, there is only one Singapore tertiary dance institution, the Nanyang Academy of Fine Arts, specifically addressing this need through offering a module in Dance Movement Therapy Performance. A case narrative by the course leader Filomar Cortezano Tariao in this volume recounts developments.

This chapter has presented some of the dance activity and special initiatives towards access and inclusion in Singapore – it is acknowledged in this case-based approach that many other impressive programmes are quietly moving on with their classes while new initiatives are being imagined and resourced. Singapore has recently started an awareness campaign in the general community to spike public consciousness about embracing access and inclusion, such as the annual Purple Parade[12] and festival. Hearing-impaired dance crew Redeafination are gaining international recognition, while local events such as lighting up the Marina Bay Sand's iconic Helix Bridge, the National Gallery and St Andrew's Cathedral in blue position Singapore as joining the international 'Light it Blue' advocacy campaign to commemorate World Autism Day.[13] Momentum is building but there remains quite a journey ahead to ensure a brighter, inclusive future for young people with special needs and their families and caregivers.

Acknowledgements

I would like to thank the National Arts Council Singapore for their support through a Research and Development grant and the dance teachers and choreographers who participated in the interviews for their generosity in sharing their process, personal views and insights.

Notes

1 https://www.moe.gov.sg/education/programmes/support-for-children-special-needs [Accessed 12 April 2016].
2 http://www.pathlight.org.sg/
3 https://aep.nac.gov.sg/nacaep/nacaep/programmes-and-schemes/NAC-Artist-SPED-School-Partnership-Programme.html [Accessed 24 June 2016].
4 http://www.vsa.org.sg/
5 http://rainbowcentre.org.sg/index.php?id=67#.V3SyZlR94dU
6 Personal interview 7 May 2016 with Very Special Arts choreographer Karen Katrea.
7 Personal interview 7 May 2016 with Very Special Arts programme executive performing arts Chok Shin Ni and dance teachers Zulfikar Ali and Karen Katrea.
8 S. Burridge 2013, http://inkpotreviews.com/2013reviews/0323,rele,sb.xml [Accessed 24 June 2016].
9 Personal interview 29 April 2016, Flamenco Sin Fronteras artistic director Daphne Huang Vargas.
10 http://www.flamencosinfronteras.com.sg/#!history/cn37 [Accessed 2 May 2016].
11 Personal interview 26 May 2016, Esplanade Theatres on the Bay sensory-friendly performances programming and production team including Chua Lik Ling, Emily Hoe, Pele Ling and Luanne Poh.
12 http://www.purpleparade.sg/
13 https://www.autismspeaks.org/what-autism/world-autism-awareness-day

References

Burridge, S. (2010) 'Platforms for change: Cambodia and contemporary dance from the Asia Pacific region.' In Burridge, S. and F. Frumberg (Eds.), *Beyond the Apsara: Celebrating Dance in Cambodia*. Routledge, India.

Dowling, William C. (2011) *Ricoeur on Time and Narrative: An Introduction to Temps et Récit*. Notre Dame: University of Notre Dame Press. Available at http://www3.nd.edu/~undpress/excerpts/P01504-ex.pdf (pp. 1–17) [Accessed 3 August 2016].

Foster, S. (1997) 'Dancing Bodies.' In J. Desmond (Ed.), *Meaning in Motion: New Cultural Studies of Dance*. Duke University Press: Durham & London.

Krishnan, K. (2014) 'Arts in community.' In Burridge, S. and C. Carino (Eds.), *Evolving Synergies: Celebrating Dance in Singapore*. Routledge, India.

Lomas Christine M. (1998) 'Art and the Community: Breaking the Aesthetic of Disempowerment.' In Shapiro, Sherry B. (Ed.) *Dance, Power and Difference: Critical Feminist Perspectives on Dance Education*. Human Kinetics Publishers Ltd, Champaign, IL.

Zongyi, Deng, S. Gopinathan, and C. Kim-Eng Lee. (2013) *Globalization and the Singapore Curriculum: From Policy to Classroom*, Springer, Singapore.

4.4

CELEBRATING DIVERSITY

A Jamaican story

Carolyn Russell Smith

Jamaica as a developing nation has ambitions for its population that will eventually put it on par with the more advanced countries. One such ambition seeks to address the diversity of creative and physical needs within Jamaican schools. The current school system endeavors to integrate dance not only as a subject, but also as an integral part of extracurricular activities, sometimes manifesting itself as school clubs that students are at liberty to join. Jamaican education policies have sought to guarantee equitable access for all to artistic and educational programs for students regardless of race, color or creed.

Khulcha Theatre School of Dance

As the founder of Khulcha Theatre School of Dance, and a dance teacher for many years, I have had to call on my garnered skills to effectively tutor students of varying age groups, skill levels, and occasionally, physical abilities, and have challenged myself to make adjustments to teaching techniques when a class includes a physically challenged student [Photo 4.4]. This narrative gives some insights into my teaching approach utilized to not only involve the challenged student in class routines, but also to maintain the interest and standards of the able-bodied students. Since the school's inception, I have had the inclusion of two physically challenged students at different periods – and surprising to say, these were the most creative periods.

Joy

My first physically challenged student, who I will call Joy, came to Khulcha at the age of six and suffered from an arm and leg impediment. The early years of her tutoring saw her blending in well with the other students and an improvement in her confidence. During a class as an early teen, I gave the students a movement phrase and she came to me with tears in her eyes saying that she could not manage the movements. I consoled her and encouraged her to do what she could manage by challenging herself. She then partnered with a particular student who helped her immensely. Her mother once attended a performance and cried

PHOTO 4.4 Khulcha Theatre School of Dance
Photographer: Shane Brown

when she saw her on stage and expressed gratitude for the care and dedication given to all students, resulting in her daughter fulfilling a dream of being able to enjoy dance and being able to fit in with other teenagers her age. It is interesting to note that no member of the audience recognized her physical condition; it was not until the performance was finished and Joy was leaving the stage, that one parent new to Khulcha commented on how well she had done, displaying more energy than the other students. Joy was included in almost every school activity, making her feel a part of the team. Reflecting on the experiences I had with Joy made me more aware and passionate about the needs of persons with disabilities. It made me come out of my comfort zone of teaching only able-bodied students and I started looking at ways to embrace the diversity of the needs of all students.

Kyla

In April 2016, I was once again given the opportunity to teach a student who was both physically challenged and hearing impaired, aged ten years. I will refer to her as Kyla. Her mother, having heard of the help given to Joy, visited the school for assistance. The parent explained that they had been living in the United States and had moved back to Jamaica and had had to enroll their daughter in a special education institution. Nevertheless, she wanted her to be involved in extracurricular activities with able-bodied students. However, when the child came for registration, it was recognized that the disability was more severe than Joy's, as she was crouched forward, unable to stand up straight, and suffered occasional muscle spasms. I was hesitant because I had never taught anyone in her condition before but was won over by her beautiful smile and the look of eagerness in her eyes. Based on her age I decided to place her in the nine to eleven age group. I explained to the parent that I would not be able to tailor the class to her, seeing as I had many other students to work with. I had forewarned the other students of her condition prior to her arrival and that they should assist in making her welcome. The first class was used to assess her capabilities. Along with her crouching disposition, her hands could not stretch out fully and she tended to be off balance. I had to switch gear and have them move to different drum beats and intermittently instruct them to freeze and find a partner at the next break. This routine continued until they were totally engrossed in what they were doing. It allowed me to assess what she could do and the extent to which she was able to keep up with the class. Fortunately, there was a student in her group who knew sign language and when she was being distracted she would be signed to in order to get her attention back on the class.

Cultural pedagogy

Having Kyla in my class along with the other students opened my eyes to different teaching methods capable of having everyone engaged in the class routines without frustration stepping in. I had to learn how to be more creative in my teaching approach to make everyone feel accepted by drawing on the various play games that the students are familiar with culturally; some of these games integrate song and dance, and all have a wealth of rhythmic movement ideas. Kyla became the star of the group; where she could not manage, they lifted her up and gave her little solos that re-merged with the group. This creative work by the students was presented at their Kids Expression concert in June 2016, which was well received by the audience. The physically challenged student did not just make friends, but was able to develop her self-confidence and take on challenges; at times I was concerned she was going to hurt herself. She was a happy child and accepted her disability, which in many instances encouraged her peers not to give up, and often they could be heard saying "If Kyla can do it, I can do it also." Kyla's crouching posture has now straightened, there is improvement in her balance and she is now capable of executing her movements better.

Conclusion

Gaining the trust of students is one of the key things needed in teaching. This emerges when you show interest in the welfare of your students; for example, noting things they like, asking how their day at school was, and most of all complimenting them when they complete their tasks. The role of the teacher is to guide and give suggestions and it does not matter if what they present is not to my complete liking; it is their creative work that is valued and they should be supported. The group interaction they experience as they work together in exploring various movement activities allows for social integration through discussion, planning, arguing, decision making and dancing their movement ideas. The dance students learn to share, listen to others, wait their turn, respect the views of others and develop their self-confidence. It is our task as teachers to find not only what enables each student to learn and feel welcome, but also what motivates them to be appreciative and respectful to all no matter their differences. If students can adjust to and accept physically challenged peers and learn to co-exist with them, we can go a long way toward achieving a more effective classroom environment and learning experience for a better world.

4.5

'I CAN ...'

A Cambodian inclusive arts project

Laura Evans

Epic Arts is an international inclusive arts organisation based in Cambodia and registered as a charity in the UK. It aims to use the arts as a form of expression and empowerment, to unite people with and without disabilities and to bring about personal and societal change in attitudes by promoting the message that every person counts. In 2015 Epic Arts received funding as part of the Cambodia Disability Inclusive Development Fund (CDIDF) from UNICEF and Australian Aid to conduct a project called *I Can* …. The *I Can* … project aimed to achieve three key goals over two years:

- To educate people with disabilities about the things they can do in their lives and within society in Cambodia, enabling them to develop confidence and self-belief through arts based activities.
- To educate community members, including key decision makers from the Department of Education, village chiefs, local school directors, teachers and health representatives about how people with disabilities can live their lives and be active members of society in Cambodia.
- To raise general awareness of the abilities of people with disabilities in Cambodia as active members of society and challenge perceptions by demonstrating that disabled people are capable of many different things.

These goals were achieved through a number of project elements, all of which were led and delivered by people with disabilities who had trained with Epic Arts on their two-year Inclusive Arts Course in Kampot Cambodia.

I Can ... Arts Activity Days

Recent graduates (with disabilities) of the Inclusive Arts Course at Epic Arts were employed to create a Community Arts Team that would deliver Arts Activity Days, which included dance-based performances and workshops at a number of disability-focused organisations across Cambodia. The Community Arts Team worked together with the assistance of a professional community arts leader to develop a performance that was based on overcoming a series of obstacles that a person with a disability might encounter in Cambodia. These obstacles came from the Community Arts Team's personal experiences of having a disability in Cambodia and were turned into positive statements that included: 'I can ... go to the hospital,' 'I can ... go to school,' 'I can ... fall in love,' 'I can ... have a job,' 'I can ... have a voice,' 'I can ... be an artist,' 'I can ... be independent' and more.

The performance was presented at a number of disability organisations around Cambodia during the course of the project. Local decision makers from health and education ministries, school directors and other community partners were invited to watch the performance along with families and local community members. After the performance, a guided question and answer session was held with the audience with the objective of starting a discussion in Khmer communities around the abilities and rights of people with disabilities and to inform the decision makers of both today and tomorrow about their potential.

In addition to the performance of *I Can* ..., the Community Arts Team also developed a movement-based workshop around its themes. The workshop included practical and discussion activities based on the United Nations Convention on the Rights of Persons with Disabilities (2006) and was delivered to twenty participants with disabilities at each of the disability organisations visited by the team. The workshop encouraged the participants to interact with the Community Arts Team and develop a short performance about their own suggestions for their families and communities regarding the things they feel they could achieve with support from, and inclusion in, their own community, such as 'I can ... go to school if there are no steps to my classroom'; 'I can ... get a job if the community supports me'; 'I can ... have a baby if I can access a health centre with my wheelchair'; or 'I can ... be a teacher if I'm allowed to take the exam'. This performance developed by the workshop participants during the Arts Activity Day was included as part of the public performance to community members alongside the performance by the Community Arts Team. This not only increased self-esteem and raised confidence amongst the participants but also gave them a space to demonstrate to their communities that other people with disabilities have succeeded and attained their dreams and so could they if they had the right support.

I Can ... viral video campaign

To create mainstream, national impact for the project and to promote inclusion of people with disabilities in Cambodia, Epic Arts created a parody of a popular music video in the country. The aim was to create a high quality music video that would appeal to young, mainstream audiences and presented people with disabilities in a way that would challenge preconceptions. The song 'Uptown Funk' by Mark Ronson Ft. Bruno Mars was selected and the members of the Community Arts Team took on the roles of the singers and performers in the original music video. Perceptions around both disability and gender were addressed within the film and a number of local Cambodian locations were selected to ensure cultural relevance. The film was produced by a professional music video company from the UK and was filmed on location in Kampot and Phnom Penh. The film was uploaded to YouTube and promoted by Epic Arts and UNICEF via social media to Cambodian nationals. It was also screened on national television in Cambodia a number of times during the project. The music video had over 175,000 views and instigated national press reports on the project. Performers in the video became national celebrities and were often stopped in the

PHOTO 4.5 *Uptown Funk*
Performer: Po Sakun
Epic Arts Cambodia
Photographer: Laura Evans

streets of the capital to be asked about the film. National press in Cambodia reported on the video saying, "Performers show disability is no barrier to grooving out" (*Phnom Penh Post*, 7 March 2015) and "Their disabilities are invisible as they lip-sync the lyrics and dance to the funky beat, and their message that 'people with disabilities in Cambodia can be valued and respected' rang true" (*Khmer Times*, 22 March 2015).

I Can ... poster campaign

To coincide with the viral video and the Arts Activity Days, a poster and sticker campaign, using a tag line from the music video, 'Don't believe me ... just watch!', was developed to promote the message of the *I Can* ... project. Posters and flyers with the key ideas contained in the *I Can* ... performance were distributed nationally to disability organisations and amongst the community in the areas where the Arts Activity Days were conducted. The posters shared the *I Can* ... message along with details of where to find the 'Uptown Funk' video on YouTube and the time and date of the performance in the community [Photo 4.5].

Conclusion

The project was a success with regard to starting a discussion around inclusion and challenging the perspectives and attitudes surrounding disability in the country. The combination of a national, mainstream approach along with a community-targeted approach that included both participants with disabilities and key decision makers, created an impact that reached far and wide. The project took a two-pronged approach, firstly educating people with disabilities on the possibilities available to them them and on their rights, developing their confidence and self-esteem, and providing them with a voice and space to share their performance experiences. Secondly it 'educated' key decision makers and the wider public about what people with disabilities can do rather than what it is perceived that they cannot do. The use of social media and video was a powerful tool that enabled cost-effective and wide sharing of the message, to both people with and without disabilities, leading to further investigation into the use of social media for challenging attitudes in society in Cambodia.

References

http://www.un.org/disabilities/convention/conventionfull.shtml [Accessed 28 November 2016].
Khmer Times [Accessed 8 March 2015].
Phnom Penh Post [Accessed 8 March 2015].

4.6

LEARNING TOGETHER THROUGH DANCE

Making cultural connections in Indonesia

Gianti Giadi

This is the story of Namira (N), a young dancer with Down Syndrome who came to my dance school in Jakarta, Indonesia. She is passionate and determined in everything that she does and is clever and assertive, with a high awareness of her image and looks. When she first came into the class, I was automatically drawn to her. I knew that there was something special about her and she has changed my own preconceptions of what Down Syndrome people are like. This narrative is an account of us growing and learning together over a four-year period.

2012–2013

K-pop started booming in Indonesia around 2012 and it triggered the rise of local 'girl bands.' From watching them on TV, N first showed an interest in dance, lip syncing and performing in front of her family members. She even asked them to take videos of her while 'performing.' The family saw her talent and enrolled her in Gigi Art of Dance in 2012, the only dance school in Jakarta that offers a class for Down Syndrome students [Photo 4.6].

The class started with five Down Syndrome and three hearing-impaired dancers. We had a trial of three months training with a performance at the end of the project called 'Danshare: Share through Dance, Care to Share.' I used the concept of 'hopes and dreams' and took inspiration from this. N's reaction was a little bit confused; at first she was not sure how to react to the other dancers, especially having the challenge of dancing with people with hearing problems. I noticed that she was taking the performing seriously and was very curious about the result of combining these two communities together through dance. There was also the question of how I was going to teach them.

The problem lay in communication. Directing dancers with Down Syndrome needs a different approach to directing dancers with hearing impairments. I tried using very simple movements (more gestural) with basic timing and musicality that were often lyrical. I focused on group work using short tasks, improvisation to give them freedom in movement and the use of imagery to inspire their creativity. The goal was for them to be able to communicate

PHOTO 4.6   Namira (centre) with Gigi Art of Dance
Photographer: Nini Andrini

better with gestures, the body and expression because, apart from N, most of the students had speech impairments.

This first project was to introduce them to the joy of moving with the music and how to 'speak' through movements. We also explored partnering work so that they interacted with each other in the hope of improving their social ability. N's reaction to the task I gave her was very surprising and she was not shy in exploring her movements. Because she was always open to challenges and enthusiastic, I gave her a solo and made her the leader in the partner-work. I was surprised how fast she could remember movements and timing. Her mother noticed at this time that her body awareness was improving and that intensive training boosted her mood and self-confidence.

2013–2014

After a successful performance in 'Danshare,' I was confident more people with Down Syndrome would join the class. We made *I'm Possible*, an inclusive dance piece about equality, to be performed in Indonesia and on World Dance Day in Singapore. For this project, we had eighteen Down Syndrome and eighteen able-bodied dancers create a choreography about their personal lives. After focusing on making them comfortable with simply moving and using their bodies expressively, we added text and voice into the piece to enable them to be relaxed when speaking about themselves. By this time, N had already eased into dancing and interacting with the others and was made the rehearsal master for this project. I gave her the challenge of being my assistant and told her that she needed to memorise everyone's dancing parts. I also gave her the task of helping me with blocking (staging) the dance and transitioning the formations. I wanted to push her more than the others because I knew that she was capable. She embraced her new challenge, took it very seriously and wanted to be in the studio full time. N became more open to others, saying 'Hi' to other students that came to the studio, and grew in confidence in many ways. I noticed that she started to be very active online, watching dance videos that she then tried to do on her own. The effect of dancing was affecting her personal life positively.

2014–2015

Reviewing major improvements in her personality, social skills and dancing, I suggested she join our typical technique classes. She only joined the classes for two months after which she became stressed in the class and could not concentrate. The level was too high for her to catch up, although the other dancers and teachers were very accepting of her. Eventually her mother decided to stop these classes to avoid her being overly stressed as it affected her mood outside of dance classes.

2015–present

N continues to be the star in and outside of her dance class. We did an interview and performance at the local TV station[1] and I noticed how she was very aware of her looks and the angle of her face. She knows how to present herself well in front of the audience and the camera. Although she was quieter than usual (she told me that she was very nervous) she and her two friends managed to make everyone proud by showing the audience about the possibility and the potential of what Down Syndrome dancers can do.

Conclusion

There are many things that N and her friends have proven me wrong about with regard to people with Down Syndrome. Initially I was sceptical about how to communicate with them and how to teach them properly. I was worried they would not understand me or learn anything from me. I am glad that the positive effect of having this programme is not only for N and her friends, but also for the parents that feel proud seeing their Down Syndrome son/daughter socialising and achieving something. N, who has minor Down Syndrome, has shown tremendous talent and potential and I hope she continues to shine and be the star that she can be.

Note

1   Tania L. Saputra (2013). 'Talk show ISDI & Gigi Art of dance in the Indonesia morning show program – net TV'. Available at https://www.youtube.com/watch?v=Piaa6SGqyw0 [Accessed 12 December 2013].

4.7

FROM THE GROUND UP

A Portuguese dance education collaboration with regional communities

Madalena Victorino in conversation with Annie Greig

Madalena Victorino is a Portuguese choreographic and community artist who works with a unique method of integrating artistic practice and life experience creating theatrical magic and enchantment. Madalena continues to create connections between art and social justice through community engagement projects that are inclusive of diversity in class, race and age. In this conversation, she and Australian dance director and educator Annie Greig talk about the *Mirage* project, a community dance initiative [Photo 4.7].

Annie: Tell me about the background to the project with the young people in the South.
Madalena: I have had a connection with the municipality of Odemira over five years and some time ago was asked to create a cultural event that was an ephemeral

PHOTO 4.7   *The Mirage Project*
Facilitated by Madalena Victorino
Photographer: Jen Brown

living museum, which could highlight the historical background of the area and bring the people together to celebrate their rich cultural heritage.

Annie: What did they propose and how did you fit?

Madalena: I am a community artist working with both professional artists and community members of all ages and I weave them together in projects that create connections between these diverse artists and audiences. They did not have a budget for a museum as we know it and thought I'd be the right person to bring together the population in a performance event and conference.

Annie: So how did you approach this project?

Madalena: Over three months we worked with local artists in film, technology, visual arts along with other key groups from the community. What we created was called *One Night in the Village* and included an array of arts experiences. I asked a local writer of fiction to select the best fragments of his work, a visual artist to put the sentences onto bed sheets for the older women to embroider and these were strung as flags in the piazza. There was a local amateur theatre group who whispered these texts throughout the night. A group of older men sang hymns of the mines in an old, dilapidated bus station that was blackened by fumes and was like a mine. Also, there was a group of fifty women prisoners who were allowed out for the night and wore coats with white lining which became a screen for a film on this new form of slavery with agricultural workers. The development process and the event itself was a wonderful experience for the people and what I have described are just some examples of the rich expressions that were facilitated by and for the local people.

The Mirage project

Annie: How did the schools become involved?

Madalena: The *One Night* event was seen as such a success that I was then asked to implement a performing arts program for the schools in the area – we called it *Mirage*. Firstly we associate the name of this project to the Mira River that flows through this village and the desire to transform school life through successive mirages of exceptional artistic experiences that have a lasting impact on all the students of this municipality.

Annie: What was the process of working with the schools?

Madalena: *Mirage* began with an experiential and analytical phase. I employed numerous professional performance groups from theatre, dance, circus and film for the students to see and the classroom was transformed into a dance theatre experience. This was something for them to receive – these objects of art.

Annie: How did you resource this project with the students?

Madalena: I wrote a book which I gave to each of the students in order to help them think critically about the arts and to create a discourse about their performance or filmic encounters.

Annie: The book set out tasks that students could complete at home or in the classroom with their teachers. It holds numerous analytical tools that can be used by students of all ages and even adults would find it a useful tool. For example, one exercise is called the x-ray of the performance and with a graphic of the body, students are asked to fill in the different body parts. In the brain, it is the ideas behind the performance; in the heart, the emotions they felt; in the ears, the music they heard; and in the belly, the underlying story brought to life in what they saw.

Madalena: This book also served as useful professional development for the teachers. Whilst the teachers were very positive about this aspect of the project, they wanted practical experiences so the second phase involved the students in creating and performing.

Annie: Can you talk about the implementation of the *Roda Atlantica* (*Atlantic Wheel*) which was the next phase of the *Mirage* project?

Madalena: There are many Guinean students in the technical college and they are often in the country without their parents. Their country and Portugal are connected by the Atlantic Ocean, hence the title. They have little or no contact with the white students at the other higher level secondary college. I was trying to bring these two groups into closer contact to gain a better appreciation of and respect for each of their cultural backgrounds.

Annie: What was your process?

Madalena: I engaged a local dance teacher and a musician to bring together these elements from both Portuguese and Guinean cultures. We offered the program to both schools and developed a working group that had predominantly Guinean participants, although my aim had been to have 50-50 representation. Marta Coutinho, the world dance teacher, assisted me in developing a performance that we could share with other schools and members of the local community. The idea of touring the group meant that more people had contact with these talented young performers.

Annie: What do you see as the key outcomes?

Madalena: For me the most obvious thing was seeing the African students grow in confidence, show pride in the culture and be able to demonstrate this in the performance. They had contact with young students as part of the show and this allowed them to share their own joy of dance, song and music. Learning professional presentation skills is an important life lesson and the discipline involved is invaluable.

Annie: Could you identify other benefits for them?

Madalena: I observed improvements in their concentration – their ability to focus on the task at hand, whether it was a choreographic task or holding musical patterns. They also showed great empathy for their fellow students. Teachers also commented on how this project assisted their verbal literacy and English language skills.

Annie: As a member of the audience at two shows of *Mirage* in Vila Nova de Milefontes, I can attest to the enthusiastic reception. The younger children were fully engaged throughout, squealed with delight from moment to moment and shouted for more. The older group really wanted to join in with the dancing and get close to the performers. Their participation at the end was difficult to bring to an end.

Madalena always brings an egalitarian and inclusive approach to all participants in her projects, no matter what social sector, age, or race. Her total respect for all allows an openness in the process and development of her projects. She asks for and incorporates the movement vocabulary inherent in the cultural groups she is working with and participants are also encouraged to offer up their ideas and thoughts about how the movement ideas are working. This brings an ownership of the finished product and a sense of pride.

Victorino sees the arts as a vital and integral part of society, another way of knowing our world and each other. She uses dance and other forms of performance as tools to connect people and she values people's experience of the arts as both audience and participants. Her book is a toolkit that assists us to unpack the layers of complexity in theatre experiences and provides a critical language to talk about the shared experience. In all the projects I have witnessed and experienced, Madalena offers rich involvement and understanding through her unique approach. She works from the ground up and not the top down and whilst she rejects the elitist approach to the arts, she works to achieve extremely high standards in all she undertakes.

PART V
Professional integrated collaborations

PHOTO *Open Space*
Choreographer and collaborators: Adam Benjamin with Integrated Dance Company-Kyo
Dancers: Maho Amakata, Shunpei Mitsuhashi, Asumi Masuda
Photographer: Adam Benjamin

5.1

PULLING BACK FROM BEING TOGETHER

An ethnographic consideration of dance, digital technology and Hikikomori in Japan and the UK

Adam Benjamin

Global communities

In the last twenty years, most of my work in Japan has been concerned with leading improvisation workshops or choreographing community projects with disabled and non-disabled dance students; my last visit, however, was to choreograph for the newly established Integrated Dance Company-Kyo, based in Tokyo.[1] The piece I made with the company was titled *Open State* and premiered at the Tokyo Arts Centre in July 2015. During the creation period, I worked with composer/architect Mathew Emmett (Plymouth University), who combined the technique of spectralism to explore the interiority of the human voice (Benjamin & Emmett, 2016). Mat magnified edited 'slices' of words spoken by the dancers to create acoustic landscapes that we could use to fill the surrounding space, and which in turn generated new possibilities for choreographic exploration.[2]

The initial voice recordings were made during a series of virtual encounters between dancers in Japan and dancers in the UK, who were able to see and comment on each other's improvisations and indeed interact with each other through live video links. It would be fair to say that as a dance maker I am, if not technophobic, then at least techno-wary. Working with Mat, however, through sound, space and multiple digital platforms, I learned a great deal and was able to extend and make many aspects of my work more accessible. We were able to extract soundscapes[3] that were rich in complexity and meaning, even when specific words and content could not be deciphered, generating new creative possibilities not only for those speaking different languages, but importantly for those with speech impediments. We were also able to explore the possibility of an international community of dance artists sharing practise around the globe without actually 'leaving the building,' and were able to bring together young people who ordinarily would never have the chance to meet.

Local thresholds

This building of connections around the globe is undoubtedly one of the extraordinary benefits to have arisen from the internet age and one I was excited to experience along with my students. Although the use of the internet is ubiquitous, and its benefits widely lauded, we are only just beginning to register the effects on the generation of young people who have grown up with, and into, this new digital age. Cultural shifts are often difficult to pinpoint or even notice while we are in the midst of them, but these changes can be marked and often quite stunning when returning to a country after a few years absence. Returning to Japan in 2015 following the initial, very positive Skype improvisations earlier that year, I boarded the subway in Tokyo to see every single person on either side of the carriage staring intently at a tablet. The silent disengagement of a whole compartment of people so thoroughly oblivious to me, and to each other, left a profound impression. Of course, customary Japanese politeness can easily be misinterpreted by a Western visitor as 'isolation,' whereas to the Japanese this is merely the conscientious observance of personal space. Even in 'pre-tablet' times, a Tokyo subway carriage (outside of rush hour) was a far more tranquil experience than its London or New York equivalent. I was nonetheless struck by the realization that the same technology so wonderfully used to connect dancers in Japan and the UK as part of a global community, was also capable of stripping people of their ability to communicate directly in real time. Though a 'gaijin' (outsider), and therefore recognizably 'other,' I felt completely invisible in a way I had never done before in that city. I will return to the notion of community later in the chapter, but first I would like to share something I wrote twenty years ago on my first visit to Japan.

> I was impressed with the students' ability to listen to each other, a quality that seemed an essential part of Japanese culture. What I offered in the workshops seemed to be quickly absorbed and understood, and yet returning to England I had the uneasy feeling that I'd somehow missed something essential. The following year, while teaching at the Aichi Arts Centre in Nagoya, I found the answer to what had been troubling me.
>
> It was a roasting hot, ozone holed afternoon and I was standing with a small group of pedestrians across the road from the centre, waiting for the street sign to change. It was some time before I noticed that the road we were waiting to cross was all of two paces wide, "A tiny-bloody-road!" I thought, as the sweat trickled down inside my shirt and I stared longingly at the cool shadow of the Arts Centre opposite. To make matters worse not a single bus, car or bicycle passed us as we slowly cooked by collective accord. Despite the searing heat, no one moved until the 'walk' sign turned green. By the time it took to cross the road, get changed and enter the studio I had formulated a response to the question that had been troubling me since the previous year.
>
> Japanese society places great emphasis on conformity and I realised that while most Japanese will do anything not to draw attention to themselves, disabled people cannot help but be different and be noticed. I realised that I could not begin to get the non-disabled dancers to understand their disabled contemporaries if they were not able to step out of line, to understand difference themselves.
>
> *(Benjamin 2002: 139)*

Crossing the Line, the score that I evolved with my students in response to this experience, still holds endless possibilities. It is perhaps the most accessible, enjoyable and, for those who like to challenge themselves, testing of improvisational scores.[4] Essentially the score explores decision making through the simplest of movement choices; those of entering and leaving a defined space.[5] The score engages the group with issues that, while individual, are at the same time reliant on an intricate and nuanced understanding of the decisions made by others. It is a score that ultimately emphasizes our interconnectedness, our power to influence, and our ability to serve. It is about communality and individuality. I could not have imagined that it would shed light on new issues and new challenges two decades later.

Life on the edge

The sad reality is that Japan is experiencing a disturbing trend among young people who have decided in huge numbers not to cross a very particular line. These young people have decided, for multiple and complex reasons, to withdraw from education and have cut themselves off from all forms of community, to remain, in the words of Hitoshi Tsuda, a researcher at Nagoya University, "on the edge of the public space" (Tsuda, 2012). For a culture so profoundly based on principles of communality, this is a deeply worrying and culturally confusing development.

While this phenomenon is still disputed in terms of its causes and diagnoses, there is nonetheless a particular term for it. The Japanese call it Hikikomori (引きこもり), from 'hiki,' meaning 'pulling back,' and 'komoru,' meaning 'together,' also known as 'hermit syndrome.' Estimates range from 500,000 to over a million students[6] who are failing to engage in mainstream education or society. The term 'Primary Hikikomori' is used to refer to those who have retreated from educational and social contact with no diagnosis of an underlying medical condition. (Suwa et al., 2003). These young people spend most of their time alone, confined to a single room, and avoid social contact other than the minimum required with family (Teo and Gaw, 2013). The phenomenon is considered by some to be 'familial' and is exacerbated by Japanese cultural mores, in that parents will often subtly re-enforce the isolation of their teenage recluse, not wanting to bring shame on the family by harboring a 'non-contributing' member of society.

The causes behind this phenomenon affecting young people are widely debated but are generally regarded to be a result of a number of factors: a school system that over-emphasizes assessment and in which failure to conform can result in isolation and bullying; a reportedly poor understanding of how to deal with bullying within the school system; and a culture in which group bullying or *Ijime* is not uncommon (Ando, Asakura, and Simons-Morton, 2005). Lastly there is intense pressure to achieve qualifications that will lead to employment and this is situated within a faltering economy in which jobs are on the decline. All of the above coincide with a period of adolescent development (which parents of teenagers will readily recognize), characterized by periods of withdrawal and re-emergence, a natural feature of teenage years and part of the 'stop-start' journey into adulthood.

These are facts, well documented and fairly irrefutable, about a cultural change happening on the other side of the world. There can be little doubt that the act of opting out, or 'pulling inward,' has been rendered more attractive in the last decade by the ubiquity of digital/internet devices. There is good reason to believe that this is not solely a Japanese problem (Wong, 2009) but its profile in Japan is more easily recognized because of the traditional collective values within Japanese culture and the consequent 'naming' of the syndrome, while in the UK and elsewhere such behaviour might easily pass as depression and therefore draw no 'special' attention, although there is a proliferation of research and reports on Internet Addiction Disorder (IAD) in the UK and elsewhere.

In the building

In contrast, what I am about to relay is an impression gleaned from teaching dance over the last eight years within the university system in the UK, as a studio-based dance lecturer but also as a tutor. It seems to me that increasing numbers of dance students are affected by stress and struggle with group work tasks within class, and that more students suffer with bouts of sleeplessness, depression, anxiety, and panic attacks than when I first came into higher education. This impression is borne out by a report carried out for the Higher Education Funding Council for England (HEFCE) in 2015. "Across the universities and colleges interviewed, there was an overwhelming consensus that both the number and proportion of students declaring mental health problems has risen" (Williams et al. 2015: 73).

Another report from the Association of Managers of Student Services in Higher Education (AMOSSHE) also found a "noticeable increase in complex mental health crises" in 2015 as compared with 2014. At my own university in Plymouth, there has been a rise of 32 per cent in appointments offered by associate counselors within the last three years.

As already stated, there is no doubt that digital devices have allowed many of my disabled colleagues and friends to communicate and participate in dialogue and debate in a way that was previously unimaginable. The internet has allowed for exchange between my students in Japan and the UK and the sharing of practise globally among myriad communities, but perhaps this new global connectivity comes with a price.

The companies behind this new technology have tapped into that profoundly human need to communicate and we have, in every aspect of our lives, bought into it wholesale. Our understanding of the effects of exposure to these new devices is yet in its early stages and, it could be argued, comparable to our understanding of the dangers of cigarettes in the early 1960s. As is now well documented, the UK government was well aware of the addictive and damaging effect of cigarettes long before any steps were taken to safeguard the public from their use; the revenue from taxes on tobacco was simply far too lucrative to be endangered. Today our reliance on tablet/internet usage is driven by huge corporate interests and is fully endorsed both by schools and universities and yet there is already good reason to believe that for those who suffer with tendencies toward isolation and depression, the internet holds serious risks:

> The rapid and unfettered increase in the number of people accessing a relatively unrestricted internet substantially increases the possibility that those suffering with an underlying psychological comorbidity may be at serious risk of developing an addiction to the internet.
>
> *(Christakis, 2010)*

Within an increasingly monetarized education system, academic departments are being encouraged toward more online lectures and submissions in an attempt to increase their reach and decrease their costs. Dance training in the UK is not exempt from this shift. Increased numbers of students equates to increased income, so larger cohorts and larger class groups are to be expected and online elements of both learning and marking (even tutorials) are being implemented widely across the system. Departments who fail to increase their numbers face being axed. Students (and staff) are thus actively encouraged to spend more and more time behind the screen as part of the educational experience.

Being present

It is quite likely that the human/social experience of students within this system will become less personal and more anonymous; there is a danger that they will be less known as an individual with a voice and increasingly be seen more as a number, one of many, being processed to meet the university's 'employability criteria.' For dance at least there is (as yet) no digitalization of the studio experience, but the drive toward increased numbers and the current obsession with employability will certainly affect the kind of teaching that can take place.

In Japan the students who have been brought to dance workshops by concerned parents and teachers over the past decade have readily responded to the improvisational setting in which error is embraced and judgment suspended; they have, with gentle encouragement, been able to play and explore and test ideas. They have been able to find themselves and make contact with others, and I have frequently wondered how such delightful young people could have slipped so silently from the system.

Sherry Turkle refers to Erik Erikson's theories of how young people form their sense of identity particularly during the 'college years' when "Relatively consequence-free experimentation facilitates the development of a 'core self', a personal sense of what gives life meaning" (Turkle, 1999: 644). She goes on to point out that Erikson was writing in the 1950s and 60s, when higher education was more concerned with growth and the development of ideas, than with pre-professional qualification. She suggests that this need to experiment and take risks is today increasingly provided via the internet but that this is a medium that precludes the necessary interaction with other human beings to test and solidify this self-identity, and that in many instances, immersion in the virtual world of the internet avoids the social learning that would necessarily accompany this stage of development in the real world. Similarly, Justin Sokol (2009) refers to Erikson's belief that the "Individual and society are intricately woven, dynamically related in continual change."

Hitoshi Tsuda (2012) suggests that a route to recovery for those caught within the Hikikomori condition is the development of "interpersonal tolerance and the rebuilding of their confidence in 'seken' (世間)," a particular Japanese term that refers to the public, communal field of relationships and awareness, that echoes, though in a very different way, Erikson's sentiment of the individual as being 'woven' into society.

I am increasingly concerned about the young dancers who, through a raft of anxiety-related conditions, struggle to attend classes at my university. While they are clearly not exhibiting the full-blown features of Hikikomori, they are nonetheless similarly struggling to cross thresholds, from private into public space, from adolescence into a confident and stable adulthood.

The HEFCE and AMOSSHE reports represent a generation of students nationally who are exhibiting signs of mental ill-health in numbers that we might ascribe to some kind of shift in cultural and social practises, and it might be argued that those of us who are teaching, particularly within higher education, may be failing to recognize these symptoms because we are similarly affected by a system that is forcing all of us to spend more time than is healthy behind a keyboard and less quality time with our students in a truly creative environment (Darabi, Macaskill, and Reidy, 2015).

Crossing the Line may serve both as metaphor and practice. The tradition of dance improvisation can trace its roots (on this side of the Atlantic) to the German Expressionists in the 1930s and in America to the Judson Church dancers who borrowed heavily from Japanese traditions such as Aikido, and from instructors whose practises relied on a deep understanding of *kumite* or 'meeting' between teachers and students, student and student. The qualities of informed touch, and the understanding of space and proxemics in my own practise, have a lineage in practises from China (Tai Chi) and Japan (Shintaido). The richness of these cultural migrations, and our ability to learn from each other through physical practises within the dojo or studio, are a reminder of a teaching tradition, imparted from person to person, that connects us as 'families' of dancers in a way that transcends national boundaries and emphasizes the real learning at the heart of the teacher-student relationship. This learning is one that has no real substance in the virtual world, and at risk of sounding old-fashioned, its characteristics are: trust, sharing, ethics, gratitude, responsibility, pride (in each other), respect, and, dare I say it, love.

In the department where I teach at Plymouth University, we have continued to hold a place for improvisation and embodied practices within our offering to our dance, theater, and acting students. In our making modules, we have recently begun a practice of giving verbal feedback particularly for group work, and we do this sometimes within forty-eight hours of an assessed performance. These sessions are recorded and available for the students to review later, but it means that they are involved in a face-to-face discussion about work, and are not alone at a screen reading their feedback in isolation. It is one of a number of strategies that we are putting in place to maintain the 'fabric' of our artistic community, the human face of learning and teaching.

If there was ever a time to ask what it is that the teaching of dance as an embodied art form has to offer, I would suggest that time is now. And if my experience in Japan is anything to go by, then the need for a physicalized, improvisational space, where risk taking is encouraged and where students can learn to value the support of others and offer support in return, has never been greater. Ironically, if the Hikikomori effect is not just a Japanese phenomenon but a condition that "transcends geography and ethnicity" (Sakamoto et al. 2005), and if it is proven to be linked to our increasing use of/reliance on/addiction to digital technology, then the experience of an embodied, somatically based, learning environment will become of increasing importance to all students of all ages and all disciplines in the years ahead. I would argue that the means by which we deliver and assess will be of equal importance to the mental health of those of us who teach, as it will be to our students, in an ever increasingly digitalized/automated world.

Acknowledgements

I would like to thank Yuko Ijichi for first inviting me to Tokyo and for her ongoing determination to develop community dance practise in Japan. To Misako Yokota for introducing me to Hikikomori. The dancers of Kyo-company. Mathew Emmett and all those involved in *Open State* in the UK. Anne Bentley, Student Counselling and Personal Development Service Team Leader at Plymouth University. All of the students and staff in the Theatre and Performance department at Plymouth who are my constant teachers, and lastly, my wife Tamami Benjamin for help with reviewing Japanese terms, and for her efforts to maintain a digitally balanced home for our own children.

Notes

1 *Integrated Dance Company-Kyo* was established by Muse Company director Yuko Ijichi and is the first professional integrated company in Japan. More information at https://www.tpam.or.jp/2016/en/?program=integrated-dance-company-kyo-workshop and https://www.facebook.com/Integrated-Dance-Company-響-Kyo-356292594582053/.
2 Emmett called this mixed-reality platform a "data specific networked environment" (see www.mathewemmett.com), as the virtual domain of the Japanese dancers was integrated within the physical environment of the UK dancers.

3   The soundscapes were created using Praat and Pure Data scripts.
4   For further discussion of *Crossing the Line* as an embodied practise with "the capacity to repair and renew our connection to the world we live in," see Benjamin 2016, in *Invisible Differences*.
5   See *Making an Entrance*, p. 139 for a full description of *Crossing the Line*.
6   The national press tends to overestimate, while scholarly articles usually state slightly lower figures.

References

Ando, M., T. Asakura, and B. Simons-Morton. (2005) 'Psychosocial influences on physical, verbal, and indirect bullying among Japanese early adolescents.' *Journal of Early Adolescence*, 25(3), August 2005, pp. 268–297. doi:10.1177/0272431605276933 [Accessed April 2016].

Benjamin, A. (2002) *Making an Entrance: Theory and Practice for Disabled and Non-Disabled Dancers*. Routledge.

Benjamin, A. and M. Emmett. (2016) 'Event spaces of infinite perspective.' In *Digital Echoes: Spaces for Intangible and Performance-Based Cultural Heritage*. Cambridge Scholars Publishing.

Benjamin, A. (2017) 'Finding it when you get there.' In Whatley, S., C. Waelde, A. Brown, and S. Harmon (Eds.), *Dance and Disability: In-Visible Difference*. Bristol, Intellect (forthcoming).

Block, J. (2008) 'Issues for DSM-V: internet addiction.' *American Journal of Psychiatry*, 165, pp. 306–7.

Correy, Evan. (2012) 'Hikikomori.' Undergraduate Honors Theses. Paper 285. DIMITRIS.

Christakis, D. A. (2010) 'Internet addiction: a 21st century epidemic?' *BMC Medicine*, 8. doi:61-10.1186/1741-7015-8-61 [Accessed April 2016].

Darabi, M., A. Macaskill, and L. Reidy. (2016) 'A qualitative study of UK academic role: positive features, negative aspects and associated stressors in a mainly teaching-focused university.' *Journal of Further and Higher Education* (In Press).

Sakamoto, N., R. G. Martin, H. Kumano, T. Kuboki and S. Al-Adawi. (2005) 'Hikikomori, is it a culture-reactive or culture-bound syndrome? Nidotherapy and a clinical vignette from Oman.' *International Journal of Psychiatry in Medicine*, 35(2), pp. 191–198. Available at http://journals.sagepub.com/doi/pdf/10.2190/7WEQ-216D-TVNH-PQJ1 [Accessed April 2016].

Sokol, Justin T. (2009) 'Identity development throughout the lifetime: an examination of Eriksonian theory,' *Graduate Journal of Counseling Psychology*, 1(2), Article 14. Available at http://epublications.marquette.edu/gjcp/vol1/iss2/14 [Accessed June 2016].

Suwa, M., K. Suzuki, K. Hara, H. Watanabe and T. Takahashi. (2003) 'Family features in primary social withdrawal among young adults.' *Psychiatry and Clinical Neurosciences*, 57: 586–594. doi:10.1046/j.1440-1819.2003.01172.x [Accessed June 2016].

Teo, A. R. and A. C. Gaw. (2010) 'Hikikomori, a Japanese culture-bound syndrome of social withdrawal?', *The Journal of Nervous and Mental Disease*, 198(6), 444–449. Available at http://doi.org/10.1097/NMD.0b013e3181e086b1 [Accessed June 2016].

Tsuda, H. (2012) 'On the edge of the public space – an existentialistic contribution to the understanding and treatment of people with Hikikomori.' *Seishin Shinkeigaku Zasshi*, 114(10), pp. 1158–66. Available at https://www.ncbi.nlm.nih.gov/pubmed/23234195 [Accessed June 2016].

Turkle, S. (1999) 'Cyberspace and Identity.' *Contemporary Sociology*, 28(6). American Sociology Association.

Wong, Victor C.W. (2009) 'Youth locked in time and space? Defining features of social withdrawal and practice implications.' *Journal of Social Work Practice*, 23(3), pp. 337–352.

Williams, M., P. Coare, R. Marvell, E. Pollard, A. Houghton and J. Anderson. (2015) 'Understanding provision for students with mental health problems and intensive support needs,' Report to HEFCE by the Institute for Employment Studies (IES) and Researching Equity, Access and Partnership (REAP).

5.2

FREEFALLING WITH BALLET

David Mead

Beginnings

Formed in 2002, Freefall Dance Company is an innovative, collaborative partnership between Birmingham Royal Ballet and Fox Hollies Performing Arts College, a local authority maintained school for pupils aged eleven to nineteen with severe learning difficulties in the south of the city of Birmingham. The seed for Freefall was sown at workshops at the school in 1992 that were designed to support The Company, Fox Hollies' after-school theatre group. Initially, Fox Hollies was just another school that the company was engaged with but the possibilities for providing a training and performing platform for some of the school's highly gifted young people quickly became clear. Since then, Freefall has become firmly established as part of the city's dance landscape, performing, holding workshops in schools, participating in conferences and playing a role in teacher education [Photo 5.2a].

Although inclusive ensembles such as Candoco Dance Company and Stopgap Dance Company, and numerous professional disabled dancers such as David Toole and Caroline

PHOTO 5.2A Freefall Dance Company
Photographer: Alex Griffiths

Bowditch, have done much to challenge perceptions, young disabled people in the UK continue to face multiple and significant barriers to participation in dance and especially to dance training and performance (Aujla and Redding, 2013; Lyons, 2016). One of these is that most dance for the disabled is aligned closely with community dance and is largely recreational in nature. There tends to be an emphasis on creativity, fun and the therapeutic benefits, the latter being common in special schools, which can lead to discouragement for students to take their interest further, notwithstanding the original positive intention (Walker, 2006). Such a focus may also suggest that dance produced by students with disabilities is somehow less worthy of being performed publically (Barnes, 2003: 7–8).

Aujla and Redding (2013: 3) highlight a clear gap in provision between recreational participation and professional companies and recommend building networks involving all types of schools, youth dance groups and professional integrated dance companies to encourage and support all young disabled people in dance. But why stop at integrated companies, and why stop at contemporary dance, where almost all work with dancers with a disability resides? What could be achieved if classical ballet, with all its associations with aesthetic purity, was put at the heart of work for such dancers? What kind of theatre could be made? These were just two of the questions Lee Fisher, then a dancer and now Birmingham Royal Ballet Head of Creative Learning and Artistic Director of Freefall, asked himself when he encountered Fox Hollies.

At the time, Birmingham Royal Ballet had a particularly visionary Director of Learning, Anne Gallacher. She removed barriers between professional and school by asking dancers or other artistic staff to deliver workshops and projects, with the learning team functioning more as facilitators. Several of those projects culminated in large-scale performances involving several schools or groups with diverse cultural, educational and social backgrounds, fully supported by the company's technical staff and usually danced on the main stage of the Birmingham Hippodrome. Bicknell (2015) says that performing can challenge typical perceptions of people, transforming the perception of individuals from passive to active members of society, particularly if artistic risks taken defy the participant and audience expectations, and make the participants' voices heard. Working towards a performance also gives creativity and shared endeavour a sense of purpose, she believes. Although Bicknell was writing specifically about older people, her comments appear equally applicable to any marginalised group within society. Gallacher also introduced a programme whereby company dancers and staff could study for a Master's degree part-time at Birmingham University. Fisher (2016), one of the early MA students, says "It broadened my perspectives about what education work could be."

He recalls his first encounter with Fox Hollies: "I found myself in an environment where I was being so inspired by the people coming out in front of me. I hadn't seen anything like it before; unadulterated passion and movement devoid of any sort of self-consciousness. So many things were coming from deep inside these dancers that I thought was exciting. I'd come through the Royal Ballet School, straight into Sadler's Wells Royal Ballet, and up to Birmingham." Fisher's experience of dance basically was that, he says. It was of an art that aimed at an ideal, with an emphasis on particular form, style and clarity of line. "Here was a different, appealing, aesthetic."

Keith Youngson (2016), then a teacher with a theatre-in-education background and now head teacher at Fox Hollies, recalls that first workshop and how Fisher was fully engaged with The Company and absolutely willing to compromise his professional practice according to the situation.[1] "He was fascinated by the young people and the different aesthetic they carried with them. He was already projecting movement to what it might become."

Youngson (2016) explains that students at the school do not acknowledge boundaries, so there have never been any issues about combining drama, singing and dancing in a single workshop or performance. "They are really up for cross-arts." Some of the students were particularly enthusiastic but many were in their final year at the school. Some had already left. It was therefore decided to open up Freefall to both Fox Hollies students and recent leavers.

Right from the beginning, Fisher and Youngson wanted to mesh their particular specialisms in dance and special education in a scaled-down repertory company, and modelled Freefall on a professional ensemble. As Fisher stresses:

> Freefall *is* a performance company. We want to put on the best possible performances we can and for people to appreciate them simply as a piece of theatre rather than a piece of disabled theatre. I want them to go away with a smile on their face having enjoyed themselves. If that happens, we've succeeded and hopefully shifted perceptions around the idea of ballet and special needs.

Technique

Although less often the case than previously, codified techniques are still often perceived as being more suited to certain body types than others, especially if they are to be aesthetically pleasing in performance. This can pose a barrier for those who do not possess such a body, disabled or not. Verrent (2003) highlights that while many young dancers with a disability wish to improve their technique, it frequently does not form part of their training, the focus instead being on a more personal, idiosyncratic movement vocabulary.

Ballet poses particular issues. In 2007, Fisher referred to it being built on "deference for tradition, passed down wisdom and loyalty to rituals," with a movement vocabulary that is both equalising and soul destroying, although also noting how its shared language can contribute to a sense of group identity and security.

Things may need to be explained in shorter sentences or in simpler ways, but the language of ballet is firmly embedded in Freefall practice. Fisher accepts that working with dancers with learning difficulties requires much more of a facilitative approach than does working with vocational students. Each session starts with a circle warm-up, a very strong, structured ritual led by the dancers. The ballet barre that follows includes all the usual exercises although they are slightly shorter than usual. "It's a way to hone fitness, to develop control, coordination and strength," he says. He is not concerned if a Freefall dancer's first position is not close to 180 degrees, or if a leg is not perfectly placed. "You have a certain different criteria. What I'm interested in is exploring the essence of each exercise." Equally important, he says, is that the barre gives them something they all do together, and gives some ownership over a dance language. Just as for a professional dancer, technique is only a starting point, though, he emphasises. "The question is, 'What can you do with it?'"

Choreography and style

Fisher insists he does not try to enforce a style on the dancers. When creating work, he works a lot from improvisation, an approach that, while not unknown in ballet, is more commonly found in contemporary dance. He constantly challenges them, 'What would you do with that? What do you like about that?' However, while repetition and muscle memory help in performance, dancers with learning difficulties often cannot remember what they did in improvisations. "Still, the iPad is a wonderful tool!" says Youngson (2016).

Fisher stresses that while always working for excellence and with attention to detail, he simultaneously tries to empower the dancers to make the work their own, which in turn allows the movement to be honest and authentic. Even after fourteen years, he admits that the dancers still surprise him. "I see some very exquisite things emerge out of improvisations; movements that just wouldn't have entered my head with my schooling."

The approach leaves Freefall's work difficult to categorise. Fisher says that humour is really important and that what works really well for them and helps the dancers really know the work is having an underpinning narrative and character. He hopes that at times there are echoes of classical form but says what is most important is that there is a particular energy behind the movement and that it's authentic to the dancers. "Individuality is not important, it's essential," he stresses. "So it does start to make the crossing into physical theatre."

Although some early pieces were abstract, quite soon the decision was made to work firmly with narrative and to pull out the different personalities of dancers. "We are highly personalised," says Youngson (2016), who says it's a question of working with the skills of each dancer while dealing with associated issues. For example, he explains, one has a great ability to know exactly where everyone should be in a piece, but can sometimes show that obviously on stage. Another has amazing comic timing and can play an audience with genius, but also tends to work well within himself when there's no-one there. Another is brilliant at playing the nasty villain.

"One of our principles is that the dancers shouldn't be dancing about cognitive things that they don't understand," says Youngson (2016). "You can't overlay on them a set of complex emotions or a complex interplay of characters, but we can get quite adventurous. Sometimes body memory takes over that cognitive middle band of brain function. So, Freefall can rattle out a 40-minute piece, whereas on paper people like them are not meant to be able to take in that much information."

A piece that is typical of Freefall's work today is *Freefalling Off the Pyramids* (2015),[2] created as a piece that could tour to primary schools. Fisher took images of hieroglyphics into the studio, asked the accompanist to play music that had some of those roots (live music is an important part of Freefall's work, in the studio, in creation and in performance), and pulled things out of improvisations that were interesting. The result is a work featuring a Howard Carter-esque type of character who stumbles across a hidden tomb. "It's great fun," he says.

Advocacy

"It's so rare for people to find lifelong access to the arts for people with learning difficulties," says Youngson (2016). Figures for Birmingham indicate that of 7,000 young people with learning disabilities, only about 5 per cent receive any kind of arts provision outside school (Hayhow, 2016). Advocacy, working to bring about change in the way people with learning disabilities are perceived and increasing awareness of the possibilities has become an important part of their work.

The company appears regularly at conferences, but the most publically visible project was *We Dance*, part of the 2012 Cultural Olympiad, delivered in partnership with

PHOTO 5.2B *Seated* (2014)
Freefall Dance Company
Photographer: Sima Gonsai

MENCAP[3] and mac birmingham.[4] Activities included dance workshops, training and development for regional dance artists, and the commissioning of a new work, *10 and ¾*. Fisher is particularly proud of the film, *Freefall: We Dance*, made as part of the project and since shown with great success at many international film festivals. More recently, the company made *Seated* (2014), a site-specific dance film directed by Sima Gonsai based on their stage work, *Chairs* (2013), and following Freefall's imagined outdoor world in a collection of locations and witty scenarios from travelling on a train to dancing in the park [Photo 5.2b].

Outreach

Although a product of Birmingham Royal Ballet's outreach programme, Freefall now has a programme of its own, taking dance to primary schools in the city. Early workshops were highly structured but as confidence grew, more freedom has worked into the delivery, says Fisher. Dancers now even lead elements of exercises (and it is 'elements of,' Fisher stresses), while he or Youngson facilitate events. Fisher says, "We are continually trying to stretch ourselves, challenge our own knowledge about how much they can deliver independently given that many of our guys are not particularly verbally skilled."

Like most things with Freefall, the build-up to dancers leading has taken time and patience. Roles are personally tailored. Youngson (2016) gives the example of a dancer who has autism. He knew the warm-up inside out and would get distressed if the order was changed for any reason. He and Fisher realised that the dancer could lead successfully if he could watch the participants and recognise they were not mirroring correctly. The process involved them joining in with the warm-up and very obviously doing things incorrectly, so he couldn't help but notice and correct. Now he scans the group as they warm-up and does give effective feedback.

Teacher training

Dance is a creative and aesthetic subject often assessed subjectively, which physical education teachers, more used to focusing on activities assessed objectively, feel uncertain about.[5] Research indicates that many students and qualified teachers find it difficult to define what being good at dance means and that dance even makes some feel uncomfortable (Wilson et al. 2008; Rustad, 2012; Russell-Bowie, 2013). Working with disabled students often adds another layer of concern. To counter this, Aujla and Redding (2013: 4) recommend that dance providers should offer disability awareness and specific teacher training in integrated practice (see also Chapter 3.1 in this volume).

Freefall offers new and existing teachers opportunities through workshops with Birmingham Royal Ballet and Freefall dancers and staff. Of most significance are the links Freefall has with the University of Birmingham's School of Education, where since 2009 it has worked regularly with final year trainee physical education teachers. Sessions are designed to help them feel more confident in their ability to teach dance in general but as Fisher says, such engagement with dancers with a learning difficulty can only encourage the students to think differently about the talents of young people with disabilities and understand the possibilities. "They will be engaging with people with special educational needs in their teaching careers. It's a fact." Feedback suggests eyes are indeed opened. Freefall also works with Central England Teacher Training, delivering training for primary school generalist teachers who are usually not physically confident, and where Fisher says the focus is again very much, 'Here's dance. Why can't you teach it? Here's how you might.'

Questions of quality

Freefall has been fortunate in that its emergence has coincided with a widening understanding of what dance can be, even in those forms of dance such as ballet with its widely perceived aesthetic ideal and the notion of its continuous search for perfection. Even so, Freefall's work, like that of other inclusive dance companies or those working exclusively with dancers with particular needs, raises questions about what constitutes quality in dance, and why some dance, or art in general, may be perceived as quality and some not; complex questions not least because, as noted visual artist Grayson Perry (2014: 10) observes, there are problems with most of the methods of judging art, with many of the criteria used potentially conflicting.

What makes a dancer really stand out is only partially quantifiable. Technical proficiency is measurable to some extent: the degree of turn-out, the position of the working foot, the height and line of the working leg, the number of pirouettes. However, technique is not absolute. Even within heavily codified dance forms such as classical ballet there are differences in style, what is perceived as excellence changes over time and as Smith (2002) observes, "Technique must always compensate for physical limitations of an imperfect instrument (the human body) and that each body is unique."

While quality can be seen purely in terms of form, Prime (2002) notes that art has the potential for the sublime, evoking a more powerful aesthetic and a deeper emotional response. The challenging of conventions or the breaking of so-called 'rules' of aesthetics or beauty do not preclude the sublime from being achieved, she says. Indeed, if that were the case, it would suggest that much contemporary dance or dance theatre could not produce a sublime aesthetic and emotional experience.

Prime (2002) considers specifically how quality is to be judged when dance is performed by an artist with a disability. She notes that ideas of what is beautiful or what constitutes quality in art are largely conditioned, a notion supported by research by Meskin et al. (2013), which found aesthetic preferences are significantly conditioned by regular exposure and reinforcement to that aesthetic.[6] Prime further observes that some audience members are likely to have a low expectation of work performed by disabled dancers, and that some may also feel uncomfortable seeing some movements performed by people with disabilities. It seems this is particularly likely to be true if someone is more used to watching dance where a given body type tends to predominate, or where there are particularly widespread perceptions of what constitutes beauty, such as in classical ballet. As Perry (2014: 14) notes, while ideas of quality are constructed, they are also built on shifting layers and can change.

The extent of the influence critics and the media have generally is debateable, but as Perry (2014: 27) says, it is undeniable that media coverage does influence opinion. It certainly increases awareness. To this end, Fisher has worked hard at keeping the Birmingham and specialist dance press informed about Freefall's activities and achievements.

Prime (2002) concludes that quality should always be judged against the sublime aesthetic rather than conventions about form. She says, "Quality dance is when I can see an emotion communicated in a way that words could not; it produces an aesthetic as well as other emotional or intellectual responses in me." As Lyons (2016), presenting Candoco's point of view, observes, disability can make for more interesting dance: "If someone can't point their toes, that doesn't need to be a problem."

Anecdotal evidence suggests audiences are similarly most concerned by the impression given by a work as a whole, and by individual dancers' expression, communication and connection with those watching. Indeed, it is these aspects that critics most frequently focus on when reviewing any performance rather than the nuances of technique, even when writing for specialist dance publications. Most will also not only avoid emphasising the disability but sometime not mention it at all, not for any political reason, but simply because it is not seen as important. There are similarities here with the way disabled sport is reported.

Youngson (2016) brings in an analogy from visual art. "Take Mondrian, who chose to work with all those lovely squares, rectangles, triangles and colour. He chose to use a different palette to be expressive. We too have a different palette to create our pictures." Fisher agrees, adding that Freefall dancers may have a smaller number of colours to choose from than a Birmingham Royal Ballet dancer, and some different shades, but at their best they move him just much as any ballet moves him.

Getting families involved

Despite Freefall's success, barriers remain. The performing arts are frequently not perceived as a viable, long-term or even an appropriate activity for people with a disability (Aujla and Redding (2013: 4). The talent development of youngsters in any field can be expensive in terms of time and finances but significantly extra support is likely to be required when a young person has a disability (Martin & Wheeler, 2011).

None of Freefall happens without family commitment. Access and transport is a particular issue. The dancers are not independent travellers and they can't get anywhere without help. "There's a lot of work around influencing their families, getting them involved," says Fisher.

The first hurdle is often persuading parents and carers that a performing arts interest is worth pursuing seriously. Youngson (2016) explains that it is essential to work on them slowly but always engage them in the process and let them see the possibilities firsthand as much as possible. To that end, meetings with parents are twinned as much as possible with performances or workshops.

Looking ahead

Dance for people with disabilities has always had a close association with community dance but Fisher is clear, "Freefall is not an inclusive company and not about anybody can come." He and Youngson are not ashamed that the company is selective. Fisher explains that they could not do what they do with an open door policy. It would lead to very different performances and less celebration of Freefall's individual and collective gifts, he adds.

Fisher and Youngson do see the benefit of opening access, however, and new strands for Freefall are slowly being established. With very little resource, there's now a Junior Freefall for eleven to eighteen year olds from which a couple of dancers have moved up to the main company. They are also keen to establish a 'Little Freefallers,' with the aim of getting primary level children excited about dance. Starting a weekly open dance class where anyone with a learning disability can come is another possibility. "Of course, each of these would allow the company dancers to continue to hone their teaching skills," says Fisher. Film must be part of the future, though, he adds. "It creates extra stimulation for the dancers and is a great way of challenging stereotypical views about people with learning difficulties; and it's a great platform to showcase the talents of the Freefallers."

The art must come first

Freefall is a one-off. Its particular circumstances, and today's situation regarding education and arts finances, render it unlikely to be a model that others can follow. Indeed, given the small number of dancers in the company, it has been a battle to even keep Freefall alive at times, says Youngson, although the fight is helped by workshops and performances touching a much wider audience. However, its approach and ethos does demonstrate what is possible, even on short-term projects.

Fisher observed in 2007 that ballet often has to justify its place in community dance. It has always struggled even more to justify its place in dance for dancers with disabilities. Freefall remains in the vanguard of challenging stereotypical views of ballet, of dance, by dancers and those who come to see it. The company shows what is possible, not only in the studio, or for therapy or to enhance personal or social skills, but most importantly through presenting performances of the highest quality. In doing so, the relationship with Fox Hollies School remains important where Youngson tells of students who aspire to join the company after seeing it in performance. "For the first time, they have role models. The importance of that is impossible to underestimate."

Attitudes and perceptions of who can dance are changing but dance for people with a disability or special need is still sometimes seen as charitable, worthy work. Lyons (2016) says that even Candoco come across with an almost patronising attitude occasionally, although more overseas than at home. Lyons (2016) says, "We are getting there, but not as quickly as we would like. Dance can be excellent regardless of who dances."

While disability cannot be ignored, Fisher believes that the only way you change attitudes is by putting the art first, and giving people a really positive, inspiring experience. As Youngson says, "We wouldn't want to be defined by what we can't do." As Hayhow (2016) says, "The arts sector needs to work with people with learning disabilities not because of a box-ticking access agenda, but because this work inspires us all."

Notes

1 Youngson's background is in theatre-in-education. He initially joined Fox Hollies to cement the place of drama on the curriculum, both as a tool and an artform.
2 Using the company name as a pun in titles is a feature of Freefall's work.
3 Mencap is the UK's leading learning disability charity. It campaigns to transform society's attitudes to learning disability and improve the quality of life of people with a learning disability, and of their families.
4 Formerly known as Midland Arts Centre, mac is an arts complex in south central Birmingham.
5 In the UK National Curriculum, dance sits within physical education.
6 Although not referenced by Prime, this idea is discussed at length by Marcel Proust (1913–1919 and 1923–1927) in his two-volume *Remembrance of Things Past (A la récherché du temps perdu)*.

References

Aujla I. & E. Redding. (2013) *Barriers to Dance Training for Young People with Disabilities*. Nottingham: Dance4.
Barnes, C. (2003) 'Effecting change; disability, culture and art?' Paper presented at the Finding the Spotlight conference, Liverpool Institute for Performing Arts, 28–31 May. Available at http://disability-studies.leeds.ac.uk/files/library/Barnes-Effecting-Change.pdf [Accessed 12 May 2016].
Bicknell, J. (2015) 'Staying healthy, being happy and pushing boundaries.' *Animated*. Autumn. Available at www.communitydance.org.uk/DB/animated-library/staying-healthy-being-happy-and-pushing-boundaries?ed=34663 [Accessed 10 June 2016].
Fisher, L. (2007) 'Participating in Ballet.' *Animated*. Autumn (pp. 12–14).
Fisher, L. (2016) Personal conversations with David Mead, 16 January and 16 May.
Hayhow, R. (2016) 'We need to do better.' *Arts Professional*. 30 March. Available at www.artsprofessional.co.uk/magazine/article/we-need-do-better [Accessed 10 May 2016].
Lyons, J. (2016) Personal conversation with David Mead, 16 February 2016.
Martin, J. & G. Wheeler. (2011) 'Psychology.' In Y. Vanlandewijck & W. Thompson (Eds.), *The Paralympic Athlete: Handbook of Sports Medicine and Science* (pp. 116–134). West Sussex: John Wiley & Sons.
Meskin, A., M. Phelan, M. Moore, & M. Kieran. (2013) 'Mere exposure to bad art.' *British Journal of Aesthetics*, 53, pp. 139–164.
Perry, G. (2014) *Playing to the Gallery*. London: Particular Books.
Prime, S. (2002) 'The Quality Question.' *Animated*. Summer, pp. 24–25.
Russell-Bowie, D. (2013) 'What? Me? Teach dance? Background and confidence of primary preservice teachers in dance education across five countries.' *Research in Dance Education*, 14(3), pp. 216–232.
Rustad, H. (2012) 'Dance in physical education: experiences in dance as described by physical education student teachers.' *Nordic Journal of Dance*, 3, pp. 15–29.
Smith, K. (2002) 'Dancing healthy.' 16th International Congress on Dance Research, Corfu, Greece, 30 October–3 November. Available at http://writings.orchesis-portal.org/index.php/en/articlesen/272-smith-karen-lynn-dancing-healthy-16th-international-congress-on-dance-research-corfu-greece-30-10-3-11-2002 [Accessed 12 September 2016].
Verrent, J. (2003) *Disability and the Dance and Drama Awards Report*. Sheffield: Department for Education and Skills.

Walker, J. (2006). Art Divisions: Arts provision for Disabled and Deaf young people in Special Education and Mainstream schools. *Research Report: The Role of North West Disability Arts Forum in Developing Disabled and Deaf Young People and their Interest in the Arts.* Liverpool: North West Disability Arts Forum.

Wilson G., R. MacDonald, C. Byrne, S. Ewing & M. Sheridan. (2008) 'Dread and passion: primary and secondary teachers' views on teaching the arts.' *The Curriculum Journal*, 19(1), pp. 37–53.

Youngson, K. (2016) Personal conversation with David Mead, 6 June 2016.

5.3

TROUBLING ACCESS AND INCLUSION

A phenomenological study of children's learning opportunities in artistic-educational encounters with a professional contemporary dance production

Charlotte Svendler Nielsen

Introduction

This chapter takes a critical look at the idea of providing access and inclusion to a broad group of twelve- to thirteen-year-old school children in a collaborative project between a professional contemporary dance company, an orchestra and educational institutions in Denmark, with the purpose of staging a public performance including eight school classes at a theatre in Copenhagen. From the viewpoint of the school teachers and dance educators, who were contracted to lead a class each, the purpose was also to explore and attract attention to how dance can be relevant from an educational perspective. These diverse purposes raise questions as to what is possible in a project that has an artistic purpose, especially in the context of the production, and as to the importance of an agreed purpose when multiple players are involved in collaboration.

From an ethnographic and phenomenological perspective, a study was done focusing on which opportunities for learning the children had in the different encounters of the production by following one of the eight school classes closely. The study took place both at the school and at the theatre over a period of two months. The lessons that the children had with their dance educator and some of the sessions at the theatre were filmed, and the children, school teachers and dance educators were interviewed while the children also did some drawing and writing exercises about their experiences. Analyses of this material using a hermeneutic-phenomenological strategy (van Manen, 1990) enable reflections on how such a project becomes relevant to the children – what is meaningful (or the opposite) to the children's learning opportunities in the different encounters of the production? The chapter thus progresses from the perspectives of the children.

Setting the children centre stage as experiencing human beings – consequences for research methodology

"Nothing about us without us"

(Charlton, 1998)

Research that aims at looking into an artistic-educational encounter cannot avoid touching upon ethical, aesthetic and political issues (Bogdan, 2003). All the professionals who are part of such an encounter (artists, teachers and, in this case, me as the researcher) have motives for being there, something which we think is important and of value. The role of the children is different as they do not have a choice regarding whether they want to take part. To be in school is mandatory in Denmark for children aged six to fifteen (unless they are home-schooled by their parents) and while in school the children have to follow the plans that the school and the teachers make for them.

The statement by James I. Charlton above originally came from the disability-rights move-ment, but has also inspired policy making related to other minority groups. The statement has been used to communicate the idea that no policy should be decided without the full and direct participation of members of the group(s) affected by that policy. If taking this statement seriously also when teaching and doing research with children, it would entail always remem-bering the perspectives of the children in the practice that we create for them. In relation to this particular artistic-educational project it is my aim to create an understanding of how such a project becomes meaningful from the perspectives of the children. In this way I intend to build a bridge between the understandings of the children and what the phenomenologically inspired psychologist Les Todres (2007: 40–41) calls "the world of shared understandings … a greater chorus of voice from others, colleagues and an existing body of knowledge about the topic area."

Meaning as a central phenomenon when studying learning opportunities from a phenomenological perspective

The concept of meaning is central in an endeavour to set the children's perspective in the centre of a research analysis, and it is also a central concept in a phenomenological perspec-tive on learning (van Manen, 2004), which inspires the analyses of the artistic-educational encounters presented in this chapter. Implicit in the analytical focus on meaning in this study is an understanding of learning as processes that are tied up in emotions, embodied experi-ences, action and creativity (Horn & Wilburn, 2005). It is hard to know exactly when learn-ing happens, but we can study the processes that lead to new experiences and new action, we can study what children are directed towards ('the directedness') and what their intentions are ('the intentionality') (Merleau-Ponty, 1962/2002). As a consequence, I focus on chil-dren's accounts of what they experience as they are able to express themselves in a variety of modalities (see Svendler Nielsen, 2009) and on the meaning-making that I can observe, which are all connected to their learning *opportunities*.

Children's learning opportunities in the different encounters of the production

The first encounter – workshop at the school:

> The 23 children from 6th grade are standing in a circle in the middle of the school gym. Today is the first time the dance educator who is connected to their class comes to

the school to start her work with them. After an introductory talk and some warm-up exercises the dance educator starts to move in a short improvised movement sequence ending with her very gently touching the shoulder of a boy beside her. He receives the impulse and creates his own movement – the movement freezes and he ends with a sharp gaze at the girl beside him – who then starts moving. None of them really have time to reflect on what movements to do – they receive a movement impulse and invent a new one… it is very silent in the room and everyone is focused on the one who is moving here and now. Their cheeks are red and their eyes are shining with an expression of 'in just a moment it is my turn.' The students are in focus one by one and they relate actively to each other's creations. When the impulse has travelled through the whole circle the dance educator moves through the circle and finishes with a movement giving the cue to the student she meets that now it is her turn to move across the floor. The girl whirls in circles that end with a jump landing in front of a boy who quickly lets himself fall to the ground to roll over to the other side where another boy reacts to the fact that now it is his turn. The dance educator at the same time starts a new movement in another direction which brings a student more onto the floor. In the end there are young people moving in all directions – jumping, rolling and almost flying across the floor. Stop! The dance educator says and immediately there is silence – both in movement and in sound, only their breath can be heard as they are almost playing in tune.

This situation is the children's first encounter with the dance educator who is to lead their group into the public performance to be ready two months from this. None of these children have had lessons in contemporary dance before or even been part of a professional artistic production. So, by being part of this project they are provided with an opportunity of getting access to an experience of contemporary dance which they otherwise would not have.

When watching the lessons, I see a couple of children who stand out from the rest, among others one girl who is very often alone and seems to be seeking the attention of the dance educator and often comes physically (too) close to her. For example, when they are sitting in a circle on the floor, she almost leans over the dance educator and looks into her notes as if she does not have a sense of personal space. The dance educator continues and does not tell the girl to move, but sometimes gently moves her by giving her a task to do. Another child I notice is a boy who is often also standing alone. He is a short and very thin child, whom I later learn is often bullied and beaten up by the other boys. He is one of seven siblings with different combinations of parents and also has a hard life at home. When they have to work in duos, these two children often end up together even though the girl is much taller.

In the situation from the first dance lesson described above, the children have to respond to other's expressions and the impulses made by their bodies, either as a certain eye contact, a small push or other kind of physical touch. They have to sense the 'intentionality' of the others and act accordingly. The structure that the dance educator has planned forces them all to follow and participate. They cannot avoid those that they normally do not engage with, because it goes so fast that there is no time to stop and think. In exercises of this kind, ALL of the children are part of the group, including those who otherwise seem to be isolated. Perhaps by being forced to communicate using their bodies they all get an experience of working together in a new way? That it is okay to give an impulse and respond to those whom they normally do not communicate with? We can only speculate about the importance that this might have for the experience of being included for those who are often excluded, and about the importance that it might also have for their relationships outside of the dance class.

The eight school classes meet for the first time in a sports hall:

> There is a lot of waiting time for seven of the school classes while one school class is practising a part of the choreography that they have to do as part of the performance. They are the only class that gets to dance that much in the whole piece. While they are waiting I see the girls from 'my' class spontaneously sit down in a long row behind each other and start massaging the one in front. The one girl whom I often see excluded from the other girls is also part of the row. As an observer I feel the empathy and care, the good things they want to give each other ... NOW the kids finally have to come down on 'the stage' which has been marked on the floor. The 200 children have to stand in a line, class by class, and then they have to start practicing walking around the stage, out through the imagined tunnels to 'the foyer' and back again as if they were in the theatre. They are walking, and walking and walking ... around and around and around ... The music is very slow and very difficult to follow when walking. The artistic director says that there are too many kids for this, so now they have to pair up and walk in twos. They are again walking and walking and walking .... At one point I hear a girl saying to another girl (while walking): Do you actually know where we are going? And I start to think that this is perhaps an important issue – do they know WHY they are walking? Has anyone told them why they have to be 200 children on stage? And why they are walking that much? What role do they play? What is the meaning of them being involved when they do not really have to dance that much? Finally all of the children have to learn a dance sequence that the artistic director and some of the dance educators who are each leading a class are showing. And then the day is over.

This situation is the children's first encounter with the other school classes and with the whole production team. The purpose of meeting today is to find out how much space the 200 children take up when they are on the stage, what it is possible to do with them all and how much time it takes to move them around. The children seem bored and through the noise they make and their running around, which becomes more and more intense, it is clear that it is not a meaningful experience to them just to be hanging around and waiting. Here they are directed towards each other and the new children that they have been looking forward to meeting. That is probably why they then find meaning in running around and playing or engaging with each other, like for example the girls in the massage row. In the activity that these girls have started, I see the girl who is usually excluded from the others included for the first time. This might already be a sign that all the work which they at this point in time have done with the dance educator who is leading their group has had the side-effect of the others being more open to including her in the group.

The next time the dance educator comes to the school, she has a long talk with the children about the experience in the gym hall. She tells them that she thinks it was hard work and a little boring because it was very practical. But, she says, this was necessary as part of our planning of what it is possible to do. She also tells them that she is aware that they need to hear about the story of what they are going to dance and that at the next meeting in the theatre they will hear more about this. Then she hopes they will be able to feel that they are also acting. She tells them that part of this project is to practise to be a performer – they have to learn to be in a role, to be focused and aware of what happens around them, to not tickle themselves in their hair or scratch their arm, because the audience will think all the movements they do while on stage are part of the choreography. She then goes on to ask the children what their experience was like. One girl says that it was boring to sit and wait, but it was nice to meet new people. Another girl says that she had a headache. The dance educator responds, "Me too, and that was because there was also so much information for all of us."

The first encounter at the theatre:

> The eight school classes that will participate in the performance are all to meet for the first time at the theatre in Copenhagen today. I meet with 'my' class in the foyer of the theatre. They are busy eating some snacks they have brought with them. They have already been there for half an hour, but some of the buses are delayed and they will probably have to be hanging around for another hour before it can start. The children seem full of energy, though, and they are excited about being here and about what they are going to do when the rest arrive.
>
> Now it is time to enter the stage and the 200 children are told to go and sit as the audience. It starts with a number of speeches. After a while many of the children start yawning and saying 'ahh' and other sounds which express that they are bored and tired. They have also been up early and some have travelled far and till now nothing concrete has really happened. Both the theatre director and the artistic director of the orchestra talk for quite a while about how wonderful this project is. They seem to try to make their speeches relevant to the children by explaining how they themselves met this piece of classical music, which is part of the performance, for the first time. But it does not really seem to resonate with these children. This is not their type of music … the director of the orchestra starts to go through the different sections of the music explaining what they mean. He asks if it doesn't sound cool? "No!" is the clear and loud answer from many of the children. "Well, but I think it sounds cool," he says. Now the floor is the choreographer's. He explains that his job is to put steps together. He asks if they would like to meet the ones that they are going to dance with. He presents the professional dancers one by one, by their name and nationality, and the dancers do a short solo each. Two of the men impulsively start to play around and for the first time the children start to laugh. And spontaneously they clap their hands. The choreographer says: "They are improvising so I don't know what they are doing!" The children seem more alert now.

The children are clearly expressing being bored and tired after long hours of waiting, and when what they have been waiting for, to enter the stage and start dancing, turns into a series of long speeches they seem to give up. They cannot pay attention to this. They have come to dance. Perhaps that is why they suddenly become alert when the professional dancers come onto the stage and start playing around. They are fun to look at and there is something about what they do that resonates with the children and their reason for being there (their 'intentionality'). While watching the rehearsals I see that only one of the school classes gets to do movements that they have choreographed themselves. The rest of the piece is based on movements that the company has choreographed and that the children have to learn. At this point I wonder what the connection is to all of the choreographic tasks they have worked on with their dance educator.

The dress rehearsal and the premiere:

> Today the children are wearing the costumes for the first time. They are wearing baggy pants and shirts that have to be bound around the waist. Each class wears a different

'earthy' colour and they have been designed for all of them, both boys and girls, to wear a scarf bound around their heads.

All of the 200 children now have to enter the stage running fast from one of the four tunnels one by one … one boy makes a mistake in the timing, but the choreographer stops and says that he actually liked that and now gives the boy the task of doing that again so that this small variation becomes a part of the choreography. The next time this boy has to do it, he runs extremely fast and is totally focused and aware in his eyes and movements.

While watching the whole performance I realise that there are a lot of children in the stage space, they almost cannot be there all of them at the same time. It looks very crowded. While following 'my group' on their way around the space, in the foyer I pay attention to a couple of children who are just hanging around on the sofas, not participating in the performance at all.

… Now the audience is seated. It is silent. The 200 children are divided in the four tunnels waiting for their turn to enter the stage. It starts now. First the company dancers, the music is on, first very light and then in a faster and faster beat. The dancers are running and coming through the tunnels, now the children start walking on to the stage. They find their places and they are all extremely focused. Their eyes are shining. They follow the music just perfectly and do what they have practised so many times. The last part. They gather up and fall to the floor. They run out. Come back in. And receive the applause from the audience. I meet them in the tunnel when they run out again. They are all so excited, it went so well. They have light in their eyes and are very happy with the result on this first evening. They cannot wait to do it again!

There are many issues to deal with when wanting to include 200 school children in an artistic dance production. The children come from diverse backgrounds, they are of different body types, have different experiences with dance and the different relationships between them all have an influence on what it is possible to do with them. All of this also influences how to make the performance both meaningful to be part of and at the same time of a high artistic quality. One issue is the costumes. Some of the children are Muslim and the girls have to wear a scarf. For this production it was possible to include them by designing the costumes for all of the children to wear a scarf around their heads. But there are some children who, for different reasons, cannot participate and would not be able to be in any production unless there could be special attention paid to their needs. I later learned that the children whom I saw hanging around on the sofas in the foyer are some that cannot manage to be part of the performance, they are children who in Denmark are called 'inclusive children.' For some years now, public schools have had to 'include' some of the children from special needs schools. Some of these children have difficulties concentrating or they are easily disturbed by others. Children who do not feel good about being part of the performance or cannot act as they are told to, have to hang out in the foyer all the day waiting for the others to finish.

A project like this, however, has the potential of giving the children who *participate* an experience for life. This is the case for many of them. They will never forget that they were on stage in a public theatre. The boy who is in focus in the description of the dress rehearsal is the boy from 'my class,' who is usually either on his own or with the girl who is also excluded from the group. In the break afterwards I ask him about this change of the choreography and he explains proudly what happened. In this situation the choreographer 'included' this boy and the others saw that he was given a special responsibility. This might help to change his social position in the class. This choice by the choreographer probably happened as a coincidence, but nevertheless it might make a world of difference to this boy.

Arts in a school context and school in an artistic context

Through the analyses of the empirical material collected around this project, some dilemmas have become visible. When children are involved, as educators we sometimes take it for granted that there is both an educational and a social purpose based on the logical idea that school is for all, so all have to be included. What happens when this context moves into the context of the arts? Is it still the overall purpose of the school that counts? Or do teachers and children then have to participate on the premise of the artistic context and the purposes defined within this? Are the two necessarily in opposition? This is a timely discussion, at least in Denmark, as a school reform from 2014 prescribes collaboration with society for schools through 'Open School' initiatives, which, for example, can entail artists coming to work in schools or schools going to arts institutions. But these initiatives still have to correspond with the overall purpose of schools and thus have a focus on learning and being beneficial to the children. Another dilemma is that there is a certain context around the production itself which determines some of what it is possible to do and how it can be done. It is like a big machine that has to work in all its different parts. When there are multiple parts of a performance and not all dancers are on stage at the same time, there will be waiting time for all included. This also counts for the professional dancers. This is different from a school setting in which children are involved all the time. Being part of an artistic production might also mean learning what it entails to work like a professional artist. A third dilemma is that it seemed to be more possible for the dance educators to create a space with their one class in which the children's perspectives came into play and their own choreographic work was in focus. There was a contrast between the work they could do and what happened at the theatre when all involved in the production were gathered together and the artistic quality, as it was deemed by the artistic directors, was prioritised. Taking these dilemmas into account, in what ways was it meaningful to the children to be involved in the production? And what could they learn?

A couple of weeks after the performance weekend I went with the dance educator to the school to have a final roundup and evaluation with the teachers and children. When we asked them what they thought, in a couple of years from now, they would remember from the project, the following were some of their responses:

> "To stand on the stage. That the audience was clapping their hands." (boy)
> "The run across the stage." (the boy who was asked to run at a different time from the others)
> "The part in which we had to improvise." (girl)
> "The exercises about relationships." (girl)
> "In the beginning I was not so happy about the project, but now I know how great it is to be part of something so big." (girl)

"I felt proud to be part of the performance … it gave something extra when we put on the costumes." (boy)

"I felt a rush in my belly when I entered the stage … the trip to get there was long, but it was worth it. The workshops were the best." (girl)

During the project, I also interviewed the children on different occasions, just after a lesson, during a break or while waiting in the theatre. These are extracts of what they said:

"The days of practising all together are a little long, because we have to wait a lot. But all in all it is good. And the music is great." (boy)

"I like the physical exercises the most, the new movement experiences and I feel a difference in my body, I am much more flexible." (boy who usually does karate at a high level)

"We have learned to be focused and keep more quiet." (girl)

The class teacher tells me that she usually works a lot with the class on giving each other constructive feedback. She thinks that this project can help strengthen this endeavour. She also thinks there is a very intense focus in the lessons with the dance educator at the school; she has for example noticed that the children do not always look at their watches during the three hours lessons they have. She has observed that they are working a lot on their coordination skills and that they can learn about communication, culture and structures. She has also observed that they have become better at keeping a focus, understanding and respecting each other's ideas, and responding to each other.

Another teacher who is involved in the project tells me that he thinks it is important because it gives each of the children an experience of being an important piece in the whole picture. They have a role to play in order for it all to succeed.

Both teachers and dance educators agree that 'timing' is one of the most important issues that the children have learned during this project. One mentions that "they have learned how to be part of a 'big machine.' This is a kind of learning that has to do with how we relate and communicate with other people. The ability to either be the one in focus or step back and let other people be in focus and watch or listen for a while. But it is also about ME being of importance to a group, it has a consequence if I am not following."

The critical issues that have become visible when studying learning opportunities for the children in this artistic-educational encounter give rise to questions at an educational-political level. Those children who seemed to be challenged to a degree which made it impossible for them to participate in the final performance of this project would probably have the same experience in other projects in which it was not be possible to pay attention to special needs. If we want to include students with all kinds of needs in schools and in projects with other actors in society, it is necessary to acknowledge that some have special needs and need special attention in order to feel good and be able to do their best.

Quality in education and artistic-educational encounters

Arts and education can be considered both as goals and means to enhance one another instead of either a goal in themselves or a means for learning something else. But artistic practice taking place in schools must adhere to the overall purpose of school. Everything that goes on in a school has an 'instrumentalist' purpose as it is a means for learning something 'bigger than the actual skill or subject itself,' as it must be useful in life. The question of quality must be considered in relation to questions of the overall purpose stated for an activity in a specific context. Is artistic quality possible without educational quality when there are children involved? The overall purpose of schools in Denmark includes: "to develop working methods and create structures that give opportunities for deep experiences and activity in order for the students to develop their cognition and imagination and trust own possibilities and develop a background for taking a stance and act" (Danish Ministry of Education, Law of Public Schools, paragraph 1.2.). Goals of artistic practice are often described as offering opportunities for engagement, deep experiences, imagination, creativity, working on life issues and being critical (see for example Dissanayake, 1995). Are the goals of artistic practice and education then in opposition? Not in theory, as they are combined in the concept of arts education (UNESCO, 2006), but it might be a challenge to let them meet in practice.

Recommendations for artistic-educational encounters

What is needed for an artistic-educational project to succeed with regards to both an educational and an artistic value?

When different institutions have to collaborate different challenges may arise. First of all it is important to be clear about the purpose that different actors and institutions might have – is there agreement on the purpose(s)? Another question is what it takes when a choreographer wants to work with children and not only dancers? Some artists work deliberately with a focus on 'inclusive dance' and what different kinds of bodies/people can add to a piece. Such work might include the children's choreographic creations to a higher degree, taking into account that the dance aesthetic might then change. It might prove beneficial to the work considering that the children's sense of ownership of the movements is important both for their experience of having contributed to the piece and in order for them to remember the material. It is also important to consider how to deal with the fact that school classes hold a broad variety of children and how the professionals around the production will deal with this in order to succeed both in the artistic and the educational quality of a collaborative project.

How can the children's perspectives in an artistic-educational encounter be included?

At the local level of collaboration between the school and the dance educator in this project, it worked well to discuss the purpose of the artistic production with the children and to inform them about the whole apparatus that they were part of in the process. They were informed about what it entails from the perspective of a professional artist to make such a production successful at times when, for example, it was boring, and this seemed to make them accept this as a premise. To take this further, the children could also be asked what they would like to gain from such a project, what they would like to experience and learn. Their responses might then be taken on for the artistic director to consider as part of 'the big machine.'

References

Bogdan, D. (2003) 'Musical spirituality: reflections on identity and the ethics of embodied aesthetic experience in/and the academy.' *The Journal of Aesthetic Education*, 37(2), pp. 80–98.

Charlton, J. I. (1998) *Nothing About Us Without Us: Disability Oppression and Empowerment*. Berkeley: University of California Press.

Danish Ministry of Education. *Law of Public Schools*. Available at http://uvm.dk/folkeskolen/folkeskolens-maal-love-og-regler/vejledning-om-love-og-regler/love-og-regler [Accessed 4 December 2016].

Dissanayake, E. (1995) *Homo Aestheticus: Where Arts Come From and Why*. Seattle, WA: University of Washington Press.

Horn J. K. and D. Wilburn. (2005) 'The embodiment of learning.' *Educational Philosophy and Theory*, 37(5), pp. 745–760.

Merleau-Ponty, M. (1962/2002) *Phenomenology of Perception*. London: Routledge.

Svendler Nielsen, C. (2009) 'Children's embodied voices: approaching children's experiences through multi-modal interviewing.' *Phenomenology & Practice*, 3(1), pp. 80–93.

Todres, L. (2007) *Embodied Enquiry: Phenomenological Touchstones for Research, Psychotherapy and Spirituality*. Houndsmillls, Basingstoke, NH: Palgrave Macmillan.

UNESCO. (2006) *Roadmap for Arts Education*. Paris: UNESCO.

van Manen, M. (1990) *Researching Lived Experience: Human Science for an Action Sensitive Pedagogy*. New York: State University of New York Press.

van Manen, M. (2004) *The Tone of Teaching: The Language of Pedagogy*. London, Ontario: The Althouse Press, The University of Western Ontario.

5.4

DANCING IN WHEELCHAIRS

A Malaysian story

Leng Poh Gee and Anthony Meh Kim Chuan

Anthony and Aman Yap Choong Boon, founders/choreographers of Dua Space Dance Theatre (DSDT), do not hurry to compose a dance for wheelchair dancers. They both observe the dancers' physical ability and limitations to avoid injury: How far can the arms reach? How far can the torso twist and tilt? Are they able to leave the wheelchairs with the support of their arms? How fast can they travel in the wheelchair?

In 2006, the founders of DSDT Anthony and Aman Yap Choong Boon were invited to establish Shuang Fu Performing Arts Troupe (SFPAT), which was attached to the Shuang Fu Disabled Independent Living Association, a non-profit organization that provides occupational training, education, and comprehensive care to the disabled, and has advocated social awareness since 2001 in Kuala Lumpur, in Penang since 2004 and in Johor since 2007. Wheelchair users were selected for this initial disabled dance program due to their strong commitment and maturity in terms of social interaction, which allows them to convey ideas and provide verbal feedback clearly, as well as to understand and interchange roles between that of leader and team member. Anthony has served as artistic director since then and started his pioneering explorations in the field of wheelchair dance at that time. Anthony does not work alone; he involves full-time dancers of DSDT, as he believes that creating access to dance is part of the dancers' social responsibility.

Both instructors and wheelchair dancers exercise extreme caution in regard to the various levels of injuries on different body parts. The safety of the wheelchair dancers is the main concern. Exploration and numerous discussions are conducted and shared before the training starts. Besides the physical aspect, insensitivity to rhythm, passiveness, shyness, and stage fright are the major challenges to the wheelchair dancers. To reduce these feelings of inferiority, weakness, and helplessness, and to ensure a supportive atmosphere, Anthony and Aman decided to join the wheelchair and able-bodied dancers together. Anthony proposed the concept of *Shang Jian Yi Jia*, literally translated as 'one family regardless of able-bodied or disabled,' for SFPAT wheelchair dance development [Photo 5.4].

Under the direction of *Shang Jian Yi Jia*, Anthony and Aman created an encouraging platform for the wheelchair dancers. At the initial stage, performances by the wheelchair dancers were led by the DSDT able-bodied dancers in order to alleviate the stage fright of

PHOTO 5.4 *Dancing in Wheelchairs*
Performance by DSDT dancers and Shen Chiu Hsiang (center)
Photographer: Dua Space Dance Theatre

the disabled, who could imitate and receive cues of movement execution. DSDT dancers can move the wheelchairs to allow the wheelchair dancers to move their heads, arms, shoulders, and torsos freely, and this also enables them to travel quickly to achieve different formations on time. In certain ways, the wheelchair dancers can be lifted, removed from the wheelchairs, and returned safely by the trained DSDT dancers. On the other hand, SFPAT must examine carefully the condition of the performance venues, which range from outdoor platforms and multipurpose halls to theatres. They must ensure that the locations are accessible for the disabled, and that the stage floor is totally flat, with a surface that is not too slippery or rough. Sometimes they need to cover the floor with a mat, or to fix some minor problem on the carpet or floor by themselves with the help of the volunteers.

Findings and negotiations on the competency and limitations of the integrated wheelchair dance are reviewed from time to time. Methods of training and various approaches of choreography that are relevant to express their feelings and emotion have been discovered and refined through action-oriented dance practises. Anthony and Aman designed specific warm-up exercises and regular dance workouts for the disabled, which contained both center work and cross–floor traveling. The training system included the exploration of spatial elements as directions, levels, and relationships; exercises for rhythmic awareness as body percussion; codified dance training with related terminologies and contextual information such as ballet arm positions; improvisation of pedestrian actions, mime, and extension of movement within and beyond the kinesphere.

Anthony and Aman are keen to find ways to utilize the wheelchair as part of the disabled bodies, not wishing to treat the machines as a burden on the dancers. The wheelchair dancers are encouraged to reach beyond the conventional response to a movement task, and to express and communicate their feelings and understanding through movement. They keep on experimenting and exploring various possibilities of wheelchair usage in dance; for example, pivot turns, self-lifting using the arms, jumps with the wheelchair, and many more movements were explored within the capability of the dancers and the affordability of the wheelchairs. Certain parts of the wheelchairs needed to be modified or strengthened mechanically.

Normally dancers of DSDT and SFPAT do warm-up and regular dance class together before the rehearsal sessions start. Both cooperate to understand their situation bodily and rehearse new forms of being and performing together. Through dance, SFPAT dancers are able to achieve their dream of performing to the general public, as well as touring performances locally and abroad.

Since their debut in 2006, the SFPAT and DSDT partnership has gained high respect from Malaysian society, especially in the Chinese speaking community. Their performance aims to raise funds and to create an awareness campaign for the disabled. Sometimes, they also perform to raise funds for other non-governmental organizations such as training centers for special children. Besides the DSDT dancers, Anthony occasionally involves the able-bodied volunteers of Shuang Fu Disabled Independent Living Association to participate together in the performances. Until now, SFPAT have been keen to develop integrated dance rather than performances solely by the wheelchair dancers.

The integrated dance works choreographed by Anthony are highly melodramatic, lyrical, and are easily accessible and resonate with the public. Both pieces, *Call Grandma Once More* (2008) and *I Want To Fly* (2008), share a common theme that seeks to demonstrate how the disabled can eventually not only gain self-confidence, but that they are also able to help and comfort other disabled or able-bodied individuals through their talents and experience. The wheelchair dancers often play characters who are initially depressed and marginalized, but subsequently cheered and encouraged by the able-bodied dancers. Anthony likes images and gestures, such as recoiling and shrinking with fear, helping each other get up after falling from the wheelchairs, pushing away obstacles aggressively, praying with faith, flying freely, and embracing each other; these motifs are often seen in the pieces. As the artistic director, Anthony decides the type, duration, and direction of dance repertoire to be performed for various occasions, from short pieces to mid-length works combined with speech and drama. SFPAT-DSDT has performed at Taipei, Taiwan as part of the disabled talent performance, 'The Beauty of Crescent Moon,' several times. Through the performances, Anthony and DSDT connected to Taiwan's Joyce-Apage Association, a polio care center. Similar to SFPAT, the Joyce-Apage Association formed Extreme Wheelchair Dance Company (EWDC), who incorporate street dance, popular dance, and acrobatic moves into their performance. However, the incorporation of such aggressive dance elements posed great danger to the wheelchair dancers. EWDC invited Anthony to train their dancers with his moderate approach, and he was commissioned to create works for EWDC. In this way, experience and skills from the making of Malaysian integrated wheelchair dance is now transferred to Taiwan. Besides EWDC, Taiwanese representative for and pioneer of wheelchair ballroom dance, Ling Siu Xia, are in touch with Anthony and DSDT for collaboration and exchange programs. Since 2012, dancers of SFPAT, DSDT, EWDC, and Ling Siu Xia meet regularly either in Taiwan or Malaysia to create and perform dance together to raise funds for several charity institutions in both countries. The production team has received critical acclaim from respected Taiwanese governmental agencies and television broadcasters. In Malaysia, they have performed in Kuala Lumpur, Penang, Kedah, Johor, and Sarawak. In 2016, an alliance of DSDT, Joyce-Apage, and Ling Siu Xia was invited to tour to South America and the group performed in Argentina, Chile, Peru, and Paraguay for charity purposes.

From the concept of *Shang Jian Yi Jia*, Anthony initially facilitated creative expression of a diverse group of people (wheelchair and professional dancers, and ad hoc volunteers) in a community. After ten years of working with the disabled, the methods of training, making, and performing integrated wheelchair dance that were developed for SFPAT-DSDT gradually expanded their influence internationally through EWDC and Ling Siu Xia. Community performance is communally created and it rests in the process rather than the product. Integrated wheelchair dance is a community performance due to its purposeful dance making process, and increases access to dance regardless of body conditions, thus embracing diversity of a community. Their performances as a manifestation of their existence in society increasingly gain a greater range of sponsors who understand that the productions are not individually authored, and who are willing to support them financially for the common good of their community.

5.5

'TWILIGHT'

Connection to place through an intergenerational, multi-site dance project

Cheryl Stock

This creative case study focuses on three of the community groups contributing to a large-scale performance event made up of twelve groups. *Twilight*, a multi-site work with the theme 'sensing sea, sky, earth through connection to place,' was performed for and with the Townsville (Australia) community across fourteen sites in Jezzine recreational park. Comprising 167 participants, the project was led by a team of professional artists and community arts leaders. Together, performers and audience members descended winding paths in a promenade performance, beginning at dusk and finishing in moonlight. Dancers and musicians, parkour performers and a sixty-five strong a capella choir performed along with senior women movers (both indigenous and non-indigenous) and an intergenerational disabled group. All contributed to a collaboration that deepened existing community relationships and built new ones through the shared experience of connecting people to place.

Importance of site in the creative process

Aesthetically beautiful and recently landscaped, Jezzine Barracks is a significant historic and cultural site spanning fifteen hectares. The site is a multi-purpose recreational park incorporating heritage elements into the design, in addition to military and indigenous elements. The site path chosen for the *Twilight* project began on the incline to Kissing Point cliffs, with sweeping views of the sparkling Coral Sea offset by the mauve-tinted Magnetic Island, and then wound down through landscaped and tree-lined sloping tracks to finish at sea level on an expansive grassy amphitheatre.

The project concept and performance material were based on the special ambience of this area at twilight, which evokes contemplation, memories and story-telling. The creative process, which occurred intermittently over five months, was one I have evolved in approaching site-specific performances. 'Scoring the site'[1] involves: participants immersing themselves in the site through observing spatial qualities, energy, sounds and movement; sensitising themselves to the surroundings; mapping the site, physically and visually, through writing and imagination; and finally, embodying the site through improvisation. Over time these site explorations are formed into structured performances. In the *Twilight* project, each group was different in its response to their site and how they worked within it.

'Scoring the site' with young dancers

The performance began, as was fitting, with a senior Aboriginal Ngulumburu Boonyah Women's Dance Group and was followed by fourteen young women who were studying dance at Kirwan State High School. Their contribution, *Ascending Twilight,* became key to the entire site experience as it was these young dancers who led the audience up several wide stone staircases in a transitional dance to the top of Kissing Point. With the encouragement of their teacher Kylie Tillack, the students undertook almost every rehearsal on site, working closely with Dancenorth choreographer Mason Kelly and Cultural Engagement Facilitator, Susan Van Den Ham (Suzie). Despite the afternoon heat and constant interruptions from joggers and dog walkers, they enthusiastically embraced the scoring concept described above, making suggestions and problem solving improvised group sections with each other. Their confidence grew as they experienced the work taking shape. Once in performance, their focus and intensity was impressive, especially when faced with people passing by at close quarters, as the young dancers framed the site with their bodies and movements in varied formal and informal configurations. Following the performance their teacher commented that it was 'a great project to be a part of' and how much 'she and the students from Kirwan thoroughly enjoyed the experience.' Importantly Dancenorth continues its workshops with the Kirwan State High School.

Starlit – inclusion and access

A palpable sense of enjoyment in experiencing the site was also manifest in the twenty or so participants from Kith and Kin, Endeavour and Cootharinga Disability Groups. Although those attending the movement workshops leading up to the performances of *Starlit* changed continually, there were regular attendees who helped build a sense of cohesion amongst the performers and their carers (who also performed). The section *Starlit* was led by Suzie, who had already built an atmosphere of trust, fun and inclusivity through regular workshops with the Kith and Kin group in the previous two years as part of the Dancenorth community programme. The age of those opting to take part in *Twilight* ranged from young teenagers to one man in his 50s, with a reasonably even gender mix.

Suzie (often accompanied by myself) worked both in the Dancenorth studio, with which some participants were familiar, and in their own space in a community centre. Since there was a range of physical and cognitive disabilities, it was not possible to take the participants through the site scoring process. They were accustomed, however, to the dance workshops in which they followed Suzie's movements. They had also previously learned some short dances. We agreed that a specific prop as part of the movement activity would assist the participants to focus on the performance in a tangible way. We settled on all the performers wearing two small LED lights on the fingers of each hand which, when massed, gave the impression of a starlit sky. The dancers enjoyed this approach and were very excited when they performed *Starlit* during National Disability Week, which was hosted by Dancenorth at their studio, two weeks prior to *Twilight*. It was also the first time they heard the music composed for them by Chor Guan. As a result of this 'pre-performance,' other disability groups wanted to participate in the project. Rehearsals (especially on site) and indeed performances had to therefore be flexible to accommodate the changing cast. This included extra costumes that were adjustable to various sizes.

It was decided early on that an ideal site was the large grassy square surrounded by a low rock wall halfway down the hill. This provided a safe and comfortable environment that was enclosed but still expansive. The *Starlit* performers took to their special space from the first visit, despite some challenges getting them to the site. Later, some were transported in a golf buggy that soon became an enjoyable part of their performance ritual, as did 'hanging out' in their designated dressing room in one of the old barracks huts.

As *Starlit* was the seventh section of the overall work, darkness was falling when the performance took place. The audience had left the site path with the sea view and were approaching dramatic Castle Hill, which dominated the city, with suburban house and road lights twinkling in the distance; the LED lights worn by the performers added to the sparkle of the night sky. Since it was difficult for many participants to remember movements from rehearsal to rehearsal, Suzie performed with the group, facing them so they could imitate and follow not only her arm movements but also where she moved spatially. The effect, as many in the audience remarked, was quite enchanting.

Surprise 'sitings' – the perfect place for parkour

We discovered that two young men regularly practised parkour at dusk around the rocky slopes along our chosen site path. Nathan and Rhys soon became a regular part of the rehearsal schedule, joined by the older and experienced international bike trail performer Borys, who became an informal mentor, especially through his example of a serious and safe training regime. These three spectacular performers were joined by Dancenorth member Harrison Hall, who had some experience in parkour. Harrison relished the opportunity to

PHOTO 5.5 *Twilight*
Parkour performers in rehearsal from left: Rhys Kirk, Borys Zagrocki and Nathan Wood
Photographer: Ashley McLellan, Dancenorth

shape the virtuosic physical feats for which parkour is known (such as scaling walls, jumping across rocks, walking on precarious tight edges, and tumbling and hurtling through small gaps) into a choreographic whole for the audience to enjoy. The unexpected appearances and disappearances amongst the lit rocks was an energetic highlight of the programme, especially with live musical accompaniment by the African Wassa drumming group. Rhys and Nathan reported to me afterwards that they were proud to be part of a professional Dancenorth production and had learned a great deal, especially in terms of how to harness their passion more effectively into a coherent performance. Rhys is continuing contemporary dance classes with Dancenorth in his desire to continue developing his skills [Photo 5.5].

Inclusion through connection to place

Whilst the three groups above did not physically overlap, they were closely connected through their embodied and shared sensing of sea, sky and earth. The most satisfying aspect of *Twilight* was the strong impact of an intergenerational shared journey which was inclusive and participatory, especially for those groups who tend to be marginalised in mainstream activities. The choice of a site meaningful to the community certainly enabled the palpable sense of a collective experience. For those of us living and breathing its magic for five months, the most significant gift the site provided us with was a recognition and celebration of difference through connectivity.

Acknowledgements

Concept and direction, Cheryl Stock.
Cultural Engagement Facilitator, Susan Van Den Ham (Suzie).
Composer and musician, Ng Chor Guan.
Production, Dancenorth.

Note

1   My own engagement with site is partially influenced by early experiences in the late 1970s with Marilyn Wood and her Celebrations Group, which worked exclusively on conceptually based site-specific urban projects in the United States and beyond for almost thirty years. In adapting her original process over the years I adhere to the major premise of immersion in site and the belief that site dance is a non-transferrable event, resulting in the site 'choreographing' the work rather than imposing pre-conceived interventions on the site.

5.6

NAVI'S STORY

Access to collective identity through intercultural dance in the Fiji Islands

Sachiko Soro

> The Indonesian dance master beat his chest
> *"Tari dengan 'Rasa!'"*
> "Dance with '*Rasa!*' – with flavor, with spirit, with *mana*
> In the mountains of West Sumatra
> In the sweet stench of clove cigarettes and dancers' sweat
> I was born.

This excerpt describes one of my personal intercultural dance experiences that has prompted me to question: what is it about being in an intercultural context that allows for poignant moments? For me, being immersed in other cultures allowed for realizations, for reflections, for personal evolution. When I decided to start VOU Dance Company in 2007 in my hometown of Suva, Fiji, I knew that I wanted to provide opportunities for these pivotal intercultural moments for the young dancers that I would be leading.

This is the personal story of Navitalai Waqavotuwale (known as Navi to his friends, family, and colleagues), a twenty-one-year-old who is a professional dancer from VOU Dance Company in the Fiji Islands [Photo 5.6]. Contemporary dance is still an emerging art form in Fiji and there are no formal institutions that one can go to to study dance, so this narrative examines how the intercultural dance experience may be a location for learning and self-realization in dance.

For instance, in 2014 VOU collaborated with the Auckland Museum and some Auckland-based artists to create a series of short films around the objects of the Fijian collection held at the museum. During the process of this project, titled *Me Vaka Duavata*, the dancers discussed cultural objects in the Fijian collection in relation to their significance, use, and symbolism. Inspiration from these discussions helped the dancers to create responses to the objects in dance. These choreographies were made into short films for the Museum and there was also a live public performance. This traditional object analysis and discussion involved various cultural experts from the museum: *iTaukei* lecturer and museum expert from the University of Auckland, Dr Tarisi Vunidilo, a cultural elder that had come from Fiji; Ratu Jone Soro; and another cultural elder that was

PHOTO 5.6 *Mataqali Drift* (Mataqali means clan)
Dancer: Navi Fong
VOU Dance Company Fiji
Photographer: Fotofusion

living in Auckland, Joana Monolagi. Navi describes the moment after performing in the Auckland Museum thus:

> At VOU we have always tried to channel the energy, spirit and 'mana' every time we perform – of what? Of our history? Of who we are and of this land? I feel like before that moment I don't know where I was getting it from, you know, where would I be getting that from? Was it real? I feel like after that moment we can start to understand where it should be coming from, start to know a little bit more about where that 'mana' is coming from, like when I go out and do 'na lotu.'[1] I know a bit more about what it was like then, and suddenly that mana has an origin.

Perhaps, after becoming more educated about the historical context of the origins of traditional Fijian dance by this intercultural performance at the Auckland Museum, Navi was able to connect with Fijian dance in a new way. Navi also highlights that in this moment of understanding he became conscious of the absence of this understanding of his culture prior to this intercultural experience, when he questions where he would have been getting the mana from before, and he asks, "was it real?" This brings forward the lack of understanding of Fijian culture within the Fijian context. It could be said that Fiji holds its own culture as "low-context culture," (Hall, 1989), where little is known about it, even within its context of origin. It could also be said that if a Fijian performer had been educated outside a detached colonial curriculum (Thaman, 2003), their intercultural dance realizations would be different. All of these ideas are trajectories that this study could take, to further understand how an intercultural dance performance might allow for access to knowing about one's own culture.

Returning to Navi's experience of the Auckland Museum project, Navi expands upon how these discussions of Fiji's history in the intercultural dance workshop made him feel about Fiji's 'selectively' remembered 'common past' (Blumel & Solomos, 1998: 827). As Navi describes:

> I was a bit angry at how ignorant a lot of people are, when we learn about the history of Fiji everyone knows almost just up to the 1600s and there are no other dates from [before] then. In 1600 Abel Tasman sighted Fiji and blah blah onwards … and before that all we know is 'oh we were cannibals,' full stop.

Navi highlights here how colonialists documented history to their own advantage. Deferring to Western perceptions, a more nuanced reality is still unexplained, and we are just left with the stereotype of the cannibal (Obeyeskere, 1998: 63). It has been discussion in the space of an intercultural dance project that has allowed these realizations of Navi's previous ignorance of the history of his collective identity to come forward. These intercultural dance discussions continue to reveal histories and information about Navi's collective identity, of his *iTaukei* culture, that he previously had not known existed. Navi explains:

> I don't feel like the colonization should be that AD/BC marker, you know it's just another part of our history. It's very black and white; here is after colonization, here is before colonization, and no one knows the before they just know – cannibal. I feel like we need to acknowledge this entire richness.

It could be deduced from the above quote that intercultural dance experiences can uncover places of ignorance in relation to collective identities and shed new light on previously unknown information. Fiji, like the rest of the Pacific, comes from an oral tradition, and British colonialists and Christian missionaries wrote the documented history of Fiji. Fiji still maintains a colonial education system that has not been seriously re-appraised since independence in 1970 (Thaman, 2003). To this day, it could be said that Fijians such as Navi are still viewing their own history of "ferocious Fiji" (Lovett, 1899: 1) through a colonialist lens. Navi continued to talk about his realizations of collective indigenous history through the Auckland Museum project. He states:

> It made me realise how much I didn't know … It took stepping away from home, it took going out and meeting other people, it took going out and seeing other lifestyles, and acknowledging other cultures and seeing that in comparison to my own, to realize just how much is here or isn't here.

It could be deduced from this quote that having intercultural dance discussions on collective identity outside the geographical context of that collective identity's origin can allow for different kinds of conversations to happen. This could be because these discussions are taking place in a context with different socially constructed rules, and the expectations of traditional Fijian roles are not as firmly rooted when in a Western museum context. In Fiji, the discussion of the pre-Christian ritual and the country's war-faring history is now seen as culturally taboo from the Christian standpoint (Kelly, 2014a,b). Furthermore, it has been said by Blumel and Solomos (1998) that "collective identity is based on the (selective) process of memory, so that a given group recognizes itself through its recollection of a common past" (p. 827).

Perhaps Navi's beliefs about his collective identity were being challenged because Fijian society had 'selectively' chosen not to consciously remember aspects of the nation's pre-Christian past. These personal experiences described by Navi illustrate the idea that intercultural dance experiences can allow for realizations of collective identity. These personal experiences are important because they contradict in an embodied way the inaccurate neocolonialist writings of foreign academics and they bring forward histories that have been 'selectively' disregarded by the effects of a colonial education and Christianity. It would be interesting to see if this project would bring forward similar realizations of collective identity if it were held at the Fiji Museum in a context that values history but shuns anything pre-Christian as 'devil worship' (Kelly, 2014: 107b).

In conclusion, this journey has identified some of the ways in which dancers can have access to self and access to collective identity through intercultural dance workshops, performances, and discussions, as detailed by Navi's personal narratives. It also highlights previous ignorance with regard to cultural histories that had been obscured by the effects of colonialism and religion.

Note

1   Na Lotu is a traditional *iTaukei meke* that VOU performs, from the province of Nadroga.

References

Bulmer, M. & J. Solomos. (1998) 'Introduction: re-thinking ethnic and racial studies.' *Ethnic and Racial Studies*, 21(5), pp. 819–837.

Kelly, E. (2014) *Towards a Generative Politics of Expression*. Doctoral Dissertation, York University, Toronto.

Kelly, E. (2014) 'The political and religious tensions of Fijian dance in Canada: renegotiating identity through affect.' In *Congress on Research in Dance*, September, pp. 106–112. Cambridge University Press.

Lovett, R. (1899) *The History of the London Missionary Society, 1795–1895*. H. Frowde, London.

Obeyesekere, G. (1998) 'Cannibal feasts in nineteenth-century Fiji: seamen's yarns and the ethnographic imagination.' *Cannibalism and the Colonial World*, 5, p. 63.

Thaman, K. H. (2003) 'Decolonizing Pacific studies: indigenous perspectives, knowledge, and wisdom in higher education.' *The Contemporary Pacific*, 15(1), pp. 1–17.

5.7

THE VALUE OF AN EXTENDED DANCE RESIDENCY

Restless Dance Theatre in a South Australian school 2014–2015

Nick Hughes, Michelle Ryan and India Lennerth

Background

Restless Dance Theatre is an inclusive company working with young people with and without disability in South Australia. Four main areas of activity include: a core performance group of fifteen to twenty-six year olds with and without a disability, who work in collaboration with professional artists; a community dance workshop program; the making of inclusive, professional works of disability dance capable of touring; and a range of one-off projects including master classes, residencies, film works, and extended collaborations. This case narrative draws on a report by a senior teacher following the completion of the second residency at South Australia School (SA) for Vision Impaired in 2015.[1] The project ran over Terms 2 and 3 in 2015 (1 May to 8 September) and featured a daylong face-to-face session once a week, with a performance showing at the end. There was a team of five Restless tutors who worked with all twenty-seven students at the school, divided into two groups.

Restless has developed a way of working whereby participants are presented with a series of creative challenges and asked to respond in movement. Dance sequences are then built up from their responses. This produces unique, distinctive, and very striking dance through a process that nurtures the creative voices of the participants. This approach is used throughout the different areas of activity. Both residencies involved detailed liaison with the school staff before and throughout the project to ensure that the outcomes were integrated within school objectives and teaching and learning aims to maximize the benefit to each student. Restless Dance Theatre tutor teams are led by experienced professionals who are highly competent in dance and working with young people and people with disability – the company also ensures that there is at least one tutor with disability in every tutor team [Photo 5.7].

Residency at SA School for Vision Impaired 2015

The residency had the project name 'Shared Visions.' The outcomes reflected observations in several key areas:

PHOTO 5.7   Restless Dance Theatre
Photographer: Andy Rasheed

a. *An increased sense of independence and willingness to participate on the part of the students*
Several students showed an increased inclination to participate in tasks unaided by teachers or tutors. There was a noticeable increase in the number of students who were working independently. Students demonstrated a willingness to try things unaided when requested to do so, which demonstrated that there was a relationship of mutual trust between student and teacher. Students were able to identify and assess challenges and strengths when creating art.

b. *Students expanded on movement vocabulary and used creative movement as a response to external or self-derived stimulus*
Tutors used real life questions and relevant scenarios to provoke a response from students via movement. Creative imagery and visualization were used to generate material. Tutors explored the use of opposition and extremes to create visual prompts for students, for instance: fast/slow, big/small, light/heavy, happy/sad.

c. *Students demonstrated greater ability to retain movement and sequences*
Restless tutors employed the use of mnemonics to help students retain movement. Chunking of sequences was also used to facilitate better retention rates. Certain numbers also acted as triggers for cues.

d. *Students worked as part of a collective*
By learning each other's movements and working with partners, students were able to better understand and appreciate different perspectives, interact with each other on a creative level, interpret and compare their responses, and give value to one another through personal conversation. The culture of the room developed to support the idea that every creative response was a valid and valued effort, which compounded the importance of acceptance and collaboration.

e.   *Strategies to clearly define space and boundaries were successful*
The use of tactile boundaries and paths on the floor of the space was a successful strategy to define areas and also worked well to give students confidence in terms of their spatial and body awareness. These boundaries allowed students to have a greater freedom of movement, as they did not require one-on-one assistance to navigate through the space.

f.   *The use of assistive technologies for the presentation showing was helpful*
Students created music for the performance using looping pedals, artworks created on iPads in response to the performance themes were projected during the performance, and a student used a CCTV Optelec during the performance, which was also projected on to the wall.

The main successes of the 'Shared Visions' project can best be summarized by breaking down achievements into the categories of physical, social, emotional, intellectual, and artistic. Overall, all students showed an increased range of movement or confidence in moving. One non-ambulant participant was eager to explore and try different approaches in her dance practice, when Michelle (the workshop leader) modeled alternatives for her to try from her own wheelchair. All participants extended their movement vocabulary and showed improved strength and coordination by demonstrating a progression in key concepts involved with dance practice. The students also showed an increased proprioceptive awareness. The end of term performance consolidated skills and contributed to feelings of independence and accomplishment.

Through dance, students were able to effectively communicate their ideas to their peers and an audience. They were able to connect with their peers on a personal level, share stories, and deepen their understanding of each other's culture and unique experiences. Students developed a sense of belonging and felt connected to the group. Relationships were re-examined through engaging with teachers and peers in a different context and students had a sense of achievement and value when presenting their ideas to an audience. Class rituals and expectations developed positive social interactions.

Working memory was demonstrated through the ability to retain movement sequences and through participation in class rituals. Creative thinking was evident through the offering of original ideas and stories. Open questioning in relation to each other's work developed critical thinking skills. Assistive technologies were used to help communicate thoughts and offer written responses. Original responses were evidence of creativity at work. Unique ideas and thought processes were communicated physically and verbally. Finally, the students' performative outcome was indicative of high levels of creative thought and understanding.

Conclusion

This case example illustrates that there are many benefits for students through working with artists in creative activities on long-term residencies in their schools. For some students these experiences can be life changing. These outcomes can be of particular use to students with disability and flow from the opportunities for deep engagement with the artists that an extended residency in a school offers. As one teacher described it, "it doesn't matter what ability or disability, it seems to be something that they can shine in and show that they are as capable as anyone else. I think it just knocks the barriers down."

Acknowledgements

Restless Dance Theatre completed five residencies in schools between 2010 and 2015. All five residencies were funded through the Creative Education Partnerships – Artist in Residence program that was an initiative funded by the Australia Council for the Arts.

Note

1   This report was prepared by India Lennerth.

INDEX

Taylor & Francis eBooks

Helping you to choose the right eBooks for your Library

Add Routledge titles to your library's digital collection today. Taylor and Francis ebooks contains over 50,000 titles in the Humanities, Social Sciences, Behavioural Sciences, Built Environment and Law.

Choose from a range of subject packages or create your own!

Benefits for you

» Free MARC records
» COUNTER-compliant usage statistics
» Flexible purchase and pricing options
» All titles DRM-free.

REQUEST YOUR
FREE
INSTITUTIONAL
TRIAL TODAY

Free Trials Available
We offer free trials to qualifying academic, corporate and government customers.

Benefits for your user

» Off-site, anytime access via Athens or referring URL
» Print or copy pages or chapters
» Full content search
» Bookmark, highlight and annotate text
» Access to thousands of pages of quality research at the click of a button.

eCollections – Choose from over 30 subject eCollections, including:

Archaeology	Language Learning
Architecture	Law
Asian Studies	Literature
Business & Management	Media & Communication
Classical Studies	Middle East Studies
Construction	Music
Creative & Media Arts	Philosophy
Criminology & Criminal Justice	Planning
Economics	Politics
Education	Psychology & Mental Health
Energy	Religion
Engineering	Security
English Language & Linguistics	Social Work
Environment & Sustainability	Sociology
Geography	Sport
Health Studies	Theatre & Performance
History	Tourism, Hospitality & Events

For more information, pricing enquiries or to order a free trial, please contact your local sales team:
www.tandfebooks.com/page/sales

 Routledge
Taylor & Francis Group

The home of
Routledge books

www.tandfebooks.com